Praise for Paula Weideger's
Venetian Dreaming

"Weideger deftly describes her quest to spend a year living in that enchanting island city. . . . The book's strength is Weideger's obvious delight with the city's beauty and rich past . . . her observations are sharp and fresh. [*Venetian Dreaming*] serves up a feast of historic nuggets, too."

—*The Christian Science Monitor*

"[*Venetian Dreaming*] appeals as a personal glimpse of one of Italy's most unusual cities."

—*Publishers Weekly*

"Here is Venice for our century where life is lived and recorded by the passionate eye of Paula Weideger. Taste with her delectable *olive ascolane,* enter with her the Jewish cemetery, watch as the elegant gondolas built in the *squero* race in the *Vogalonga* and join her for a Christmas party at *Palazzo Donà.* This is an enchanted world and you're in it the moment you open *Venetian Dreaming.*"

—Nancy Milford, author of *Savage Beauty: The Life of Edna St. Vincent Millay*

VENETIAN DREAMING

Paula Weideger

WASHINGTON SQUARE PRESS

New York   London   Toronto   Sydney   Singapore

Washington Square Press
1230 Avenue of the Americas
New York, NY 10020

ISBN: 0-671-04729-9
       0-671-04730-2 (Pbk)

First Washington Square Press trade paperback edition September 2003

10 9 8 7 6 5 4 3 2 1

WASHINGTON SQUARE PRESS and colophon are
registered trademarks of Simon & Schuster, Inc.

Manufactured in the United States of America

For information regarding special discounts for bulk purchases,
please contact Simon & Schuster Special Sales at 1-800-456-6798 or
business@simonandschuster.com

To Judith Curr

Contents

Preface

I got out of the train, passed through bland, 1950s Santa Lucia station with its shops selling newspapers, knickknacks, and chewing gum. I walked down the broad, shallow steps to the pavement and was surprised by what I saw; surprised by one of the most often reproduced views in the world; a sight I myself had seen ten years earlier. Nothing—not photographs or movies, memories or paintings, nor all the words of Henry James—is a match for Venice in person.

Straight ahead was the sunlit blue water of the Grand Canal. Men in flat straw hats rowed standing up in the back of black gondolas. White vaporettos, the city's public transportation system, came and went from the docks. I walked over and boarded one of them and, as the boat pulled away, a big, goofy smile came on to my face.

One fantastical building after another rose up at the water's edge. I was tickled and impressed. I was also a little wary. Was this a fairyland or a trumped-up stage set, this small city with so very many lavish palaces? Later when I learned that it's both, I didn't feel put off. I liked Venice even more.

On my first visit to Venice I'd been too tired, too sweaty, and too befuddled to be charmed. I even lost weight on that trip because by eight every night I was so tired that sleep was more tempting than dinner. Now the weather was as hot as it had been then and the vaporettos were just as packed, but I was enchanted and didn't care. A decade hadn't changed Venice, but it had changed me, domestically and geographically.

A New Yorker at heart as well as by birth and upbringing, I now made my life with a Londoner. Henry had lived in New York before we met and didn't want to do it again. I knew how he felt. There are people born elsewhere who seem to feel their "true"—that is, their more graceful, amusing, discerning selves—when speaking French, say, or just walking down a Paris street. London did not have this effect on me.

Neither Henry nor I wanted to move to the other's hometown. Then H., who is a fair-minded fellow with a belief that fairness can be quantified, came up with a plan: We would divide the year into equal shares.

Soon I was "bicontinental" (this learned from a woman who shuttled between California and New York and called herself "bicoastal"). It may have seemed glamorous to some people but I wasn't one of them.

I found dividing the year tricky; what with my dog in New York and the unyielding characters who made up my Manhattan apartment's co-op board. Then there was Christmas. It fell during the six months we had decided were mine. But Christmas, it turns out had to be spent in London.

It seemed as if I was always sitting down and getting up again. Yet in order to feel I could do my work, I needed to have the illusion that time was just rambling along with no roadblocks in sight. The airline ticket tacked to the bulletin board made that impossible.

This awkward if numerically equitable arrangement continued for eight years. Then I made a tactical mistake. I started to work on an English book.

There was no time to be in New York, not even for Thanksgiving. I didn't mind, really. I was smitten by my subject, the National Trust, Britain's largest public charity with more members than all its political parties put together, and an abundance of treasure houses, great gardens, romantic landscapes, and aristocrats. There is nothing like it anywhere else in the world. Only later did I realize what I'd done.

While I'd been absorbed by research, touring the countryside, meeting foresters, farmers, gardeners, and baronets, and then later when I was up at the top of the house writing, Henry had dug in. After the book was published and all the carrying on had stopped, he did not want to go back to the previous regime. And I?

I was in a muddle. By now my giant, curly poodle had endured quarantine and had joined us in London. He was not only my companion, he was an outpost of New York. It helped. So did living in a house and having a garden. While my patch was tiny, I felt like a Bronx Vita Sackville-West about to create another Sissinghurst as I brooded about which roses to order and wondered whether or not peonies would thrive.

Public politeness was something I came to appreciate, too. In London, even a fellow with studs in his lip says "Please" when asking for stamps at the post office, having first stood in line for ten minutes, silently, along with everybody else. But I could not get used to the dark. In winter the days were so short and gray that it seemed as if all the shades had been pulled down and would never be raised again. And then there was the mismatch of temperaments.

In London a cough can be a way of communicating disapproval; the flutter of an eyelid a sign of welcome or even affection. In both cases the action is assumed to be quite sufficient. I went around twitchily alert trying to pick up signals that usually I failed to detect until it was too late. As for my own efforts at friendliness, these were seen as pushiness or an attempt to ingratiate myself.

In the beginning I was miserable, then I graduated to detachment. This state of being had its advantages and in time I came to savor and maybe even fancy them. I even appropriated a few of the natives' techniques. For instance, when asked a question that I did not wish to answer, I learned to sit still and not say a word. There were a few other diabolical delights in the English social arsenal that I managed to make my own as well. But often I felt I was shriveling up in what appeared to be a normal temperature to everybody else but for me was a terrible chill.

I couldn't live in London full time. A return to the restless life of being bicontinental was not appealing either. In this uncomfortable condition I set out for my second visit to Venice.

It was June. A painter I knew was representing Britain at the Biennale and I was joining the group of friends gathering in Venice to celebrate this honor. I had left the train and boarded the vaporetto.

The sky was sunshiny, the water sparkled. Pink and white and terra
cotta buildings lined the Grand Canal as the boat chugged along and I
grinned my dopey grin. I was still beaming when I left the boat and
walked to the only campo in town called a piazza.

There, sprawling across the top of the grandest square in Venice like
the sultan's favorite odalisque, was the pride and prize of the
"Serenissima," San Marco. Everything about the church was mar-
velously, absurdly glorious. The pale yet colorful stone columns out
front (once carried as booty or ballast in ships returning from the republic's overseas outposts), were so different each from the other that they
seemed marked with their own swirling fingerprints. The pastel pillars
standing before me had become a three-dimensional encyclopedia of
marble patterning. The golden mosaics over the arched front doors,
warmed by the setting sun, seemed to turn a molten orange. As for the
roof, the basilica is the most feminine of churches in a city everyone
refers to as female, yet its many domes reminded me less of breasts than
a platter of gigantic, feather-light profiteroles.

On that June evening standing opposite San Marco, I fell in love. I
couldn't know it, of course, as I stood gazing at the basilica's radiant
beauty, but the pleasure I felt, aesthetic yet also sensual, is both an
extraordinary and an everyday thing in Venice.

"Good night," Italians say, *sogni d'oro,* "golden dreams." During that
first week in Venice mine were, even when my head wasn't on the pillow. I kept feeling happier and ever more besotted. Not only was the
city afloat, my spirit was too.

Lovestruck, I longed to get to know this exotic, astonishing,
labyrinthine town better. I wanted to learn everything I could about her.

Millions of people travel to Venice each year and thousands confess
to the same passion as my own. "Oh, if only I could live there," they say.
The odd thing is that I managed to do it. Or maybe it isn't as odd as all
that since, you might say, I did it for love.

I had settled down late-ish, following years in which I had not been
romantically idle. I was both old enough and had fallen in love often
enough to be convinced that Cupid can send his arrows flying all day
long and if you're not in the mood, they bounce off your heart and fall
to the ground.

Or, to put it another way, while it may not feel like it, falling in love always has a practical, solution-to-a-problem aspect. Nevermind that it can make a problem worse.

It was my inability to manage life as a transatlantic commuter or a full-time resident of London that made me ripe for love. But above all I have Venice to thank for being Cupid with a quiverful of arrows, and so very much more.

By the time I had to leave for London I was determined that I would be back as soon as I could manage it, with Henry, to stay. Surely he would agree; the English after all, have been in love with Venice for centuries.

VERO E REAL DISEGNO DELLA INCLITA CITA DI VENETIA

TRAMONTANA

MVRAN

FONDAMENTE NOVE

POINTS
ON THE
COMPASS

1

A Dice Game

How was I going to find a place to live in Venice? I didn't want to go to a Venetian real estate agency. Ciao and buon giorno was all the Italian I knew. Either people wouldn't understand me or, if they did, they'd assume I was after one of those apartments especially done up for Americans. I could do without the power shower and the inflated rent.

Then I learned that there are freelance experts in Venetian rentals who run their businesses from offices or kitchen tables in London, New York, Paris—and, for all I knew, Berlin and Tokyo. By fax or e-mail or on their Web sites they give out details about properties, complete with color photographs. I got the name of one of these cottage industrialists and called to ask for her list.

A week later it came. I sat at the breakfast table, looked at the professionally produced brochure and drooped. I might as well have been studying a catalogue of mail-order brides. I couldn't connect the pictures and the descriptions with me. Or with Venice.

While there was a certain amount of variation in the size, fanciness and price, all of them had the homogenized look of photographs in glossy travel magazines. I wanted something else.

I tossed the booklet on the table, hrumphing.

I got no sympathy from the man across the table.

"I'm not going. I never said I would," was Henry's response.

I reminded him that we had agreed to spend half our time in his hometown and half in mine. But I'd been in England for ages and had accumulated quite a stack of fair-is-fair days, say a couple of years' worth. I wanted to start drawing on them. It was only right.

Henry saw my point. Unfortunately, he was more convinced than ever that life was meant to be lived in his house in London with all his papers, his books, his things.

We made a deal. I could have my way. Gradually.

We would go to Venice for a month. Then, if I still wanted to, we could go again, trying a different season, maybe staying a little longer. You get the idea. He wasn't promising anything, but . . .

Now all I had to do was to find us a place to live.

"You can't expect me to be involved if I don't want to go," was the message from across the table. The conversational circle was complete. The search for an apartment was to be mine and mine alone.

We had no friends in Venice. In fact, we didn't know anybody there. And, most inconveniently, I'd concluded that real estate agents, amateur or professional, were not for me.

I had little choice. I would have to trust to chance.

I do not mean that all of a sudden I turned passive. I told every person I met, every stranger and friend, that I was looking for a place to rent in Venice. I rolled the only dice I had. I rolled them again and again.

I had been back from the Biennale more than three months. It was autumn and I wanted to return to Venice in the winter or early spring. Nothing was happening on the apartment front so I put my energy into what I could do something about. I prepared myself for our eventual return.

Diligently, one hour every day I labored at a home study course in Italian. I listened to the tapes, read the grammar book and did the written exercises. Just me and the course. I didn't have to suffer by comparison with the faster learners. I could stop, rewind the tapes, and repeat the lesson as many times as I needed to get the exercises right. I would never master Italian in two months or whatever absurdly breezy estimate the company had dangled before me, but I was learning something. That was progress enough given my history with languages.

I understand some Yiddish because my mother and hers spoke it when they didn't want me to know what they were gabbing about. And in high school and college I had taken French. Too little stuck. Even a spell living in Paris did not result in much improvement.

This time I was determined to stay with it. Knowing Italian seemed essential if I was going to get close to Venice. For that reason, too, I studied Venetian history.

Blessed London Library. The unaired paper smell of its stacks and the reverberating ping of the wobbly, openwork metal steps as I clambered from history to typography to literature are part of the pleasure of spending time there. But above all, of course, there were the books—books that I could take home.

I had piles of books on my desk. I did my Italian lessons, read my books about Venice and I waited. Then, at last, I got lucky.

My friend, "the garden designer to stars," called one night from New York. I'd known Debby when she was an architectural historian who longed to create gardens but was doubtful she could earn a living doing it. Now, she was overseeing everything from the placement of instant, mature apple orchards to the creation of ornamental vegetable patches on the grounds of ranches, haciendas, country estates and oceanfront cottages. Debby was forever flying around the United States or to her clients' hideaways offshore.

It wasn't strange that she called instead of sending a letter. Debby's life is so frenetic that she doesn't have time to sit down to write her friends. Yet unusually for someone who is so rushed that her own mail often piles up unread at home, she told me that she'd just been browsing through the classifieds in *The New York Review of Books*.

"There's an ad for an apartment in Venice," Debby said. "Are you still looking for one?"

"Yes," I answered.

"I'll fax it to you," she replied.

Minutes later the ad came chugging through my machine:

RENT AN APARTMENT IN A VENETIAN PALACE FOR LESS THAN THE COST OF A MOTEL ROOM IN KANSAS CITY.

The ad was cute, astute and effective. I was convinced this place wouldn't be too expensive and, with such a canny, funny person promoting it, the apartment probably would be sympathetic, too.

Immediately, I wrote asking for more information. As I was about to send my fax, I noticed that the phone number was for Brooklyn, not Italy. Was this an apartment owned by some American who was now trying to pay off his/her mortgage via short-term rentals? I felt a little bit let down.

One week went by. No response. Then two. Since I'd decided that I'd found the place I was looking for—and because I had no other leads—I was desperate.

Hoping that the Brooklyn fax was also a telephone, I dialed. It was. In my antsiness, however, I'd muddled the time difference. The woman who answered sounded groggy. I apologized for waking her.

The apartment did not belong to her, she told me. She was only taking messages for her friend. She would pass my query on to him. He was home, in Venice.

I perked up on hearing the owner was Venetian.

I didn't want to be in Venice only to be enveloped by her beauty, I wanted to become as intimate with the city as I could. It seemed to me that renting an apartment from another American would keep me at a remove. Maybe this was sentimental, naive and/or romantic, possibly even bogus, yet the funny thing is it did make a difference to be dealing with a Venetian. For one thing it meant that our business was conducted in Venetian time: His reply to my first fax took five and a half weeks. This was not a sign of disinterest on Filipo's part.

His faxes to me always began "Dear Ms. Weideger." To me he was always Mr. Pontini. This was lesson number two. Venetians are formal people.

The apartment Mr. Pontini wished to rent was in Palazzo Dolfin, he wrote. It had two bedrooms, two baths, a living room and a good kitchen. The rent was $1500 for the month.

"I'll take it," I shouted to the fax machine.

To ensure that I would be satisfied, Filipo Pontini suggested I telephone the current tenants. They were American, too.

The woman who answered the phone was a New Yorker in fact.

And enthusiastic. She described the furniture, pictures and layout.

"The place has everything you'll need," she told me. "The only thing I had to bring was my kitchen knife."

While I was turning this one over, she amplified. "I'm a cooking maven," she announced.

My mavenhood is more in the department of views. "Can you see water?" I asked.

"The apartment *is* on a canal," she said, sounding guarded. "If you look straight down, out of the window, you can see it." She was speaking so slowly, I imagined she was sticking her head outside to double-check before committing herself. "But you can hear gondoliers singing all day long," she added in a rush. This, she seemed to believe, should do the trick. After all, where there are gondoliers there must be water, so it was practically the same thing.

I faxed Mr. Pontini as soon as I hung up. I said I would like to take the apartment for the month of November, or February if that was not possible.

His reply came in the form of a contract for November. (February was already spoken for.) This document was not a stock item purchased from a legal stationery store but a personally crafted, exceptionally detailed list of my obligations and the monies due. There was information about the security deposit, telephone charges, cancellation fee. It was so detailed that I realized I'd been wrong when I'd taken Mr. Pontini for an advertising copywriter. Clearly he was a banker, accountant or stockbroker. (A long time passed before I discovered that Filipo is a radical, left-wing journalist. I enjoyed the joke, although he did not, when I let him in on it.)

"Shall I send the security and rent by wire transfer?" I inquired.

"No, that's not necessary," Mr. Pontini replied.

I was to mail it. Again I received explicit instructions about what to do.

With care I followed every one. Then I double-checked that the account number and the spelling of the name of the man at the bank was exactly as he'd told me. I took the letter to the post office. The deal was done.

But I wouldn't believe it until the check was safely deposited.

The silence which followed was terrible. The closer I came to getting what I wanted, the more anxious I was about losing it.

More silence. Finally, shaking a little, I telephoned Venice.

"Ah hello," said Mr. Pontini, in a guarded if cheerful voice. Then he paused. It was a long pause.

"There has been a problem," he said.

He did not sound chirpy anymore.

"What problem?" I asked tensely.

"Someone else has taken the apartment for November, December and January."

"How could they?" I bleated. "I sent you a check immediately, exactly as you asked."

"Um, yes," he acknowledged, "but the money from the people in Canada got to my bank first."

"I hadn't realized it was a contest," I said sharply.

Obviously the Canadians contacted him after me and, not wanting to lose a three-month rental, he'd had them cable money to his bank.

If I had still been living in New York this would have catapulted me straight into battle. Well I wasn't. So I employed a tactic I'd picked up from the English: I climbed onto the moral high ground. Venice wasn't London but you never could tell.

"How can you go back on our agreement?" I asked Filipo Pontini in what I trusted was a deeply affronted voice. "I did everything you asked. I followed every instruction."

"Don't worry," he said, soothingly. "I have a solution. I have arranged for you to rent another place. It is the apartment of my sister. It is comparable in every way—except there is only one bathroom. But the view is even better," he assured me.

I did not feel trusting, but I could hardly call his sister and ask "Is your apartment nice?" Either I gave up the plan to spend November in Venice or I accepted his offer.

"Okay," I said. "But since there is one less bathroom, how about subtracting a hundred dollars from the rent?"

Starting out life as a Jewish girl in New York had certain things in common with being born and raised a Venetian, it seemed. Mr. Pontini and I had made a deal.

*   *   *

HENRY AND I FLEW TO MARCO POLO AIRPORT. Marco Polo. Even the name of Venice's airport sounds romantic. (Now that I think about it, that's probably why local people insist on calling it Tessera, the name of the district where it was built.)

The airport, on the mainland directly across the northern lagoon, is so close that people in Venice can almost see the planes touching down. However, getting from the airport to the city by public transportation is hardly speedy, whether by land or sea.

We had been advised to take the blue bus to Piazzale Roma. The bus doesn't have outside storage bins so we hoisted our heavy suitcases on board. For ten minutes we sat and waited and then with a jolt we were off. Two hours earlier in London the grass was green and a few delicate pink roses were still tossing their heads in my garden. But all along this route the fields were brown and the trees bare.

The houses and factories we passed, together with the flatness of the terrain, made me think of New Jersey. They'd reminded Hemingway, a Midwesterner, of Hammond, Indiana. Much the same, I imagine: blighted, ungainly, sad. And so was Piazzale Roma, the last stop for the bus that crosses low over the lagoon on the causeway that connects mainland Italy to Venice. Piazzale Roma is a large, asphalt-covered, open space with a row of grim, gray, multistory parking garages at one end. We were entering the city through its scruffy back door.

Ah but once we passed through it, there was Venezia. . . . Pink and ocher against the slate blue gray sky, its palaces standing erect or listing slightly on both sides of the Grand Canal, Venice became Byron's "fairy city of the heart."

We followed Mr. Pontini's instructions and took the vaporetto to the Rialto stop.

Henry is usually our navigator. But I'd found the apartment and I was responsible for us being in Venice, so I was going to lead the way.

I wish someone had told me that it's possible to hire a porter at Rialto (also at San Marco). He would have stacked our luggage on a dolly and taken us to our new home. It wouldn't have cost more than ten or fifteen dollars. A bargain. Instead we pulled our heavy suitcases along, heading inland from the Rialto vaporetto stop. Fortunately, there was plenty to distract me as we walked: the narrow streets, the canals and the furs.

Never before had I seen such coats: Long, short, fingertip length. There were furs with ruffles, furs with pleats or gathers; deep cuffs, double collars. Furs with swing, others belted and straight hanging. There were furs that looked like ski parkas and others modeled on a general's overcoat, complete with hairy epaulets. Some furs climbed up and down while others ran around the body horizontally. As for the colors: there were blue coats and mauve ones, maroon furs as well as those that were in such approximately natural tones as tawny, toffee and chocolate.

I did not have a fur coat of any sort or shade. I came to Venice from London where even cloth coats with interlining are scarce. (England has two fashion seasons: summer and the rest.) But for the moment I didn't notice how cold it was. The labor of carrying my bags through the streets kept me all too toasty.

I'd worked out where Campo Santa Marina was on my street map and I'd planned a route. In a few minutes we came into a square lined with shops selling dresses, suits and linens. This was Campo San Bartolomeo just as it should be according to the itinerary in my head.

At the center of the square was a statue of a man in a frocked coat and tricornered hat. He was standing on a tall plinth. When we got closer we discovered that this was Carlo Goldoni. Not long before we'd seen one of his plays in London—in Venetian dialect. Not that I would have understood it in pure Italian. But it was one of those plays that you can follow, broadly, without knowing the language. Everybody had carried on with such gusto that even when, supposedly, they were suffering, I felt buoyed up just watching them. I was feeling much the same right now.

Clumps of people were milling around Goldoni. Teenagers, scraggly and smart; mothers with babies in strollers. There were carefully dressed men in soft camel's hair coats and slicked-back gray hair. Matrons, too, had congregated. Most of them were wearing suits; a few also wore buttery gloves. But what struck me most was the marvelous noise.

Everyone was babbling away. We had traveled south over the Alps. The city of heavy silences was now far behind us. I wasn't merely pleased, I was thrilled.

Feeling bouncy, I led the way out of Campo San Bartolomeo. Not five minutes later, we were in hell.

"You said you knew the way," Henry remarked, grimly.

"I thought I did," I answered weakly. Evidently somewhere between my scrutiny of the map and our setting off, the route had run away from me. I had no idea which way to go next.

Henry glowered. He opened his map and began studying.

From San Bartolomeo with its jaunty statue of Goldoni and its lively Venetians, we had marched off in the wrong direction. We would have to backtrack and set out again.

My suitcase was stuffed with books and winter clothes. I was also carting a carry-on bag holding both my laptop and camera. All this would have to be hauled back over the terrain we'd just negotiated. I huffed and lugged, going up the steps of bridges and then struggling to keep control of my suitcase as it bounced and twisted wildly down. By the time we found Campo Santa Marina we were red-faced, tired and late. We were also not speaking.

Entering the square I noticed a small white poodle standing outside a pet shop. He seemed a comical circus performer compared to our serene giant Zephyr. But I took it as a welcoming sign just the same. A stack of birdcages was piled up behind him. In one of them there was a restless mynah. Many mornings during the month that followed, I was greeted by its metallic ciao.

2

The Launching Pad

The door we were looking for was in a narrow alley leading out of the campo. In my communications with Mr. Pontini, I had not thought to ask for a description of the building and he had not volunteered one. Now, even before we rang his sister's bell, I could see that while the apartment we were about to occupy might be the equivalent of the one we'd lost, architecturally we hadn't been winners. His place was in a palace; hers was not.

The building was part of a row of houses which were all three or four stories high. When the buzzer sounded, we pushed open the door and came into a small lobby. It was damp and grimy and looked as if it hadn't been painted in years. A straw basket dangled on the end of a string in the stairwell. I'd grown up on a block where most of the buildings were six-story walk-ups and had often seen baskets just like this being lowered by a mother from her top-floor window. Sometimes she was sending keys down to her children so they could open the lobby door, sometimes the basket was empty, waiting for the bottle of milk or loaf of bread brought from the store.

Were we about to dislodge the owner of this basket? I steeled myself for a trek to the top of the house.

Mr. Pontini's sister was waiting for us at the first landing. She was tiny and slim with short red hair. Antonella looked bewildered and doubtful. Who were these foreign creatures about to take over her house? I suspected she'd never rented her apartment before.

We introduced ourselves. She knew about as much English as we knew Italian so the three of us communicated mainly by pantomime.

There was no escaping the first "feature" of the apartment. A room divider, all too cleverly designed, stood a few feet in from the door. It was about five feet wide. Shaped like a half moon, sturdy and breast high, it was covered in industrial gray carpet. An identical half moon curled behind it. Sunk into the small gap between these heavenly bodies was a thicket of plastic philodendrons and ferns.

Obviously the idea was to carve out an entrance hall. The concavity of the arc, which faced the door, sheltered boots, umbrellas, coats and shopping bags. The whole business looked like a castoff from a dentist's waiting room. Mercifully, once we passed this eyesore, the place improved.

The layout of the apartment was simple: The central room into which we had walked was a long, generous rectangle running from the front door to a wall of windows opposite. The space between the door and the divider became the foyer; the remainder was the dining room, which was mostly given over to a highly varnished dark wood table and matching sideboard. All the other rooms opened off this one.

The kitchen, then the bath and finally the bedroom were to the left. On the right was a small study and then, at the far end of the apartment, the living room. Apart from the dining room, most of the furniture was modern. The seats and backs of the kitchen chairs, for example, were made of strings of black rubber. By far the most stylish room in the house was the bathroom. Its walls were lined with rich, tobacco-colored cork—except for the wall behind the toilet, bidet and sink which was covered with mirrored tiles. From the burled wood cabinets under the sink to the curved glass of the shower door, the bathroom could have come from a first-class cabin on a 1930s ocean liner.

WE WERE IN THE BEDROOM, at the back of the apartment, looking at closets hung with tiers of Ms. Pontini's beautifully pressed clothes, in which a small but adequate space had been made for us, when Filipo

Pontini arrived. He was in his forties and wore one of those German or Austrian pea green loden coats with a pleat down the back, which many Italian men favor. The frames of his glasses were translucent, icicle blue plastic. He looked both eager and tightly sprung.

Our conversation was amiable, if strained.

In spite of the ghastly divider—I couldn't wait to start yanking out its artificial foliage—I liked the apartment. The bathroom with its SS *Normandie* chic appealed to me; the bedroom, dining room and living room were all light and airy; the kitchen was both larger and better equipped than mine at home; the studio was supplied with an entertainment center and stacks of CDs. But the main thing was the place had a good feeling. And it had a view.

According to Horatio Brown, who early in the nineteenth century lived in Venice, "the two great constituents of the Venetian landscape, the sea and the sky, are precisely the two features in nature which undergo most incessant change." Here we were going to have a ringside seat for this never-ending show.

We didn't know how fortunate we were. It was a while before we realized that a large number of Venetian houses overlook buildings you can almost reach out and touch or have windows facing a *cortile,* a courtyard so small that in New York it would be called an air shaft. Such places are dark and life is turned inward, by necessity. But from this apartment we could see water everywhere we looked. And the sky too.

Antonella's building was on a corner. If we continued walking past her door, the street became a bridge crossing the Rio Santa Marina. That rio slapped up against the back wall of the house as it cut through from the Grand Canal to the Arsenale in the east of the city. We could see it from our bedroom, dining and living room windows, if we looked straight down. Those windows, in fact, overlooked a T-junction. The Rio Santa Marina along the back of the house was met, perpendicularly, by the rio delle Panada which seemed to head straight for our dining room.

On the right of the T-junction stood a decaying ancient palace. From our books we learned that this was Palazzo Pisani. Or one of them. Evidently some old Venetian families had been "unimaginably rich," as one historian put it, with money enough to build a number of palaces in Venice and fill all of them with lavish furnishings and works of art. This place was grand in its decrepit way, yet it was not the most magnificent of the houses in town the Pisani built and for that matter it wasn't the grandest palace we could see from our windows.

A sidewalk followed the left side of the canal leading away from our house. (Such a pavement is called a *fondamenta* I later learned.) It ended at the entrance to an even more splendid building, Palazzo Soranzo–Van Axel. Sitting at the dining table we could plainly see "the only remaining Gothic wood door in all of Venice," or so our guidebook said.

But we had only just arrived, we hadn't yet consulted our books. Henry and I still were chatting with Antonella and Filipo, each hoping to reassure the other that all would go well. At this moment, the actual subject of our conversation was food shopping. I asked for tips and listened to Antonella's suggestions but I was also busy staring out the windows. We were in Venice. I wanted to see.

Antonella recommended a store called Aliani in the Rialto market. "It is very good for cheese," she said through Filipo who translated. "It's expensive but worth the extra money." I scribbled this down quickly, but was far more engrossed watching an old man outside who had just moved into view.

The man was sitting, half reclining, on a chair made of wooden slats. He wore an overcoat, a knitted hat; his neck was swathed in scarves while blankets enveloped the rest of him. A pair of heavy wooden poles extended in front of and behind the arms of his chair. These poles were gripped by men wearing identical, bright blue coveralls.

All of a sudden the old man listed backward. He and his electric blue escorts were mounting the more distant of the two bridges over the rio delle Panada.

These details, simple enough to describe, added up to something so strange and unfamiliar I had trouble making sense of what I was seeing. Could it be that this elderly fellow was ill? Were the men in overalls stretcher bearers carrying him to the hospital? This must be an ambulance—on foot.

I was looking out over the dining-room table into the Middle Ages. I

felt as if I were hallucinating. But nobody walking along the street outside appeared to take any notice.

What a place we'd landed in. This romantic, medieval, modern-day
Venice.

AS SOON AS THE PONTINIS LEFT, I got to work on the philodendron. My
plan was to put the stuff in a closet and throw a cloth over the divider.
However makeshift the result, it would be better than living at the
dentist's.

Damn! Only half the greenery was plastic, the rest was, so to speak,
real. There were glasses filled with water slotted into the divider at
irregular intervals. I couldn't very well yank these out, too. Where
would I hide the evidence? How would I remember the order of actual
and artificial? What if some of the hideous plants died? I put back what
I had already removed. I'd live with it. I had to.

After unpacking, we went to the nearby minisupermarket called
Full. Its windows were papered with signs advertising the week's spe-
cials but we were not capable of bargain hunting. We bought a box of
penne, a can of tomatoes, a bottle of white wine, olive oil and some sort
of cheese, I wasn't sure quite what. The fruit and vegetables looked
wan. We'd get our vitamins from a carton of grapefruit juice.

We were too tired and too keyed up to be ambitious about cooking.
Anyway we wouldn't have known where to buy the ingredients, never
mind what to call them. Nor would we have known where to find the
pots, pans, spatulas or wooden spoons.

However limited the menu, it was with a sense of accomplishment
that we went into the dining room and sat down to a warm meal. We
chatted and watched night fall. The street lamps came on and their
light was reflected on the water.

IN THE MORNING I LOOKED OUT THE BEDROOM WINDOW. I'd half forgotten the "oldest Gothic door," the bridges, the ever-changing sky and
water. And now, in addition, a wrinkled gypsy woman was sitting on
the steps of the bridge across Rio Santa Marina.

The gypsy held out a shallow bowl. She was, it transpired, our resident beggar. Every weekday she sat at this same spot. And every day, late in the afternoon, a man would come along and relieve her of the money people had deposited in the bowl. You couldn't properly call him a pimp, I suppose. But is there a word for he who lives off the takings of a begging ring? What I wonder was the beggar's cut? Did she get one?

Right after our first breakfast we set out as planned for Venice's main tourist office on the *bacino,* the old harbor at the mouth of the Grand Canal. We wanted to find out where to get a Carta Venezia.

Somewhere, in a newspaper or magazine or guidebook, I'd read that you can save a lot of money on transportation in Venice if you acquire a Carta Venezia. Not to be confused with the Venicecard sold to transient tourists, this item was for people who were staying put. To get one you have to have two passport-sized photographs and a Venetian address. The card, though not very expensive, is good for a couple of years. Once you have it, you pay much less for every vaporetto ticket and, better still, you can buy an *abbonamento,* a monthly ticket which can make traveling even cheaper and easier.

Holders of an abbonamento don't need to stand in line to buy vaporetto tickets. Nor do they have to get a ticket validated at one of the small, yellow machines with their rectangular lipstick-red mouths that bite down on the paper, leaving an impression of the hour and date. With a monthly ticket you can just rush ahead and jump on board.

Henry, now chief navigator, led us along the left side of Campo Santa Marina. "Ciao," rasped the mynah bird, thereby unleashing a chorus of cheep cheeps from his neighbors the parakeets. Left, right, over a bridge, right again. In a couple of minutes we were in a campo, much larger and more impressive than our own.

The church of Santa Maria Formosa was in the far right-hand corner of the square. Squat, with a low dome, its brick walls plastered over and painted white, Santa Maria Formosa looks like one of those poor but honest Spanish mission churches in southern California. It is sober, fine and earnest but not captivating. I'd fallen for a gorgeous, splendid Venice and was not impressed. But in time I would walk into this campo and feel warmed and welcomed by Santa Maria Formosa's gravity and grace. And much later still, on Palm Sunday of the following year, I would find myself catapulted into a grove of waving palm fronds undulating to the singing of a congregation backed by fifty or more enthusiastic, one-chord-only guitarists. Santa Maria Formosa then showed itself to be a mission church after all.

We were eager to get our vaporetto passes, our admission tickets to Venice, as I'd come to think of them, before everything in town shut down for lunch. But "never pass a church without going in" was a rule I'd been taught in my late teens when, with a painter friend from college, I'd tootled around Florence.

Henry, even earlier in his life, had adopted the "don't skip a church" rule. Both of us wanted to see all we could of Venice's art and architecture. We'd never been inside Santa Maria Formosa, so in we went.

I'm afraid I cannot tell you the number or layout of Santa Maria Formosa's chapels. And it's a good thing I am not going to try because I was a teenager before I ever dared enter a church. I'd grown up thinking of them as "enemy territory" where "god knows what" would happen to me if I went into one.

What first struck me now was how cold the church was. True, this was November and outside it had been damp and chilly. But this place was frigid. I was not going to sit down and wait for Santa Maria Formosa's atmosphere and paintings to impress themselves on me. Sit? In this icebox? I walked briskly.

Then Saint Barbara nabbed me. Standing before a tall brick tower, her left hip jauntily tilted, she wore a not quite floor-length burgundy dress knotted at her waist, with little bows down the sleeve. The bodice was draped with stiff white ribbon and on her shoulders rested a soft pink robe. Barbara was a sturdy, moody-looking woman with a small sweet mouth and long pale hair, tied back but refusing to stay put. It was her presence that stopped me, the strength of her character which infused everything from her stance to the expression on her face, which was at the same time guileless and resolute. The painting was by Palma il Vecchio.

Who was this woman? I had no idea. I later learned that Saint Barbara was a "martyr" who was said to have been a great beauty. Her father locked her in a tower to keep the boys away but when she then became a Christian against his wishes, he tried to murder her. Barbara got away, only to find herself in worse trouble—this time with the emperor who fancied her. He intended to marry her but first she had to give up her faith. Barbara stood firm. Enraged by this, the emperor sentenced her to death. Diabolically, he ordered her father to behead her. As the grisly deed was done, Poppa was struck by lightning and turned to a pile of ashes. My dictionary of saints calls the story a "pious romance." But if there is no evidence that this woman ever existed, she certainly lived as the object of a cult, with the tower as her emblem. For centuries people have prayed to her to protect them from lightning—if she could bring it on, she could keep it away.

Whenever I passed Santa Maria Formosa, I dropped in to see this dreamy-eyed yet steadfast beauty. But Barbara was just the beginning. All of Venice, inside and out, is a stupendous art gallery. For the whole of the month that followed I was giddy with pleasure as I stumbled from church to palace to museum.

We left Santa Maria Formosa and continued on our way to those abbonamentos. This, it turned out, was not so easy.

The tourist office had directed us to the offices of the ACTV, Venice's public transport company. Its glass-faced, double storefront is in one of the city's busiest shopping streets between the Campo Santa Maria Formosa and San Marco. There were, however, only two other people trying to do business when we went in—and three men sitting behind a shiny blond wood counter.

"Carta Venezia," I said. I didn't want to say more lest it be too obvious that I couldn't speak Italian. Naturally the only person I was deceiving was me.

The man I spoke to was plump, graying and in his late forties, I would guess. He looked glum. And shook his head.

"You cannot have one," he said.

"I was told I can," I said firmly. (By whom? Where? I wished I could remember.)

"You have to live in Venice."

"We do," I replied. I gave him our address.

"You have to speak Italian," he said.

For that, I had no comeback.

If I wasn't so sure we were entitled to the cards, this would have been the end of it. But I believed we had a right to them. This man just didn't feel like being bothered by foreigners and I wasn't going to be stopped by that. I didn't budge. I was determined to get the cards, but how was I going to convince this fellow who didn't want us to have them to change his mind? I couldn't suddenly produce a string of sentences in Italian.

"Lots of Italians come to stay in New York without being able to speak English," I argued. "And they are given the same privileges as the people who live there." I had no idea what I was talking about.

The man across the counter and I looked at one another. Each of us had run out of gas. He sat. I stood. We stared.

The fellow sitting next to him now piped up—in English—"I have a cousin. He lives in Brooklyn."

"Really? I'm from the Bronx myself," I shot back as if that were the same thing. (This was no time to reminisce about the Yankees beating the Dodgers or how in other ways, too, Bronxites loathed Brooklyners— and vice versa.)

For a couple of minutes we chatted about New York, which the fellow with the cousin had once visited. As we talked it slowly dawned on me that the process was beginning. Henry and I were to hand over our small color photographs. Next forms were being pushed across the countertop.

We filled in everything as fast as we could—in case somebody changed his mind.

Then we sat and waited. When we were called to the counter again, our photographs looked up at us from our very own Carta Venezias.

The card, valid for three years, cost five dollars. We then added twenty-five dollars each to pay for a November abbonamento.

We'd done it! I felt terrifically proud. Henry was proud too. We felt we had taken our first step into Venetian life.

In fact, I at least had taken two. In our dealings with the men of the ACTV, I'd had my first exposure to the Italian gift for choosing accommodation instead of confrontation. How different from the way I'd been brought up: In Italy compromise need not be the same thing as caving in.

What a novelty. And what a relief. The streets where I grew up were a fight-for-what-you-want training camp. You either put up your dukes or were yellow. Girls of course were excused from the pugilistic manifestation of this. That was fortunate because I lacked muscle power and am a physical coward. Spiritually speaking, however, I was a natural. From both sides of the family, I'd inherited willfulness. It can get tiring.

I found myself feeling quite perky as we left the offices of the ACTV.

3

In a Fog

"Not along the Grand Canal do you find the essential Venice," Max Beerbohm wrote in his reminiscences. "The beauty that is hidden away, not the beauty that is revealed, is the city's essence." How could I fail to agree with this exquisitely perceptive man? Campo Santa Marina is too plain to be included in coffee-table books and rarely appears on a tourist's itinerary, so it was flattering to think that we were living in the essential Venice. It even turned out to be true. Antonella's apartment was in Castello near its border with Cannaregio, a district that is both central and still Venetian. It was just the right neighborhood for us.

More than ten million people visit Venice each year and most of them go straight to Piazza San Marco. Or, if they walk from the station, they may pause for a look at the Rialto Bridge on the way. We were only ten minutes from this crowded route but we lived in a world apart. Yet our world, too, was filled with treasures.

Within a few minutes' walk from the apartment were two very different but equally exceptional churches: Santi Giovanni e Paolo and Santa Maria dei Miracoli. The first, known as San Zanipolo locally and as Saints John and Paul in English, is an enormous and solemn, red-brick Venetian Gothic edifice that looms up from the large square which it fronts. Inside the fifteenth-century church, to the right of the high altar, stands a carved and gilded throne, its upholstery covered with finely worked small, glass beads. It was used by doges when they visited. And when doges died, many were buried here. In fact, there are so many extravagantly carved funerary monuments to various doges on the walls of the church that it is called the Pantheon of Venice. One of the more flamboyant tombs, however, is the statue of a warrior on horseback who is a bizarre dead ringer for an Indian chief in full feathered headdress straight out of the black-and-white movies I watched as a child. But for me the church's main attraction was the handsome, anguished St. Sebastian in the altar painting by Bellini.

The Miracoli (Saint Mary of the Miracles) was even closer to our house. It is a diminutive, Renaissance jewel box of a building covered in marble inside and out—white and pink, blue veined, dove gray, creamy yellow. Framing the luminous slabs of stone are figures of angels and bands of carved foliage entwining fantastical beasts, the work of architect and sculptor Pietro Lombardo. While church services are no longer conducted under its gilded wooden ceiling, weddings are. And there are concerts, too, given by touring college choruses from all over North America and Europe, which, understandably, want to perform in Venice.

Only a small fraction of tourists, the most art and architecturally keen, I suppose, have room in their schedule or energy enough to visit either of these churches. It was wonderfully luxurious to know that I could return in a few hours or days to look again at anything that appealed to me or to wander elsewhere if I was in the mood. At the beginning, however, it didn't feel altogether wonderful; it felt terribly pressured.

Would I get lost? Yes, without a doubt. Could I make myself understood in Italian? With such a limited vocabulary and a poor aptitude for languages, the question was rhetorical.

But I had to try to speak. If I didn't, I would never learn. I knew this was true, yet it was as a timid, tongue-tied soul that I patrolled the *calles,* as Venetians call their alleyways. I tried to force myself to say something, anything, while being aware that whatever came out of my mouth would make me seem a fool. It was an unending tug of war between wanting to remain silent and knowing I had to practice if I was to improve.

On top of all this was my inevitable confusion about money. A lettuce surely cannot be the same price as a handbag. No it cannot. Quickly I could see I was mixing things up. But were Wolford's velvet opaque tights half or twice what they cost in London? I was stumped by that one. And by many of its friends and acquaintances.

I was so overwhelmed that at first I couldn't see the beauties of our neighborhood. Tension had made me as blind as Mr. Magoo.

Venice was a Technicolor blur as I walked the alleys leading out from Campo Santa Marina. I went on blundering. I could barely speak. I kept getting lost. Shopping was an ordeal. I might know what I wanted but where could I find it?

For example, white bread was everywhere yet I wanted something else. Focaccia with rosemary and ciabatta dipped in olive oil are all very well and heaven knows, voguish. But for breakfast? At last I discovered that wholemeal exists in Venice. But the few shops that stocked *pane integrale* seemed to bake it only in the form of very expensive brown rolls. I wanted a loaf.

Finally the yen to ingest burned through the fog in which I walked. The first words I'd learned to read were CANDY and SODA printed on the striped awning of a Bronx sweet shop. Max Beerbohm, when he wrote of Venice's hidden treasures, may not have had pastries in mind, but it was Didovich, a most superior pasticceria, that became the first of our neighborhood's secret delights that revealed itself to me.

Near the middle of Campo Santa Marina was a freestanding *edicola,* a kiosk selling magazines and newspapers.

"Buon giorno," I risked not so very daringly as I walked around the front of the dark green shed hung with periodicals, CDs and toys. Raffaello, the newspaperman with spaniel eyes (I overheard people calling him by name though I never dared), held out a copy of the *International Herald Tribune* for me after the second time I showed up. I could not possibly have made my way through even the first page of *Il Gazzetino,* Venice's daily paper, though I longed to.

Didovich, ten paces beyond the newsstand, is where I began my eating and speaking adventures in Italian. It was there, also, that I was given my first lesson in Italian etiquette.

A pair of shops knocked together, the wide front of Didovich is all glass. However, they didn't choose to flaunt their goods. Instead, autumn leaves and yellow mums decorated the shallow windows when I first went there. Through the foliage I saw a small bar.

Men, women and small children would stand at the counter and have coffee, tea, mineral water or hot chocolate. In one hand they usually had a small, scalloped paper napkin cradling something to munch. Everybody was always gabbing, of course. Between the bar and the window half a dozen tables were jammed together for those patrons who preferred to sit. But standing at a bar is always cheaper—and faster. Bars may be the only locations where Venetians like to be quick.

On my first visit I didn't risk the bar. Instead I went to the right side of the premises where tall display cases were filled with pastries, four tiers deep. Didovich sold savory as well as sweet treats. There were light puff pastry rounds in which sautéed radicchio or melted cheese and spinach nested. To begin with, I stuck to my number one weakness.

"Mi dica," said the trim woman with dark wavy hair and inquisitive brown eyes. "Tell me, what do you want?"

Some of the pastries looked like pretty petits fours but I was more attracted to the miniature open pies. I tried to get away with ordering by using the point and grunt method.

The woman behind the counter was not only attractive, she was also one of life's teachers. She gave me a look through her maroon-framed eyeglasses. Muteness would not do.

"Una tartina," she said with care.

Of course. These rows of dainty little cakes in their white pleated paper cradles would be feminine. How could I have not worked that out for myself?

Desire overcame shyness.

"Una tartina," came out as a whisper.

That, however, was not sufficient. What kind of tart was it that I wished to try?

The tartinas filled with chocolate and topped with shaved almond slivers were called "mousse." The ones with a translucent honey-colored syrup binding together honey-colored lumps were "marrons glacés." Between the chestnuts and the base, I was to discover a thin layer of bitter orange marmalade. *"Limone"* was straightforwardly bright greeny yellow.

"Una mousse," I ventured.

"Per portar via?" the woman behind the counter asked.

"Si," I shot back. I'd gotten it. Per portar via, to take away.

My chocolate tart was covered with a piece of tissue paper and gently placed in a small white paper bag.

"Arrivederci," I tossed off, almost casually, as I headed into Campo Santa Marina.

"Arrivederla," my teacher corrected me firmly.

Suddenly she didn't seem so nice looking anymore. She began to remind me of Miss Horn, the white-haired, red-faced witch who taught me in second grade.

I'd transgressed. I was being told that Didovich and I were on formal terms. My arrivederci had been too familiar. I was embarrassed, but also confused. I'd heard that Italians had stopped using the formal construction almost completely; that these days it's only the uptight or the ancient who use it. Well at least I hadn't come out with "ciao."

In Venice ciao turned out to be safe to use only with children, dogs and very good friends. But when was I supposed to use arrivederci? I mean with whom? How was I going to develop a feeling for when to use arrivederla instead?

Though my first visit to Didovich ended awkwardly, that didn't stop me from going back. In fact, shopping there became part of my routine. One evening I decided to splurge and order six tarts for Henry and me to share over the long weekend ahead.

"Due marrons glacés, due mousse e due limone. Per portar via." I'd gotten the whole thing out. Not bad. I mean the woman seemed to understand me.

Three rows of two tarts each were laid out on a gold foil tray. Over this a blanket of clear cellophane was lightly draped. Hoops of stiff white paper formed two arches over the top. Finally, a sheet of blood red paper was wrapped around the entire business. Didovich in gold script was printed on it along with floppy golden bows scattered in between. Gold paper ribbon secured the parcel. A knife was then applied to the ends of the ribbon, producing springy curlicues.

I carefully carried my prize back to the house. I cherished the splendid wrapping paper. With it I covered my copy of *Il Gattopardo* (though *The Leopard* turned out to be too advanced for me to read—yet).

Whenever I was on my way out of the shop, I worried about what to say in farewell. Anywhere in Venice it would seem rude to enter or leave in silence. I had to say something. But Arrivederla didn't want to come out of my mouth. I took to saying Buon giorno and I stuck with it.

LEARNING TO FIND my way around and shopping, with its tensions and pleasures, was inevitably part of my daily life. But looking at art became my main occupation. In order to gaze at paintings and frescoes, statues and mosaics, it was not, thank goodness, necessary to speak. In pursuit of art I no longer felt like Ms. Magoo.

Josef Brodsky, who was captivated by Venice and who was adored by quite a few Venetians in return, got it right: "After a while—on the third or fourth day here—" he wrote, "the body starts to regard itself as merely the eye's carrier, as a kind of submarine to its now dilating, now squinting, periscope."

My legs carried my eyes into museums, churches and scuolas. Scuolas? I had no idea what they were, but I knew that a few of these buildings were filled with work by some of the greatest Venetian artists.

I consulted my copy of Lorenzetti and *The Rough Guide,* too. A *scuola,* (literally, "school"), I discovered, is a uniquely Venetian institution.

By the seventeenth century there were more than one hundred confraternities, or brotherhoods, in the city. Each had its own headquarters, or scuola. A confraternity might be a guild of craftsmen, goldsmiths for example, or an association of men whose forebears all came from the same place. The buildings were used for prayer, as administrative offices from which charity was given out, and as social clubs, too, presumably.

Most of these societies, and the buildings in which they met, were small. But if the society was prodigiously rich, and some six of them were, it desired a headquarters, a scuola grande, that broadcast this, both inside and out.

Today there are probably dozens of scuolas still scattered around Venice. Some are derelict, some are used for other purposes. For instance, the former Scuola Grande Santa Maria della Misericordia for a time was used as an indoor basketball court. But three of the scuolas are now extraordinary museums, each housing the works of a single, masterful Venetian painter.

The Scuola Grande di San Rocco was the headquarters of an especially rich society. When their building was finished in 1560, they commissioned Tintoretto to cover the walls with paintings. He filled the interior with some fifty biblical scenes both upstairs and down.

I felt pummeled by the dark and often violent mass of pictures. To start with, it would have been better to concentrate on only one: the tremendous, engulfing Crucifixion upstairs.

The extravagantly rococo Scuola Grande dei Carmini ("Carmelites") was excessive in an altogether different way. The staircase walls are madly sumptuous. Every inch of them is encrusted with thick, limey twists and swirls, as if an army of barnacles on LSD had camped here for a couple of centuries. I was punch drunk by the time I got to the top.

The great room was a letdown after this sensational approach. At first, its atmosphere seemed stiff and dull. But then I raised my eyes and saw the ceiling painted by Tiepolo.

Tintoretto, blackened and bombastic, I had to work at. I could see they were good paintings, even great ones, but on the whole my appreciation of them was theoretical rather than visceral. Tiepolo reached right out and lifted me up into his blue sky world with its chubby white clouds. He created some of the eighteenth century's most exuberant and luscious painting and I loved every airborne minute of my heavenly trip.

A few days later I approached the Scuola San Giorgio degli Schiavoni ("Saint George of the Slavs"). I might never have gone there if I hadn't borrowed a very detailed map of Venice from our friends Susan and Patrick in England. They had placed an "x" at the edge of a canal in Castello not far from the church of San Francesco della Vigna. Because Patrick is a painter, I felt I ought to have a look at the place nearest that mark, San Giorgio degli Schiavoni. (Only when I was back in England did I find out neither of them had any idea why there was a mark at that spot on their map. They had never heard of the place.)

Before I could enter the building, I had to pass through a thorny hedge in the form of a hulking, dour ticket seller. He was very likely a member of the Slavic confraternity that still uses the scuola as its head-quarters. No doubt he welcomed the admission money we outsiders pay but he certainly did not seem to welcome its bearers. My entry was unpleasant but what I found inside was both a marvel and revelation. In the seventeenth century, the scuola had commissioned Carpaccio to decorate its walls.

The large room I entered was lined with built-in benches. Wood paneling covered the walls three-quarters of the way to the top. What little natural light there was, filtered through the curtained windows at the front. With all the dark wood, the narrow beams of the ceiling high-lighted in gold, and the richly colored paintings above the paneling, the room had a subdued splendor. I stood surrounded by some of Carpaccio's greatest paintings.

The rearing horses, fiery dragons, bloody corpses and enormous swords of the scenes from the life of St. George immediately demanded my attention. But it was two paintings from the life of the fourth-century St. Jerome that held me: One was the embodiment of stillness and the other of agitation.

A lion, it is said, came to the learned, if irascible, monk during his long retreat in the desert. The lion was limping, in pain from a thorn stuck deep in his paw. Jerome removed the thorn and healed him. In gratitude, the lion stayed with him, becoming the monk's watchful companion. In the first of the scenes pictured here, it is evident that Jerome had become so used to his lion friend that he'd forgotten other people might not consider the creature a pet. The lower left side of the painting shows Jerome walking peacefully into his walled monastic vil-lage. With him is the lion. Clearly, Jerome had failed to warn anybody that he was going to turn up with the king of beasts in tow. When they saw who was visiting, all hell broke loose.

Every living creature apart from Jerome and the lion—and there are many—from monks to peacocks and deer, seems to have taken one look at the pair and panicked. All of them are in flight. Priests, their robes flapping out behind them, scamper across the campo trying to escape.

Some of them are running up a ramp toward the church at the back of the square. They are so terrified they seem about to dive headlong into the church through its windows. It is the most convincing portrait of fear I have ever seen.

The last in Carpaccio's series of paintings hangs next to the door of the scuola and is equally moving. In it a monk sits at his desk on the right side of the room, the floor beneath him a slightly raised and carpeted platform. The room's only window is just beyond him. The room is large and painted in bluey greens, garnet red, and ocher. It contains many opened books, a gyroscope and other implements that indicate this monk is an impressive scholar. He is St. Augustine, in fact.

On the left side of the painting, a small white dog, very like a Scottie, sits on the floor. His ears are pricked up as he looks alertly toward his master. Augustine, a pen in his raised hand, is also looking attentively to the left. Through the window, he is seeing what we cannot: the image of his friend Jerome.

In this instant, everything has come to a stop. The wagging of the dog's tail, the movement of pen across paper, the wind, time. And, as Augustine now knows but we do not, the breath of Jerome has stopped, too. Augustine has seen a vision telling him that Jerome is dead.

DURING THESE FIRST WEEKS IN VENICE, I wanted to roam the streets, look into churches, visit museums, snoop around in shops. I wanted to be enveloped by Venice. I, who had longed for companions in London, now had a positive desire to be on my own. I didn't want anyone to come between me and my beloved city.

Even telephone contact with other people was difficult. Once a week, as always, I talked to my mother in Florida. Whether I was in London or in New York I had enjoyed our conversations, with the usual exceptions and disclaimers. But now the mixture of caring, closeness and exasperation, which was the cement that bound me to her, had turned powdery.

"I hurt my elbow," my mother might say. Or, "Harry and Fay and I are going out to the Wild Rose, for dinner tonight." Whatever the topic, I could no longer understand what my mother was talking about.

The familiar had become foreign to me. I felt estranged from what I knew best. And I wanted to stay that way.

While my mother talked, I would look out of the dining-room windows onto the canal and its bridges. This was my world now, this dream city with its palaces and waterways, its medieval calles and its unending mysteries. I didn't want to be nasty, but I longed to get off the phone and be back, undistracted, in Venice.

Every day, all day, Henry and I, separately or together, went exploring. We began to realize that even after a month of nonstop visits to churches, museums and scuolas, we would not have looked at everything. So while no one was making either of us keep to a schedule, we kept at it, eager to discover what would come next. Until I was forced to stop.

One morning I sat on the bed pulling on tights when I dropped back onto the mattress. I wasn't able to finish dressing.

"In winter," wrote William Dean Howells whom Abraham Lincoln had sent to Venice as America's consul, "the whole city *sniffs*. . . . Fell influenza lies in wait for its prey." He observed that the churches were colder than the streets and that the Gesuiti was the coldest of them all. Howells deferred his church visiting until spring. I, who had been spending hours in the lacerating cold of Venice's churches, didn't have that option. And the Gesuiti was one of my favorites.

The church was nearby, just off the Fondamenta Nuove. Its interior was the product of a fantastical, decorative conceit. The walls were inlaid with deep green-and-white marble which was cut and pieced in such a way that it looked like heavy, undulating silk damask instead of stone. And in a chapel near the door of the church there is Titian's painting of the martyrdom of St. Lawrence. This portrayal of the saint on a bed of flaming coals is a terrible, powerful and moving hint of what transcendence may be and what it can cost to achieve.

The Gesuiti's floor, like its walls, is made of marble. There is clearly a reason that in the days before refrigeration people chose marble when they built dairies. In August, Venetian churches must be refreshingly cool, but in November they are Siberian. I had been spending day after day in one religious refrigerator after another.

Now I got back under the covers and, with glazed eyes, turned toward the window. Before I could feel sorry for myself, I sat up again, smiling.

It was snowing. It never snows in Venice, they say. But here was snow, magical and gorgeous. Creeping out of the bedroom I found my camera. I threw open the dining room window wide and took some snaps. Then I shuffled into the study, turned on the entertainment center, chose one of Antonella's tapes and went to bed again.

A Mozart quartet played as the snow fell in front of the ancient palace opposite, vanishing into the canal below, and my fever cooked away—what a wonderfully romantic way to be ill.

The next day the snow had melted and so had the romance. The flu was worse. It was a week before I could get around again and then I was wobbly. It was during this spell of illness and recuperation that, for the first time in Venice, I began to have the impulse to meet people.

BEFORE WE LEFT LONDON, we met the childhood companion of one of our artist friends at a party he gave. "I have a sister living in Venice," she told me. "You might like to meet her." I had taken down the phone number. Now I telephoned Vivian and introduced myself.

"Come around for a drink," she proposed. Her place was in Cannaregio, she explained, only a few minutes' walk from where we were living. And with Henry doing the navigating, so it was.

Vivian lives in a large, rambling nineteenth-century house. The front door is heavy, carved wood. "A copy of the door at Ca' d'Oro," she told us. This did not make it beautiful, but, if it is my nature to be critical, I was at least able to keep this opinion to myself.

We entered a small hall and climbed a handsome curving staircase to the main floor. The living room was spacious. There were lots of books, two soft sofas, several comfy easy chairs and a huddled group of dark-defying plants.

Like me, Vivian has graying dark hair and I reckoned we were about the same age. Her mother, she told us, was Venetian by birth, her father Hungarian. Vivian and her sister had grown up in London. At seventeen, she came to Venice to study. She soon married an Italian and raised their three children in his country. Vivian had never settled in

London again. She'd recently divorced and was now the proprietor of this establishment, a bed-and-breakfast.

There was a copy of the *Daily Telegraph* on the coffee table. Most of the books on the shelves were in English too. Her guests, she told us, mainly came from Britain. I sensed she was less comfortable with the demands, or should I say requirements, of Americans.

She served us bubbly wine poured into tall, straight-sided glasses from a transparent pitcher. It was Prosecco, made in the Conegliano hills northeast of Venice. "I have my own supplier," Vivian told us.

Thousands come to Venice convinced they must have a Bellini at Harry's Bar. And that concoction of Prosecco mixed with the juice of white peaches is lovely (though it's best in June when the peaches come fresh from the tree and not the jar). But for anyone sticking around longer than a weekend, my guess is that it's Prosecco that enters their album of Venetian memories.

As we chatted, I told Vivian I wanted to find another place to rent. Somewhere for two months or so, in the spring. Then, after that, a place for a year. I explained that Antonella was not going to give up her apartment again and Filipo had told us the apartment in his palace wasn't going back on the market. I had no idea what to do.

Vivian swung from saying that we'd have no problem finding what we wanted—to remain in Castello or Cannaregio in a place with charm at a reasonable price—to announcing that it would be hopeless.

"Everything is so expensive now. . . ." she said, her voice trailing off. "You will be in London. You won't be able to pounce if something good comes up. And in Venice, there's so little, you have to act fast."

Her reasons for being negative were convincing. Then, too, I didn't know anybody else to give me a different story. But by this time I had read enough to understand that there were even more reasons why finding a place to live in the city might be hard.

The historic center of Venice may consist of more than one hundred islands but it is a pretty small area overall. New building is almost non-existent. And while the population of the city has dramatically declined—from 180,000 at the end of the Second World War to less than 70,000 now—the number of outsiders who want a part-time home in Venice, and who can pay a good deal for one, has done the opposite.

I told Vivian that we probably didn't want to buy a place. Not only was Henry reluctant, I had a hunch that we could become owners of a château in the south of France for much the same price as a poky apartment in Venice.

Yet so many palaces looked unoccupied, it gave me hope.

"Do you think it might be easier and cheaper to rent?" I said tentatively.

"Oh, they all have places to let," Vivian replied, nodding.

I looked skeptical.

"Yes, yes . . . ," she assured me, laughing. "They are all in the real estate business here."

So my hunch that there would be more choice—and therefore better value for money spent—by renting in Venice rather than buying was correct.

It seems that the tax laws have helped bring this about. You don't have to pay inheritance tax on a property left to you by a blood relation, second and third cousins included. Furthermore, real estate taxes are based on the number of rooms in an apartment, not on its overall area or its location. A person scraping by on a government pension in a warren of six dark, tiny rooms near the ghetto will get the same real estate tax bill as a member of a noble family who owns six vast rooms in a palace overlooking the Grand Canal.

In Venice, there is little reason to give up an inherited apartment even if you don't want to live in it. After all, one day your children or theirs might like to have it. If not, you could sell it later when its value will very likely have gone up. In the meantime you can earn a handsome income by renting the place to foreigners. So if you already have enough money to live on, it's easy to keep a place you've inherited.

The supply was there and plenty of local people were engaged in matching it up with demand. Contessas, architects, dress designers, the fruit and vegetable seller; everyone it seems knew somebody with an apartment that might be available, including Vivian.

"I have a friend, an architect," Vivian told us in a reassuring voice. "She sometimes hears about apartments for rent or for sale. I'll keep an ear out and let you know if I hear of something."

She was being kind; she did not sound hopeful.

That evening, our first social outing in Venice, was enjoyable. Vivian was a woman we might see sometime again. But by the time we said good night and goodbye, I was depressed.

"So Venice is a *locanda,*" Henry said ruefully as we walked home.

Yes, it did seem that the whole of Venice was for rent—with hundreds, maybe thousands of innkeepers, from princesses to porters. But I had only a single contact. How was I going to find us another place to live?

4

The Bronxness of Venice

Because Didovich was practically around the corner, I had no trouble exchanging my money for its delectable calories. But too much of the time I was still confused. My diary for this period is filled with exasperated reports of unsolved riddles.

"Set off for the Rialto market," begins one entry. "All the shops shut. Why? I thought early closing is Wednesday. I suppose it's because today's Saturday. . . . Spaghetti again."

Eventually, while looking up something else in my guidebook, I discovered that the stalls in the Rialto market are closed all day Sunday and Monday and that, winter or summer, Tuesday through Saturday they finish selling at one.

Now I could start learning about Venetian fish—and the men who sell them, the *peschivendolo*. Most of what I saw was as foreign to me as I was to the market: coda da raspo, orata, branzino. Gamberi—small, sweet, pink shrimp—soon became a favorite because there was no mystery about how to prepare them. They were marvelous sautéed with garlic in olive oil and tossed with pasta.

By my third expedition, I settled on a particularly large, ice chip–covered stall near the far side of the fish market. I never took my business anywhere else, unless for some reason I had to have something—tuna it generally was—and they had sold out. Their stock was always fresh, sometimes even "*vive*," still breathing, and their prices were good.

Of the four or five men behind the long counter, one of them—a balding fellow of thirty with liquid brown eyes and a gentle smile—always acknowledged that he'd seen me before. He even volunteered recipes. It made a difference. Not only did it give me the illusion that I belonged, it meant that I wasn't entirely overlooked in the crowd waiting to be served. Besides, I had enough adventure every day without trying out a new fish seller every time I shopped.

I still could not stop getting lost. I'd happen upon a church, for example the peaceful San Giacomo dell'Orio with a wooden ceiling like a ship's keel, and decide to go back another day with my guidebook. In the interval, San Giacomo disappeared.

To me, Venice had become the gorgeous backdrop to a perpetual game of pin the tail on the donkey in which I was forever "it." There had to be a way to find my way around without getting into such a mess.

Even such straightforward, well-known ways to find what you're looking for weren't necessarily helpful. Take, for instance, using a telephone book.

Someone we knew in London had given us the names of Venetian restaurants she liked and one day we decided to try one for dinner. I went to look it up in the phone book.

Right away I had a problem. Was it an osteria, a trattoria or a ristorante? Each category is listed under a separate heading in the directory. But that's not all. I was also expected to know if the full and proper name of the eatery began with Di or Da or Do, Al or Alla, not to mention such refinements as Vecchio or Antica. I tried every combination I could think of before, finally, I found what I was searching for.

I wasn't intending to telephone the place. I would never have been able to book in Italian or understand directions. My idea was to get the address, then in the evening we would walk over and try our luck. However, the address wasn't much help after all. The directory said Santa Croce 3122. This referred to the *sestiere* (district) and the number of the building. Evidently, the name of the actual street was thought to be irrelevant.

There are very clear maps of Venice in which every campo and calle is drawn and labeled. I had one. But how can you use such a map, if you don't know the name of the street you are looking for? I was stymied. I couldn't figure out how to make my way around this city and frustration was making me cranky.

I wanted to drift and dream. But instead of losing myself, I kept losing the places I was looking for. Getting around had become a job. True, I might, by chance, come upon a new pasticceria or a shop where I could watch as pseudo-antique tables were gessoed and gilded. But however picturesque the streets, there was no pleasure in setting off for the bakery only to arrive five minutes after it had shut for lunch. I was late because I'd taken a few unplanned detours along the way.

The bakery would be closed for the next four hours and I didn't even know if they'd have any brown bread left to sell when I went back.

I'd had enough. I wanted to be able to get from Campo Santa Marina to the Carmini, say, or to the Frezzeria, or anywhere really, in a time I could calculate, give or take fifteen minutes.

I had better apply myself to these sestieri. What were they—and where?

I could count in Italian. *Sei* is six. *Sesto* means sixty. But it didn't occur to me that these words had anything to do with sestieri, which they most certainly do. For those lucky enough not to know from experience, this is what having a negative aptitude for languages means.

While some cities have boroughs and others have quarters, Venice has sixths. It was divided into six parts—three on each side of the Grand Canal—in the year 1171. Doge Vitale Michiel, then the ruler of the almost 200 islets forming the city, calculated that by carving up the city into these administrative segments, it would be easier to collect taxes, for example.

Other groups of islets in the lagoon, among them Murano, Burano and Giudecca, along with swodges of the mainland such as industrial Marghera and sprawling Mestre, are now also a part of the municipality of Venice. But from the twelfth century until today no additions and no subtractions have been made to Michiel's sestieri. While this certainly didn't solve the tax collection problem, the creation of sestieri must have proved to have its uses.

I wasn't worried about how to find my way around Murano, Burano or Giudecca. For one thing, they are small. It was the medieval maze where I was living, the historic center, that I was desperate to get a grip on geographically.

Looking at a map of the city and starting at the bottom, the sestieri on the right side of the Grand Canal are San Marco, then Castello and Cannaregio. On the left of the Grand Canal, Dorsoduro is at the bottom, then San Polo and finally Santa Croce in the north.

All the sestieri border the Grand Canal but each is a different size and shape. It was all very well to read that Vini Bottigoni, both a bar and a good wine shop, is located in Dorsoduro. Knowing that, I could rule out trekking through the five other sestieri in the effort to find it. But Venice is only a small city if you know it intimately or are a seagull. The tangle of calles, rugas, salizzadas, campos and cortes that make up each sestiere multiplies the distance you have to patrol and the wrong turns you can make. Even if you have narrowed down the search to a single section of the city, there remain too many opportunities for getting lost.

Quite a large number of alleys suddenly ended in canals; rather too many streets kept changing their names or lurched left when I was positive they should go right. And if nobody can miss the Basilica of San Marco—just follow a crowd led by an uplifted but unopened umbrella—where does the avid window-shopper find Bottega Veneta in that same sestiere, or Do Mori in San Polo, which has some of the best of the tapas-like Venetian bar snacks known as *cicheti?*

To make things even harder, each sestiere has its own, independent system of numbering. Say, for instance, you are walking along a calle and pass building number 2023. You then cross a small bridge only to notice that the very next number is 6814. What happened to the buildings in between?

The answer is: there are no "buildings in between." What happened when you walked over the bridge is you left one sestiere behind and came down into its next-door neighbor. Since we lived near its border, we were always passing between Castello and Cannaregio. The building numbers were forever jumping around like the splinters of glass inside a kaleidoscope. Only in this case, it was I who was shaken up.

Learning about the sestieri wasn't a waste of time. But it didn't stop me from getting lost. However, by the time I'd got the hang of them, I had also noticed that in addition to, or sometimes instead of, the name Dorsoduro being painted on the corner of a building, I might see the words "San Trovaso" or, if in Castello, looking up, there would be "San Luca." One part of the pair was the sestiere. And the other?

These were Venice's parishes, her *parrocchias*. It was when I started to learn about them that the layout of Venice became less mysterious. I still got lost, of course, but I was often able to sort things out more quickly. And in understanding something about her parishes, I began to make sense of the city in other ways as well.

Venice, I came to understand, is a series of small hamlets each with its minuscule, if also sometimes extraordinarily grand, hub. These hamlets are its parishes.

Depending on who is counting, Venice is made up of between 117 and 200 islets that one by one developed and became a city. Venice grew island by island and parish by parish. Early in the ninth century, there were already more than a dozen parishes; by the turn of the first millennium, more than fifty. In addition there were convents, monasteries and scuolas. By the year 1300, there were 120,000 people living in Venice, more than in Paris. But as the Serenissima developed into a world power, the parrocchias remained what one scholar calls "the foundation stone" on which the increasingly rich and mighty city was built. Eventually there were sixty or seventy in all. Even today when the historic center of the city has a population of less than 70,000, there are about thirty parish churches still functioning.

As the city prospered, the richer inhabitants of a particular islet would pay to have a church built. The site chosen was almost always along a canal, facing onto an open green space. (*Campo* means grassy field.) There a bell tower would be erected and a well sunk. Palaces might take up one or even two sides of the campo, while the houses of more modest folk would crowd together in what space was left. Very often a shopping street led off this hub, streets with names like the Calle Lunga San Barnaba behind Ca' Rezzonico, for example, and the Salizzada San Lio which links San Marco with Rialto, the original main drag of the city. Little wooden bridges connected one islet parish with its neighbors. And there were *traghettos,* gondola shuttle services, crossing the Grand Canal. A few traghettos are still in operation. The tradition is to travel in these gondolas standing up.

Each parish had its rich families, who dispensed patronage and exercised other forms of economic and social clout. And each provided men to fight for the Serenissima. A Venetian's overriding loyalty was to the republic but to some degree a parrocchia was a world in itself and those living in it, a coherent, tightly knitted group.

Today the parish churches of Venice have small congregations and, in many parts of the city, they no longer seem to be at the center of a cohesive neighborhood. You can sense that just strolling around.

In San Marco, to take the most well visited example, most of the parishes are now filled by offices and shops and hotels aimed at transients. In other words, there are very few Venetians in residence. Dorsoduro, which at the end of the nineteenth century was populated by fishermen and craftspeople, has been so gentrified that the rather well-to-do folk who now live there brag if they are near a butcher or grocery store—as if this proves their district hasn't yet lost its neighborhood identity. Shutters cover the windows of many, maybe most, of the palaces along the Grand Canal because here, too, the owners or renters spend the greater part of the year living someplace else.

The University of Venice seems to occupy a huge number of buildings in San Polo. Its more than 25,000 students have created a new, always changing and not exactly religious neighborhood. It is mainly in the parishes of Santa Croce, Cannaregio and Castello that the Venetian heart keeps alive a city that for a millennium was the formidable Most Serene Republic.

In the streets around Campo Santa Marina, I passed children marching off to school every morning suited up with their pink-and-tangerine backpacks. White-haired men and women chatted on the streets and passed hours in caffès or bars. Shoes were mended, ironwork wrought, nightgowns purveyed, butchers, bakers, fruit and vegetable stalls were busy serving local customers. Shoppers and vendors knew one another—and their dogs. Cats patrolled the rooftops and neighbors kept an eye on each other's "activities." Venetians love to gossip and all that talking in campos and calles requires material.

I was later told by a sophisticated, intelligent foreigner who had spent years living in Venice, "Yes, they want to know everything that's going on in your life, but they don't care. They don't stand in judgment." Like almost everything else in Venice, this also had a long history.

The celebrated Venetian writer Alvise Zorzi observes that

> *it was in the Senate that Venetian ambassadors, on their return from their assignments, would read the famous reports which represent for the modern scholar the richest existing sources for dates, details, judgements and evaluations concerning most of the great European states and many eastern countries. . . . The despatches are so detailed that some have felt that in their precision (and no item of news is neglected, however intimate or private it might be, regarding kings and queens, ministers and their favored women and everyone concerned in the power structure of the country to which the ambassador was attached) they reflect the Venetian passion for gossip.*

Politics wasn't the only department in which gossip was useful but not judgmental. Business was another. The wealth and power of Venice was built on trade. Unlike England or France, for example, here the noblemen were merchants. You could look upon the façades of the great palaces along the Grand Canal as one of the most impressive lineups of shops in the world. Each palace advertised the success of the trader who built it and gave customers a foretaste of the splendid goods stored in the warehouses on the ground floor.

The questions that must have concerned those canny Venetians who bought and sold the goods that brought them such great riches were, "Will they deliver on time?" "Is the quality good?" "Will they pay— and not take too long about it?" When the answers are yes, the shrewd merchant does not occupy himself with preaching. The market is amoral, as today's investors sometimes point out.

LEARNING ABOUT THE PARISHES OF VENICE didn't only satisfy my desire to know more about the city. It actually helped me find my way around. Now whenever I had a fixed destination, I always asked what church was nearby. I'd then head for the church and choose a street leading from its campo. If the numbers didn't run in a promising direction, I'd return to the church and set off along another calle. Provided I could find the church in the first place, and usually I could, this worked.

I began to feel less befuddled. I was more relaxed now as I explored the town and that allowed me to become even more attached to it. I now, however, became aware of a jarring emotional hum in the background as I wandered around. Its monotonous message was: Where are you going to find another place to live?

Vivian had been so pessimistic, I thought I'd better get busy and try somebody else.

Before we'd left London, I'd asked my friend Gillian if she had any ideas about how I could find a place to live in Venice. She suggested I contact Lady Frances Clarke, president of Venice in Peril, an English charity that contributes to the restoration of artwork and monuments. The two women shared an interest in John Ruskin.

I decided now to phone Lady Clarke. I explained the who and whys. She in turn gave me the names of Lady Rose and Peter Lauritzen. "They might be able to help you," she said. "They sometimes know of places for rent."

I rang them. The woman who answered the phone had an upper-class English drawl so extreme I felt I'd crossed wires with a P. G. Wodehouse talking book.

Lady Rose asked us to come over. There was an apartment in their palace that might be available. She lived in Cannaregio, she said, in the parish of Sant' Alvise. The house was just outside the ghetto.

Henry the navigator and I arrived in the late afternoon. The building was a double palace with two separate doors. We rang the Lauritzens' bell, were buzzed in and stood in a square, not terribly large but very high entrance hall.

Lady Rose was coming down the wide curving staircase. She looked even more extraordinary than she'd sounded. Rose Lauritzen has the flat face of a Pekinese, the thinness of a whippet and the gait of a giraffe. Her hair was pale brown and shoulder length; it fell in not at all natural waves. In fact there was little about this woman that appeared to be natural. Both breeding and the choices she'd made had fashioned her into a creature simultaneously bizarre, glamorous and not quite of this world. I took to her immediately, in an appreciative and impersonal way.

We followed her as she walked to a door behind the stairs. So it wasn't true when people told me that since the flood of 1966 "nobody" in Venice lives on the ground floor.

The small square windows of the apartment into which we followed Rose were barred and looked straight into a canal. Only later, after we'd left, did I let myself understand why there was also chicken wire over the grilles. But rats are very determined and I doubted that chicken wire would stop them.

We stood in the long narrow kitchen chatting. A framed photocopy of the *New York Times* bestseller list hung above the stove. *Midnight in the Garden of Good and Evil* was circled with three exclamation points drawn by its author, their friend John Berhendt who had stayed here.

Rose had the offhand attitude toward the use of her title that English aristocrats frequently do. More often it's the newly minted Sir John and Lady Joneses who tend to be touchy about proper forms of address. With apparent casualness, Rose underlined the various good points of the place—the huge number of books in the sitting room beyond, for example; its proximity to the railway station—when a racket began outside that was not only loud but also peculiar.

Already certain sounds seemed to belong to Venice. Besides the hum of human chatter there is the noise from motorboats exceeding the speed limit and the ping of chisel against stone from masons' yards. For punctuation, depending on the weather and time of day, there are also foghorns and church bells. At night, most streets are empty by half past eight and the canals have little traffic. Then the only noise is of footsteps as the odd person walks by. The racket we heard was from none of the above. And it was persistent. No, it was not a platoon of rats.

Pulling back the kitchen curtain, we looked out. Fog had drifted in since Henry and I arrived. Sky, water, street, everything was gray.

This palace came straight up out of the water but on the far side of the canal there was a fondamenta. Through the misty monotone we saw a band of small children, boys and girls, marching along it. Bundled up in their winter coats, they were not so tightly swaddled that their little arms were immovable. On the contrary. Each of them appeared to be holding some sort of cooking pot and they enthusiastically banged away with wooden spoons on these improvised drums.

The troupe was proceeding along the sidewalk. Then the children stopped and went into a food shop. Two minutes later out they came again, beaming. Moving on, marching and drumming, they arrived at the door of a pasticceria. It too swallowed them up, although in fact it was the kiddies who did the swallowing. When they appeared again, their hands were filled with slices of cake. Only when they'd licked away the last trace of sticky icing did they begin again crashing spoons against saucepans as they marched on.

No wonder they were parading with such gusto on this damp, chilly afternoon. Though this was not Halloween, the children across the canal were paying calls on all the neighborhood storekeepers who were rewarding their small visitors with bags of treats.

I asked Rose what it was all about.

"It's San Martino's Day," she said, mumbling something about a horse.

To her this was explanation enough. I didn't press it. At least I had solved one puzzle.

For a week, I'd been noticing that the windows of Venice's pastry shops were filled with big flat cookies cut out in the silhouette of a man on horseback. Each shop had its own version. I had bought one that was completely chocolate covered and then piped in pink and decorated with a rainbow of M&Ms or whatever they're called in Italy. I suddenly understood—my cookie was a portrait of San Martino.

"Would you like to come upstairs for a drink?" Rose asked.

We followed her to the *piano nobile,* the principal floor of palaces. The apartment was light and airy, furnished in comfortable English country house style. The windows in the center of the living room were tall and wide and faced the broad canal and the modest buildings opposite.

"You should never have invited us up," Henry said to Rose. "Now we'll never want the apartment downstairs." It was meant as a compliment but I knew it was no joke.

We sat down and Peter, Lady Rose's husband, came out of his study. Peter Lauritzen didn't look like someone who had just been writing, he looked more like a character in somebody else's book—say a novel written in 1912.

His ginger hair and mustache were graying; he was dressed in a pale tweed suit with nipped-in waist, a matching vest, a white shirt and yellow tie. His brown shoes were highly polished—though not to the same degree as his English accent. Peter Lauritzen is American, from Chicago I believe, who was a star student of literature at Princeton. He has never made his life in Britain. He must have been working on this characterization for decades.

They were a perfectly matched pair: Lady Rose who seemed artificial but was the real thing and her Edwardian husband from the Middle West, who wasn't.

What had caused an intelligent, privileged American to turn himself into this facsimile of an old-fashioned Englishman? Maybe like the mustache, he thought it gave him added gravity. And maybe it did in some people's eyes. Luckily, I found it comical because Peter, I was finding out, could be rather cutting. Since I was unable to take him with anything like the seriousness with which he took himself, the wounds didn't go deep.

Peter who had begun his Italian life in Florence had come to Venice more than thirty years earlier. Rose arrived slightly later. They were figures on the Venetian scene—both indigenous and expatriate—so in time I heard a fair amount of gossip about each of them. Of Rose, who had been the deb of the year back home, there were whispers of a wild past, though what might have shocked the readers of *Tatler* then surely would not now. Some of the gossip about Peter was vintage, too, but it had not dated. And whether old or new, always his pretensions were a feature of these stories told with bitter relish. Clearly, I was not the one he'd cut.

In his pre-Rose days, it seems that Peter owned a beautiful camel's hair coat. He would, I was told, keep an eye on the death notices in the paper and, whenever a nobleman died, Peter would appear at the funeral dressed in this luxurious garment. In time, the living nobility began to assume that this smartly dressed American was a rather well connected chap and part of their set. In this way he began his climb.

If he'd had social ambitions of that sort, Peter had done well in marrying Rose. I am not suggesting, however, that he married her for that reason. The one thing about him that didn't seem in the slightest degree contrived was his devotion to his wife. Well, there was another thing that rang true and clear: he was also genuinely in love with Venice.

With the help of a bottle of claret that Rose provided, we were soon chattering away. At one point Peter turned to me and asked why I was looking for a place to stay.

"I'm in love with Venice," I answered. "Like everyone else."

"Oh no," he corrected me crisply. "Many people say they love Venice but they don't. They're glad to get away." (I had by this time quite forgotten that on my first trip, I had been one of them.)

Peter was passionate about the city. I knew he'd written a couple of good books about its palaces and their restoration. But he seemed to feel that people ought to be asking him to write more. Instead, I was told that he was making his way in the world as a five-star culture-tour guide. He seemed bitter.

With a wife who appeared to be related to half the English aristocracy, a large, attractive piano nobile to live in, a son who'd done his degree at Oxford and contact with a number of noble Venetian families, Peter might have been more relaxed, if not contented. He certainly wasn't.

Even before I'd felt their prick, I'd sensed that I'd better watch out for those thorns.

Rose, the most exaggerated English upper-class creature, was adept at being charming and I enjoyed being charmed. Mr. Lauritzen seemed like a cartoon snob. Peter snubbed and Lady Rose dabbed the wounds. We all smiled as we said goodbye.

Henry and I both had found the apartment for rent disappointing. For all its well-stocked library, it was dark and surely would be damp. But Peter and Lady Rose, that curious hothouse pair, were subjects less quickly exhausted. Nevertheless, as we walked back to our place in Castello my mind was occupied with something even more arresting, something I could not have imagined nor earlier would have believed: I had discovered the Bronxness of Venice.

Those ragazzi I'd seen trooping around banging on saucepan drums had revealed to me how much Venice is like the place where I'd grown up. It was at this intersection, where Venice met the Bronx, that my love flowered and found its mooring.

LIKE THE CHILDREN I had seen from that Cannaregio kitchen window, I also grew up in a neighborhood.

Morris Avenue near 182nd Street in the Bronx, and the two or three streets and four avenues which bound it, was small as any islet. It was the center of my world. I went to P.S. 79 near 181st Street. The grocery where my mother sent me to buy slabs of white farmer cheese cut by Mr. Titinski was on our block but up toward 183rd Street, next to the candy store where the grown boys hung out drinking egg creams. Our synagogue was on Walton Avenue, one street to the east. The Jerome, the movie theater I went to every Saturday with my brother, was one block beyond that. If you went any farther east you fell off the edge of the known world as far as I was concerned.

My grandparents on both sides lived within a five-minute walk from our house; my uncle and aunt and two cousins lived around the corner. Another aunt lived in an apartment directly across from ours. The fancy folk lived along the wide boulevard of the Grand Concourse where the Yankees had their victory parades, the western edge of our turf.

The relatives I felt close to (not only because of their physical proximity) as well as the girls I played with and whose houses I went to after school all lived in the neighborhood.

Not everybody was nice. Or kind. Or gentle. Boys, generically, were a nightmare because they thought they owned the streets where they played stickball. It was the sidewalk—or else—for us and our games of potsy and jump rope. Naturally, like every other little girl, I was taught not to talk to strangers. Or take their candy. Evil lurked. But as far as I knew that's all it did.

Inside the neighborhood I felt safe. Danger was someplace else—most immediately in the bordering territories where, from what I overheard, there was big trouble waiting.

The Italians had their own enclave nearby, the Irish another. In both cases Jews were the enemy. You could be stoned if you walked there, people on my block said. My cousins told me this was true. Since Elizabeth Barrett Browning High School was out of our neighborhood, I was nervous about what would happen when the time came to leave P.S. 79 and transfer there. But before I had to brave the stones, we'd moved.

Outside, beyond the neighborhood, was also the land of excitement, of course. There was a huge avenue, Fordham Road, where Krumm's shone like the Tiffany's of candy stores. Alexander's had acres of clothes. There was the big movie theater, Loew's Paradise, with a ceiling painted dark blue and covered in planets and stars. It had two balconies and boxes along the sides. No matter what was playing, going there was, in itself, a very special outing. The children's library was even farther away on Webster Avenue. I went there on the bus with my big brother. Most distant, and most exciting of all, there was "downtown," Manhattan. The Roxy. Radio City Music Hall. My father's office.

The neighborhood where I was born and raised is gone. The buildings remain but the courtyards are filled with garbage now. The windows of the ground-floor apartment where we lived are boarded up, although it is inhabited. It is not the South Bronx with its burned-out buildings, but the sense of neighborhood as I knew it might as well have been torched.

I took the memory of the coziness that never was gingerbread cute, the solidity and the unself-conscious sensation of alrightness that came with belonging to my neighborhood with me when we moved out of the Bronx just before I was ten. But it never became anything other than a memory in any of the places I have lived since.

Hemingway noted approvingly of the Venetians he knew: "The people are very tough and they give less of a good goddamn about things than almost anybody you'll ever meet." Elaborating on this toughness he said, "I suppose it is a man who makes his play and then backs it up." He could have been writing about my Bronx.

Hardship makes survivors tough. In the Bronx, and I think in Venice, too, a sense of humor kept this toughness from seeming brutal.

After such a very long time, I once again felt both cocooned and free.

Whether it was because of their outlook or character, their pride or nosiness, the behavior of those parents, relatives and neighbors of the ragazzi on San Martino's day, like that of Venice's storekeepers and garbage collectors and mail deliverers, made me believe that I, too, could wander around their city freely, just as the children in Venice did.

Of course Venetians would not feel as protective toward me as they would toward one of their own. But they would see it as their rightful place to come to my aid. I might be able to give the bloodshot eyes in the back of my head a rest.

The more I began to find out about Venice, the more it reminded me of the Bronx of my childhood. You might think that with a church at its heart, a parrocchia in Venice could not be more alien to me. Nevertheless, it was in the neighborhoods of Ss. Giovanni e Paolo and Santi Apostoli that, while I felt an outsider of course, I felt at the same time somehow I belonged.

I SPENT MY ENTIRE CHILDHOOD waiting until I was old enough to leave home. I did not yearn to leave the neighborhood. The Bronx, for me, was graced even if to others it was a symbol of rough-around-the-edges dreariness well before it became the archetype of urban decay. My Bronx had died. But now, in a town so splendid it is the envy of the world, it came to life again. I was comforted, if also astonished, to feel connected so intimately to what after all is a unique as well as a most beautiful city.

Good luck had led us to a neighborhood that remains Venetian. Even in glorious Venice, I found myself, again, at an unfashionable address.

The most glamorous avenue in Venice has always been the Grand Canal. "It is the fairest street I believe that may be in the whole of the world," the French ambassador wrote in 1495, "with the best of houses, and it goes the whole length of the city." The men who built those houses were flaunting their wealth and clout, and their desire for such display did not die with them. Although these days, foreigners with social ambitions have also made the rents go up in the sestiere of Dorsoduro.

"Don't you mind living so far away?" people in Dorsoduro inevitably asked.

Don't you love questions like that?

Of course there was no reason for these people to suspect that I did not long to move to the Grand Canal or Dorsoduro. People who want a chic address couldn't be expected to grasp that I didn't want one myself, that I really liked it better where we were.

To me, nothing could have been better than living in a Venetian neighborhood. In spite of the fear of Italians I'd had when growing up, the people in our corner of the city seemed kind, patient, tolerant and made of solid stuff as well as fast on their verbal feet.

Henry grew up in London's leafy Hampstead and sophisticated, metropolitan Mayfair. Yet he too was partial to our neighborhood. As it happened, separately and then in our life together, we've not lusted after addresses. The fact that we did not now have one was irrelevant. No, that's wrong. Every day in Venice was turning into a charmed one and our living where Castello borders Cannaregio is one reason why.

5

Lost and Found

With my abbonamento, I felt as if I was riding for free. I loved taking the vaporetto; there were such terrific opportunities for people-watching and palace-ogling.

Taxis are expensive, the opening fare is about $50 so only the splashy rich, VIPs, the ill and, above all, tourists who often feel they are spending Monopoly money, use them to get around town. With the exception of Venetians who have their own boats, everybody—from matrons in sables to mothers with baby carriages, from courting couples to briefcase-carrying executives—uses the vaporetto. It is a most democratic mode of transport and a noisy one. Unlike London or even New York, where bus riders are often silent, vaporettos hum with the sound of people talking. Should a passenger find nobody on the boat to chat with, he often claps a mobile phone to his ear so that this opportunity for conversation doesn't go to waste.

While the boatmen (some of whom are female), who tie up the heavy ropes when a boat approaches a *pontile,* or dock, and who slide back the thick, round, chrome-colored gates, can sometimes be short-tempered or abrupt, far more often they are exceedingly courteous. If an old person needs an arm to lean on when getting on or off, the boatman is almost always there with his or her elbow crooked. In New York or Paris or London, a helpful bus conductor is a welcome exception. In

Venice, despite the enormous number of passengers piling in and out, it seems to be the rule. I was learning that kindness was not limited to my neighborhood and this made me warm to the city even more.

Eventually I realized that most local people walk around their city. Unlike the slowpoke tourist who sidles up to every shop window and studies even the peeling paint on walls, residents of Venice stride at top speed through their calles. If you know your way through the city and go at a good clip, it is often quicker to get around on foot. There came a time when I, too, was able to get from Campo Santa Marina to the Accademia Gallery faster on foot than by vaporetto. The boats, after all, must slowly follow the Grand Canal as it curls and uncurls, making its way toward San Marco, whereas a walker can follow a more direct path.

I, however, had my monthly ticket and I used it.

I'd get on board and for the duration of the ride I was on vacation from being lost or worrying that soon I would be. Somebody else was doing the steering. If the weather was fine, I stood outside. The astonishing, pinch-me-I'm-dreaming beauty of Venice was passing in front of me and all I had to do was look. Sometimes I went around the whole city by boat, just for the hell of it. My favorite pleasure trip was to go down the Grand Canal from Rialto to San Marco and back again, after dark. I would look into the few palaces with open shutters. Chandeliers, their arms heavy with dangling crystal, cast a weak yellow light in otherwise dark rooms. I might catch a seductive glimpse of paintings on a wall, or the corner of a candy-colored frescoed ceiling. For a few seconds it was as if I was inside one of these bewitching places.

I also liked the mini-cruise to Murano. The vaporetto left from the Fondamenta Nuove ("new," because it was built on landfill when Venice expanded into this region of the lagoon toward the end of the sixteenth century). The route between Antonella's and that boat stop was pretty simple and I was able to memorize it fairly quickly—though the first time I set off I wondered if somehow I'd managed to get things all wrong.

No sooner had I turned left into the first calle, than it looked like a dead end. Directly ahead of me was a heavy wrought iron gate. Through it I could see a courtyard filled with plants in urns, a rather attractive sight if I hadn't felt like a trapped hamster. It was only when I was very nearly nose to nose with the gate that I realized the calle made a sharp right turn. After this, the route became less tricky.

I came out into Campo Santa Maria Nuova near the small, exquisite Miracoli. From there, after a little judicious zigzagging, I saw the white-on-blue street sign pointing in the direction of the lagoon. The street I followed was Calle del Fumo. Dear Calle del Fumo: There is not one single tiny bend from its start to the Fondamenta Nuove where it ends.

Shops line both sides of the street. I was not tempted by the premises of a painter who produced outdoor art show–style sketches of Venice nor by the vendor of tiny blown-glass squid, bumblebees and daisies. However, on the left side of the street, behind a window covered with a crisscrossed metal grate, there was a shopwindow that demanded further study.

Ranks of glass shelves displayed samples of writing paper, business cards, personalized notes. Much of the paper was a thick, creamy white and often had a decoration as well as a name or address. These seemed both individual and artful. I felt rather pleased with myself for making such a discovery.

Putting on my glasses, I studied the items more closely. On one of the calling cards I saw the name Hugh Grant. The actor had chosen a winged lion of St. Marks, inked in red, as his emblem. A veterinarian in Vienna had picked a hunting dog snoozing on top of an antique column for his. At the upper right of one sheet of stationery was a tiny drawing of a palace with its address below. Next to it was another showing a house in London with a Chelsea address. I laughed out loud. Both were homes of the cantankerous American mother of a London friend. Embossed on a stiff card near her stationery was a name with a pointy crown above it, the device of countesses and counts. It belonged to another of her daughters who in true Henry James fashion had married a Venetian nobleman. Some discovery I'd made. Half the people in town had been here.

So I wasn't going to be original. Nevertheless, I wanted some of this special paper, too.

Peering through the glass door I could see old-fashioned, hot type printing presses and the tanned, fit, black-haired man whose shop this was: Gianni Basso, *stampatore*. He is not only the printer but also the designer, salesman and shipper.

I didn't know Gianni Basso's name until I went along to the Calle del Fumo with Henry. Together we were going to choose stationery. I was also going to order note cards of my own. While Gianni Basso, with his wide if cunning smile, knew only a few words of English, I was not the first eager foreigner to come in off the street, and he managed well.

In a concoction of pidgin English and Italian we jointly considered a variety of typefaces and emblems. For my own note cards, I was partial to the image of a milkmaid on her stool yanking away at a big cow. I would have preferred Bertha the sewing machine girl (the archetypal toiling pieceworker whose name was often mentioned as I was growing up), but there wasn't a single stitcher at her treadle in Gianni Basso's book of prototypes.

"You'll get tired of that very soon," said H. when I showed him the milkmaid. I had to agree; there was a minimum order of a hundred for each size of paper.

For our stationery, Henry chose a finely drawn pear with a jaunty leaf at the top. I liked it too. The address and telephone number of our house in London would be included, also. "And I'd like the return address printed on the backs of the envelopes, please."

I was no less intent on moving to Venice than I had been, but stationery isn't chocolate. It keeps. Wherever else we might alight, and however long I could arrange for us to be away, we would always return to London. Henry's house there was for life.

It would be ten days before our paper was ready and I would have to hand over a suitcase full of banknotes. It is just as well I wasn't entirely clear how much all this was costing in pounds or dollars because Gianni Basso is not where you go for bargains. At least I don't think so. In truth I did not do any comparison shopping. The three of us shook hands and said arrivederci.

H. went off on his own and I continued on to Murano.

The sting of cold air, as always, announced my arrival at the Fondamenta Nuove. Turning left, I came to the flower seller's kiosk just before the pontile. This was not a typical Venetian sight. Venice is a poor city for flower buying. There are few vendors and most sell chrysanthemums. However at this stall I also saw midnight blue, long-stemmed paper roses sprinkled with silvery blue glitter. They were my kind of kitsch, but I didn't succumb.

Boats going to Murano first stop at San Michele dell' Isola. Behind its high redbrick walls is Venice's island cemetery. Sometimes only one person got off there; sometimes a dozen did. Often people carried flowers to leave at the graves. That of course was why a flower stall was strategically placed at the Fondamenta Nuove dock.

I left the boat at Colonna, the first stop on Murano. I enjoyed walking around because, provided that I kept to the fondamentas, I never got lost. Following the canals, I toured the periphery of the various small islands that make up Murano. Churches, shops, restaurants, everything I might like to look at and a great deal I didn't, was along my route. There was nothing to take me into its hinterland. It was only when I got a little too confident and thought I could figure out some clever cross-island shortcuts that I was back playing pin the tail on the donkey.

Murano is often described as a miniature Venice. I didn't see it that way. There is a wide canal which curves through its middle with palaces alongside it, but there are many fewer of them and none so grand as in the historic center. At one time these islands were filled with gardens and the charming villas of Venetian nobles who would be rowed over when they felt they needed a refreshing vacation. Murano has since been built up. But it lacks the dense, gorgeous urbaneness of Venice and feels more like a semiindustrial suburb, if a rather special one. It is dominated by a single, superior craft, the making and selling of hand-blown glass.

Because it was getting on toward winter, there were few tourists on the streets. Mothers and grandmothers shepherded small children along the fondamentas; men tended their boats. People shopped from the large fruit and vegetable boat moored in a canal but also at the Co-op, Murano's only supermarket. One day while passing in front of the Co-op on my stroll around town, I noticed a man intently looking up to the fondamenta from his boat. He shouted out to someone

and waved. It was his wife, loaded down with the week's groceries.
He'd come to pick her up and drive her home.

The salt-tinged, self-contained, small-town feeling of Murano
appealed to me. Everybody looked as if they were related to everyone
else, as if they'd been inbreeding for centuries. And without the fear of
getting lost, it was a pleasure to wander around and look at the older
buildings, many with overhanging upstairs porches. I did not like looking in the shopwindows, however, because I did not like what was in
them. To my relief, after a couple of cruises to Murano I discovered that
not every emporium is stuffed with tacky glass trinkets—handblown
ladybugs and miniature rearing horses in a choice of lurid green or
blood red. There are furnaces, as the glassblowing factories are called,
where even today master glassblowers create chandeliers that seem to
float in the air and wine glasses with stems of colorful flowers.

Eventually I found my way to the showrooms of Venini, Moretti,
Barovier and then to the half-hidden doorway of Murano Collezioni,
where these three top makers have joined together to sell their sophisticated wares. The interior of the shop is hung with chandeliers and has
bright blue and yellow vases and round, oval and square glass bowls
arranged on its countertops. Among the various drinking glasses,
Moretti's champagne glasses with green-stemmed red tulips blown into
the tall flutes called out, "Buy me." The whole place had a charged elegance. Spaces were defined by vast sheets of burnished copper. The
paintwork was matte gray.

This commercial collaboration of the glassmakers is quite an act of
faith, cooperation tentatively triumphing over centuries of secretive-
ness. There was a time when Venetian glass was the most sought after
in the world and, to keep it that way, betrayal of the recipe was punish-
able by death.

One afternoon I walked past a palace on which there was a sign reading "Museo Vetrario." I didn't feel excited at the thought of visiting a
glass museum but this was Venice and I didn't want to pass up anything. In I went. The garden in the back looked uncared for, even dilapidated. Upstairs, the building was deserted. But case after case was filled
with the amazingly light creations of the wizard glassblowers starting
with the sixteenth century. In the twentieth century, architects began to

create designs which the masters then blew into shape and the museum displayed many of these heavier, more vigorous and brightly colored pieces, too.

From that time on, I positively resented the rearing glass horses displayed along every fondamenta in Murano. Had the master glassblowers lost the gifts that had been the pride of Venice for centuries? Wouldn't tourists rather take home a single, exquisite flower of the sort that decorates eighteenth-century chandeliers than the dopey, trashy items on sale by the thousands? I resented all those identical horses even more because I knew the answer. When more than half the visitors to Venice are day-trippers, cheap goods are made because it's cheap goods they buy. Almost all the fine glass in Murano is made for sale abroad.

I hadn't set out to explore Murano because of an interest in glass, the fate of its makers and the boundaries of human taste, however. I'd never had any interest in glass, handblown or otherwise. To me it was another subcategory of tchotchkes, dust collectors, old people's clutter. I first went to Murano to see the Church of Santa Maria and San Donato.

Clad in intricately laid red brick, and bulging outward toward the canal onto which it faces, Ss. Maria e Donato was built at the opening of the twelfth century on the site of a still earlier church. Originally, it was dedicated solely to the Virgin; San Donato came into the picture in 1125 when the doge arranged for Donato's remains to be taken from Cephalonia and brought to Venice. The Venetians seem to have had more than the usual keen desire to house holy remains in their churches: those of Mark the Evangelist were audaciously whipped away from Alexandria circa 829 and he has ever after been the city's patron saint.

The explanation usually given for this Venetian fever to acquire holy relics is that Venice, a city with no ancient Roman past of any consequence, was a relative youngster compared to the other ambitious, powerful city-states with whom she was vying. Important relics helped justify her claims to grandeur.

But just as I didn't go to Murano initially to see the glass, I didn't go to the Church of Ss. Maria e Donato to see what might be left of the saintly remains. I went to see its floor.

Constructed at the same time as the church, its mosaic floor is a mar-

vel. Its only rival in Venice is the one in the Basilica of San Marco. The
Murano church is smaller, of course, but its floor is easier to enjoy
because there is no rubber carpeting. They don't need to protect it from
tourist feet because there are no crowds. Often I was the only visitor.

The ground under the church has shifted a fair amount in nine hundred years. The mosaic surface looks like the swelling sea on a breezy
day. But while gazing at the floor is like looking at waves and there is
the sensation that it's undulating as you walk across the rises and dips,
the stuff of which the floor is made is solid and grand.

Thousands of pieces of semiprecious stones and marble—lapis blue,
viridian green, coral pink and pearly gray—along with fragments of
milky glass, were cut and pieced together to create a carpet of geomet-
ric patterns. Scattered mosaic images of animals, flowers and fish are
embedded in the overall design. One of these shows two roosters
marching off, sharing the weight of their captive—a fox who hangs
down by his paws from the pole resting on their muscular, feathery
shoulders. The congregation might ponder on this too clever predator
during the more tedious sermons.

At least twice a week I would set off on a Murano cruise. I'd trot
along the Calle del Fumo and wave to Gianni Basso. We exchanged a
"Ciao." (No arrivederla complications with him.) Instinctively, I
reached for my scarf and wrapped it tightly around my neck when I got
near the windy and cold Fondamenta Nuove.

As the vaporetto noisily revved its engines and moved out into the
lagoon, I tried to find the most protected place on deck so I could stand
outside and watch as the boat pulled away.

I enjoyed seeing Venice growing ever smaller. I'd tease myself, pretending I was going away forever. I enjoyed the sense of loss, since I
knew that in an hour or two Venice and I were going to be reunited.

Watching the shrinking outline of the town, there was no escaping
the sight of a house off to the right. Apart from the nearby Church of
the Gesuiti, the house—a palace in fact—was by far the biggest and
most impressive building along the waterfront. Goethe on his visit to
Venice found the wide stone Fondamenta Nuove "particularly agreeable," and it still is. But a person could call the entire length of it architecturally undistinguished and not be thought hypercritical or a snob.

The Grand Canal is famous for the impressive number of elaborate, sumptuous palaces that rise seemingly straight up from the water—a "chain of marble cliffs," Proust called them. And in my efforts to find my way through the interior I'd had plenty of time to notice that in Venice palaces push up against one another all over the place. Whole alleys are filled with them. Some are marble covered, some are faced with the durable white stone from Istria farther along the Adriatic, others were once covered with frescoes and Ca' d'Oro had famously glittered with gold. Almost all that sort of decoration is gone now, though many of the artful and ancient stone reliefs called _patere_ can still be seen on palace façades. My favorite is the one of a camel set into the canalside façade of a house near the Church of Madonna dell'Orto. These objects, whether brought home from foreign conquests or carved locally, were applied to buildings with apparent nonchalance, as if they were so many candied fruits squished down in the thick icing of a festive cake.

The odd thing about the house set back from the edge of the lagoon which caught my eye when I rode the vaporetto to Murano was that it lacked the splendor everyone associates with Venice. This house was dead plain.

The three windows of its piano nobile were topped with a bit of modest stone tracery, but the design was so restrained that this seemed to be little more than a decorative exception proving the dominant rule of austerity. The house, which was very big, was not clad in marble but was covered in plaster painted a murky pink.

Some writers claim that Venice never had fashionable neighborhoods (at least not until long after the death of the Republic and the arrival of rich part-time residents), but one look at the Grand Canal, and another at the Fondamenta Nuove, makes this seem doubtful. Or, in my case, impossible to believe.

I was curious about the man who had chosen this spot for his palace. Why had he built such a big house all by itself? And why, since he must have been very rich, had he wanted such a very, very plain one?

Color aside, this was no sugar plum fairy castle, yet I was attracted to it. Its starkness and size, its lack of palatial companions or competitors, appealed to me. And, though it didn't look like a fortress with towers and crenellations, it nevertheless seemed like a building that would protect all who were inside.

"I wonder if I'll ever meet the people who own it?" I thought to myself more than once as the boat shook its way across the lagoon. "I wonder if they ever let strangers rent the odd corner?"

The house certainly was big enough for its owners to have tenants without themselves feeling cramped. And many Venetians appeared to have more property than cash. Who could tell? Maybe one day.

While I had noticed the house and had fantasies of living there, I wasn't obsessed with it. As the boat headed toward Murano, my mind would move on to something else. Maybe to lunch—there was a bar near the Co-op with a very tasty fish antipasto. There was, always, the glorious floor of Ss. Maria e Donato. And there were presents to buy now that I'd found a few places where the handblown glass did not make my teeth curl. I wanted to give something especially nice to Sheila who was looking after Zephyr.

One afternoon I stood warmly wrapped up on the deck of the vaporetto as it pulled away from the Fondamenta Nuove heading for Murano and I nodded my greeting to the big pink house. With a weight on my chest, I watched Venice get smaller and smaller. This time my sadness was for real.

Henry was standing near me. And so were our suitcases, the boxes of handsome Gianni Basso stationery making them that much heavier to haul.

The month was over. We had said goodbye to Antonella and Filipo. We were on our way to the airport.

BACK IN LONDON, part of me still turned toward Venice. I was sure we would return—and for a longer stay. I set out to be ready for it—whenever it would begin and for however long it would last. I signed up for a course at the Italian Institute in Belgrave Square and once again I stalked the stacks of the London Library looking for books about the city I loved.

I concentrated on history and then architecture in my library searches; the latter I hoped would be a way of making the former more palatable.

While all sorts of subject matter took on a fresh, sometimes lively attractiveness after the end of my official education, history still seemed like boys' true adventure stories and often put me off. For the sake of Venice, I would try again. Very soon, however, this resolve was put to the test.

A Venetian Family: 1500–1900 sounded as if it would be more personal and therefore easier to penetrate than the usual rundown of battles, dates and places. The cover, however, was not reassuring. The book was bound in a repellently institutional, shiny gray, its title printed in a dull red. The author, James C. Davis, was one of the many historians about whom I was ignorant.

In some of the other books I had piled into the basket of my skittish old bicycle, I found accounts of the wars between European kingdoms and between the city-states of Italy. I read about Venice's empire; her republic; the booty the Serenissima used to embellish her houses, churches, monasteries and convents. In the book about a Venetian family, I found something of all this—and something tantalizingly different.

The family studied by Professor Davis was named Donà, or Donato. During the course of the tale Davis tells, the branch of it he follows became known as Donà dalle Rose, *rose* meaning roses.

They are a very old family and, most unusually, they managed to hold on to most of their papers. Davis had a rich archive to work from. While many noble Venetian families have died out, it seemed that the Donà are still around. In fact, in the early 1970s, when Davis's book was completed, they were one of the very few remaining Venetian families to have continuously occupied the palace built by their forebears.

Davis was a scholar and researcher. His focus was on the support this material gave to his argument about the methods Venetian families used to conserve their wealth. This was not a subject I had any interest in to start with and the author was no popularizer, yet very soon I was hooked.

The book had only a few black-and-white reproductions of maps and engravings and I flipped through the pages to have a quick look at them before settling down to the serious business of trying to get through the text. One of them was a revelation.

The Palazzo Donà dalle Rose, built at the instructions of Doge

Leonardo Donà between 1610 and 1620, was constructed along the northwestern edge of the lagoon in the sestiere of Cannaregio. It was built on the Fondamenta Nuove, which had been created not many years before. A single drawing of the house was reproduced in the book.

Big and plain, it was my house.

The text droned on and if sometimes my eyes dropped shut, I never skipped a word.

Davis followed the history of the family for four hundred years. He stopped, however, before describing the affairs of the living members of the Donà dalle Rose family. There were few words about Count Lorenzo, to whom the palace then belonged, or his wife Celia or their sons Nicolò and Luigi. Of their wives and children, there is nothing apart from a family tree compiled in 1971, just as the book must have been going to the printers. The tree records the birth of the most recent addition to the family: Nicolò Donà dalle Rose's third child and second daughter, Gaia.

Many of the details I read did not stick in my memory. But a few words written near the start of Davis's book remained vivid: "This building is so large," he wrote, "that today it contains, beside the two large floors used by the present day Donà as living quarters, servants' rooms and offices; ten apartments occupied by other families."

Ten apartments. With tenants.

Though I was excited when I'd read these words, I calmed down very fast.

In Venice, tenants who are residents of the city are protected. Vivian had told us that after four years, a Venetian has the right to remain forever. The landlord can do nothing about it except make an offer to buy the person out.

Surely anybody fortunate enough to be renting an apartment in this palace wasn't going to give it up and couldn't be forced to. The fact that there were ten apartments, besides the ones used by the family, was at once provocative and meaningless.

SITTING AT MY DESK ONE AFTERNOON, tapping away on my computer keyboard, no closer to having made arrangements for our return to

Venice, I was interrupted by the phone. It was Vivian. We hadn't been in touch and it was good to be talking to her again now.

"I've heard about an apartment," she said. "I haven't seen it yet, but my friend Constanza the architect has. She's the one who told me about it. It's in Cannaregio."

That was good. I grunted.

"And she says it's very nice. It's not far from here. I can go and have a look for you, if you'd like."

I thanked her for her offer, which I immediately accepted. I said I'd phone back in a couple of days, after she'd had a chance to see the place.

"I think you will like it," Vivian reported when I rang her next. "It's very Venetian, with stucco decorations. There aren't many rooms— kitchen, sitting room, study, bedroom and bath—but they're big."

"Can you see water?" I asked.

"I think so," she replied. "The apartment is at the side and to the south but you can see the lagoon by looking out the windows. And you can see it when you go up the stairs."

"Is it light?"

There was a pause.

"The windows are good-sized but not enormous . . . ," Vivian answered, sounding tentative. "But it seemed light enough."

"Where in Cannaregio is it?" I asked. After all, the sestiere runs from very near where we had lived at Antonella's, which I thought of as central, on to the ghetto and beyond it, the railway station. Even the ghetto was too far from the center of town, as I conceived it.

"It's at the Castello end," Vivian told me. "Very near here."

The Castello end of Cannaregio, my favorite part of Venice.

"It's on the Fondamenta Nuove," she then added.

On the Fondamenta Nuove?

"Where exactly?" I asked, trying to keep my heart still.

The apartment was in Palazzo Donà dalle Rose.

Then, just as I was about to grab the brass ring, the merry-go-round gave a shudder.

"The family wants to rent the apartment for a year," Vivian now told me. And, almost as upsetting, she now mentioned the price. It was more than we'd set as our maximum.

"Impossible," I said.

There was no need for reflection. Henry would never agree. First of all he had said that my year in Venice had to be approached gradually. On this he wouldn't budge. He and I had known each other for a long time: I knew that no performance of mine would make a dent. It was pointless to worry about the high cost of the apartment. It was out of the question.

I told Vivian I'd sleep on it. But I knew very well that what I was going to sleep on was a pillow of disappointment.

In the morning I woke up thinking, "What do I have to lose? I might as well try to get what I want."

I phoned Venice.

I asked Vivian to find out if we could take the apartment for three months instead of a year. That was more than Henry wanted, but not criminally excessive. And I proposed a figure midway between what they were asking and what, until the day before, had been the upper limit of what we wanted to pay.

I couldn't face losing my house so soon after finding it. I wanted it so much, I'd manage to come up with the money somehow.

"I'll telephone Gaia," Vivian said.

Gaia. I recognized the name from the family tree in Professor Davis's book. Gaia Donà dalle Rose was three when that book was published. Now she was handling the letting of its apartments.

A few days passed. Vivian was on the phone again.

"I think they may accept a shorter rental, after all. But you should discuss the rent and so forth with Gaia directly."

Vivian gave me the telephone and fax numbers. I telephoned immediately.

Gaia Donà dalle Rose sounded amiable. I was so relieved. And she was forthcoming. She explained that the apartment for rent belonged to her mother, she was only acting as the agent because her mother lived and worked in Paris.

We talked for a few minutes. I explained my situation and I made my offer.

"I will phone my mother," she told me.

I was to call again the following day. And I did.

"We will rent the apartment for June and July," Gaia said.

What fantastic good news.

"Gas, electricity and telephone will be extra," Gaia continued.

Should I take this to mean we had agreed on the rent? Yes, evidently, we had. I was to send a fax confirming the terms. Gaia's mother would send me a color brochure of the apartment from Paris.

"Please fax me back to say you have received my confirmation," I said.

I was thrilled and sent my fax at once.

There was no reply. Was this going to be a repetition of what had happened with Filipo? Only this time with an unhappy ending?

After a week I telephoned.

"My mother was very angry with me," Gaia now told me. "The price has to be more. I am very sorry."

She sounded as if she meant it.

"My mother is very nice," Gaia rushed on. "But she's French. She's hard."

This candor was engaging but the message was not. We had a deal. Now there was this shifting about. I didn't like it. Yet I longed to live in that palace on the edge of the lagoon.

I proposed that we split the difference. I would pay a sum halfway between what we had agreed and what her mother now demanded.

Gaia accepted. Henry and I would move in June first and stay two months.

That afternoon a fax came. Our agreement was confirmed.

6

Arrival

On June first, with Zephyr in the English countryside with his foster family and their dogs, cats and tortoises, Henry and I took off for Venice. We'd already passed Ostende, Stuttgart and had crossed the Alps at Salzburg, the captain told us in Italian and then in English. Even I could now understand both. And I knew the temperature in Venezia. It was a bellissimo 76 degrees.

I was in love with Venice. I was infatuated with Palazzo Donà dalle Rose, though I couldn't have said why and didn't inquire. Did Cinderella put her finger to her chin and say, "Now what is it, really, that I like about the Prince?"

About the apartment in which we were going to live for the coming two months, I still knew almost nothing. The promised color brochure never found its way from Gaia's mother in Paris to our house in London. James Davis's book about the history of the Donà family had no illustrations of the palace's interior. Smitten and stubborn, I had decided to gamble. I wasn't feeling altogether calm about this now. I did not believe that two months in Palazzo Donà dalle Rose had to be wonderful no matter what.

There is plenty I can ignore but when it comes to the look of things around me, I am, alas, a delicate flower. Forced to live in a visually blighted zone, I do not rise above, I wilt.

During an earlier trip to Chicago I'd rented an apartment for ten days that had been highly recommended by a dear relative. It turned out to be dingy, dirty and stuffed with stuff. No surface, vertical or horizontal, had been spared. The woman who owned the apartment had not stopped with superficial clutter. She'd moved on to layering. There were crocheted doilies on top of place mats on top of tablecloths. It was gruesome. There were sixty-five wedding photographs in the bedroom alone. Each morning I'd tried to keep my head down and my eyes barely open until I was finished dressing and out the door.

Of course I wanted to believe Vivian's judgment was sound. But what did she mean when she described the apartment as "very Venetian"?

Italy is famous for sharp, modern design but Italian ambition in interior decorating can also produce gilt-encrusted, marble-floored mausoleums that are heavy, highly polished, very clean and creepy. The closer we came to Venice, the jumpier I felt.

My anxiety only increased once we landed at Marco Polo and took the bus to Piazzale Roma. Within minutes a nasty argument erupted.

The supposed subject was the proper way to use vaporetto tickets.

During our last stay in Venice we'd each had an abbonamento. We were going to buy one for June later in the day, but right now we needed vaporetto tickets to take us to the Fondamenta Nuove.

Henry was insisting that a ticket was good only for a single ride on a given line. I believed it was valid for an entire journey, including any transfers. Since we were taking one boat to the railway station and another from there to the Fondamenta Nuove, it made a difference. If he was right, we each needed two tickets; otherwise we needed only one.

It was high season. The pontile was packed. There was a long line of people waiting to buy vaporetto tickets. It was hot—much hotter than it had been in London. Both of us were overdressed. And there we stood sweating and arguing about boat tickets.

Laugh and say, "What the hell," were not options that occurred to either of us, ridiculous though the situation was. Neither of us was going to be flexible. And then, whoosh, Henry disappeared.

"Fine," I thought. "He's gone to buy tickets."

I went to the pontile and I waited. The 82 came and left. Five minutes later, another pulled up to the dock. I looked all around but there was no sign of Henry. The ticket line couldn't be that long. When the third boat came I thought I'd better take it as he'd probably marched off in a fury and walked to the station. I was sure to find him waiting for me there.

It was one stop to Ferrovia, the railway station. I would change there for the number 42 vaporetto, which leaves from a pontile at the opposite end of the pavement. I was exhausted when I got there. Then alarmed. Quite a few people were waiting at the dock but not my Henry.

Could he have been so angry that he was stubbornly walking all the way to the Fondamenta Nuove? With his suitcase, his computer and all those bridges? It would take ages. He'd be so tired.

Compared to the giant water buses, the number 1 and the 82, which work their way up and down the Grand Canal and the various express boats shunting tourists from the train directly to San Marco, the 42 is tiny. It has to be because it crosses to the northern lagoon along the Cannaregio Canal. Both bridges over that canal are low and when the tide is high, clearance is even less.

The vaporetto was crowded. I stood on its small open deck leaning against my suitcase.

The boat swung out wide and blasted its horn. We had come to the blind corner where it would leave the Grand Canal. On our left, as we entered the Cannaregio Canal, was Palazzo Labia. The looming, white stone palace had blue-and-white cotton awnings shading each of its windows. This was the Venice headquarters of RAI, the state-owned radio and television station.

We had visited Palazzo Labia during our last stay in Venice. Its ballroom has frescoes that were done by Tiepolo soon after the palace was finished in 1750. Tiepolo took Cleopatra, Queen of Egypt, as his subject and portrayed her wearing an eighteenth-century silk gown. Ever since, to me, Palazzo Labia was Cleopatra's house.

I could still see her sitting in a large chair, her skirt billowing out, with a tear-shaped pearl, big as a pigeon's egg, in her hand. In the painting, it provocatively dangles over a cup filled with vinegar. All eyes are on the Queen of Egypt, including those of Antony. Will she drop that moon-mysterious, magnificent object into the liquid that will dissolve it, as proof to Antony that she is the richest and most audacious as well as the most beautiful woman in the world? For more than two centuries, that pearl has dangled, the anticipation of the deed magnifying the Queen's daring over time.

The vaporetto passed under the Ponte delle Guglie (taking its name from the spires that decorate it) and was heading for the bridge with three arches, Tre Archi, near the far end of the canal. Beyond the fondamenta, to my right, was a narrow alley that leads to the ghetto and its synagogues. I intended to visit them soon.

We came into the open water of the northern lagoon. We might be moving slowly but we were in the home stretch. The vaporetto headed toward land, stopping at Sant' Alvise, then out into the lagoon again, then back to the pontile at Madonna dell' Orto.

Nearly thirty minutes after I'd left Piazzale Roma, I saw Palazzo Donà dalle Rose, hunkered down on the corner of the Fondamenta Nuove and the Canal dei Gesuiti.

"If you cross the bridge over the canal, you've gone too far," Gaia had said.

UNTIL THE NINETEENTH CENTURY there was only one bridge across the entire length of the Grand Canal—the stone bridge with shops built into it—at Rialto. While there were many small wooden bridges across the rios, Venice was a city created by and for people who went around in boats. It's the view of a house from the water, therefore, that is intended to impress. Even if the rio on which a palace faces is very narrow, its "front door" is its watergate. Friends would arrive in their gondolas and tie up at one of the barber pole–striped wooden posts painted, like a jockey's silks, in the family's colors. They would step onto a wooden pontile, the palace's front porch. In the days when Venetians made their fortune through trade, ships loaded with merchandise would also tie up at these docks. Their goods would be taken in to the ground-floor warehouses, called *magazzini*.

Deliveries of everything from pianos to groceries are still made to the watergates of palaces. Friends still come calling at the watergate if they travel by boat, though more people now use the land entrances to palaces. Palazzo Donà dalle Rose's watergate faced the Canal dei Gesuiti but it was provided with a large, heavy door on the Fondamenta Nuove. However, according to Gaia's faxed instruction, we were not to use it. (Nobody else did either, I discovered.) Instead, I was to turn right from the vaporetto, walk back to the corner of the house where there was a caffè called Algiubagiò. There I was to turn left into the calle.

On the caffè's terrace everybody seemed so relaxed. They were sunning themselves, eating pizza, drinking wine and looking out over the lagoon. With my suitcase making an incredible racket as I dragged it over the big, hard stones, I tensely turned into the narrow street.

Running toward me was Henry, red-faced and upset.

Wonderful!

I admit I was glad to see him looking anxious. It served him right after taking off the way he had. But how had he managed to get here first?

According to him, he had told me at Piazzale Roma that he was going to walk to the station and would meet me there. He had waited but, finally, he'd given up and taken the boat. It must have been the one just before mine.

At first he didn't believe that I had not heard him, or that I had been waiting for him at Piazzale Roma. But each of us had to agree that we'd given the other the only plausible explanation for the mix-up.

Relieved to be reunited we headed inland together.

On the left side of the calle was an unbroken row of small houses. On our right, once we passed the back of Algiubagiò, there was a low building, a stonecutting workshop. So much marble dust stuck to its windows that we could only just make out the men working inside. They were wearing folded newspaper hats—the kind you see in old Italian movies.

We were following the perimeter wall that encloses the palace's garden. The mason's yard was built into the wall; so was Algiubagiò.

We turned right at the first opportunity. The words "ramo Donà" were barely legible on the wall of one of the houses opposite. This alley was short and a dead end. If we had kept walking, we would have found ourselves in the Gesuiti Canal. To the left were more small houses. On the right was a high brick wall. Then we came to the garden gate, the entrance we were looking for.

Straight ahead was a path covered by a leafy pergola. It led to a pair of gigantic, dark green wooden doors. They were open and lay flat against the pink walls of the palace. Just inside them was a flimsier door made of wood-framed glass panels. It was shut. The gate was locked.

On the right of the gate was a large rectangle of brass in which were three tiers of three push-button bells. A round brass arc on which names were engraved was below each one. We pressed "G. Donà."

A buzzer sounded. Success. But not so fast. . . . Though we gave the gate a shove, it didn't open. So we rang the bell again. Again came the buzz and again the metal gate didn't move. It was obvious we couldn't get in. Why didn't somebody come and open the door?

We stood in the calle, bags on every side. We were hot and tired. It seemed an awfully long time before a woman appeared in the doorway. She was in her twenties, slim but sturdy, dressed in close-fitting short cardigan and sarong skirt. Her eyes were blue gray fringed with dark lashes, her long, dark blond hair was pulled straight back into a coil at the top of her head. She looked both fashionable and artless. Gaia had a clear, open face. She wore no makeup and didn't need any. I wouldn't call her pretty, but she could light up with beauty, though that was not obvious at first. As she approached us, her face was tight with annoyance.

However, when she said "Hello, welcome to Ca' Donà," her voice sounded genuinely warm.

Gaia came through into the calle. She shut the gate behind her. With endearing concern she wanted to understand why we'd had such trouble trying to open it.

"Ah," she said after we had shown her what we'd done. "First you must pull the gate toward you, then you give it a push."

Smiling now, she shut the gate behind us and to the echo of its clang we followed her toward the house.

BEFORE GOING FURTHER, let me say something about Venetian nobles and names.

During the millennium-long history of the Most Serene Republic, only one person in Venice was titled. He was its duke, duce or doge. But there was a class of nobles numbering in the thousands. The name of each of these patrician men was preceded by the words Nobile Homo or the initials N.H. while each of the women was a Nobile Donna, N.D. Similarly, just as only one square in Venice was called a piazza, only one grand residence was called a palace: the Palazzo Ducale, where the doge had apartments and the government met. Every other dwelling was a casa, a house, ca' for short.

When the Austrians occupied Venice not long after the conquest of the Republic at the end of the eighteenth century, they offered nobles the title of count or countess. Presumably this linguistic aggrandizement was supposed to make them feel better about losing their liberty and worldly power, a glitzy booby prize you could call it. Counts and countesses duly sprung up all over town but there were exceptions. Even today among the Venetian nobility there are those who prefer to have only N.D. or N.H. attached to their family names. The same sort of thing happened with houses.

Without changing his address, a newly created count now called his home a palace. Yet here, too, there were holdouts. Ca' d'Oro, for instance, and Ca' Rezzonico where Robert Browning lived. There's tiny, pretty Ca' Dario with its many colored marble insets both much admired and said to be cursed. These buildings, all on the Grand Canal, are the best-known examples of the impressive buildings that do not style themselves palaces. The Donà, too, have kept the old tradition. Gaia called her home Ca' Donà and almost immediately I did too.

THE VINE ON THE PERGOLA that ran from the garden gate to the door of Ca' Donà was intended to shade the path below but it was too scrawny to do the job. And to judge from what I saw as I looked to my right, straggly seemed to be the horticultural style throughout. Beyond the wire mesh that topped a low brick wall, I saw anorexic roses and floppy hibiscus bushes. The grass was as wispy as a thirteen-year-old boy's beard. In the distance, I saw some large white hunks of stone—a helter-skelter pile of marble. There was something about them that made me think they might be antique Roman capitals. The garden, which managed to seem both grand and derelict, was el-shaped and the larger part of it was around the corner of the house, out of sight.

On the left side of the path, also beyond a low brick wall, was a good-sized rectangular area ending at the Canal dei Gesuiti. It was filled with water. This was Ca' Donà's boat garage. There was a low fence of metal stakes closed by a heavy chain and padlock between it and the canal; it was, in effect, the garage door. Two motorboats were bobbing up and down inside. Later I learned this shelter is called a *cavana* and later still, that the boats belonged to Gaia's brother and her boyfriend.

Such off-street parking is as much a luxury in Venice today as it would be in New York. In Venice the problem isn't that there are so many more boats than there used to be, but that land is scarce and therefore valuable. Most of the water garages were long ago filled in.

I don't know if boat insurance is cheaper if you have a cavana, but it should be. Venice during the long years of the Serenissima was known not only for its power and its splendor but also for its safeness. And Venice is still a safe city. Motorboats, however, seem to be the exception. If an owner parks overnight in a canal or rio, he is liable to need oars by morning. Or so I was later told.

As we approached the house, I saw that the glass-paned door was in fact the wall of a small lobby which had been built just inside the entrance. To its right was a storage area that was plain, serviceable and without any pretensions. There wasn't a hint of carpeted half-moons topped with philodendrons here, though there was a motley assembly of boots, umbrellas, baby carriages and shopping carts visible through the glass.

The lobby was intended to keep out wind and rain when the magnificent heavy doors were open. But wind and rain were only words on this hot June day. One of the many lovely things about summer in Venice is that you feel certain winter will never come.

"Chiuda la porta piano, per piacere" was printed on a sign taped to one of the panes of the little lobby's door which was on our left. And, light in weight though it was, if it wasn't closed "softly," the door banged with a crack like a gunshot.

Now, at last, we were inside Ca' Donà. But in the abrupt shift from bright light to almost none, we couldn't see it. I could feel it, however. Whatever else this room might be, it certainly was cold.

THE GROUND-FLOOR HALL of a palace in Venice is called the *androne*. As palaces go, Ca' Donà is large and its androne was gigantic. Hugely long and wide, it was, I would guess, something like twenty-five feet high. As my eyes adjusted to the darkness, I saw that I was standing on a chessboard; one vast enough for a game using life-sized kings and queens and knights. Alternating squares of rich brown and creamy marble covered the entire floor, which stretched from where we were standing all the way to the door that never opened onto the Fondamenta Nuove.

I saw lots of doors, in fact, and all of them were closed. A single naked bulb halfway down the room gave out a smudged yellow light. If it was 40 watts, it was a lot.

In the murky distance I began to make out large, dark shapes. As we walked deeper into the room I saw what these were. They were boats. Gondolas!

There were six, or was it seven? For all I know there were eight, maybe a dozen. Here. In this room where I was standing, in this house where I was going to live.

The boats were sleek and black, beautiful and old. And the androne was so big, it didn't even look crowded.

As I pulled my heavy suitcase across the marble chessboard, lugging my computer and pocketbook in my other hand, I passed through the smoky light as if I was sleepwalking. Cocteau, if he'd been born Venetian, might have come up with a setting like this. Only the androne was more incredible, more romantic and packed more of a wallop because it was not a movie set. It was real.

And there was more.

Now I took in the source of what little light there was. The pathetically inadequate naked bulb hung at the end of a long cord inside a transparent glass lantern, a lantern big enough to help a giant find his way home through the forest at midnight. Holding the lantern out from the wall was a bracket made from a thick piece of strong wood. It was carved in the shape of a human arm, a giant's arm. The bottom of the lantern rested in the curled fingers of his hand.

It was not the only such lantern. As we moved farther into the androne I saw that there were three others. Each was colossal and each was attached to the wall by a more or less identical wooden arm. All contained a dangling light bulb but none of the others was lit.

I must have looked as amazed as I felt because Gaia stopped and began to explain what we were seeing.

"They are ships' lanterns," she told us. "They were tied high on the masts to light the way in the dark. This one," she said, pointing to the first one I'd seen, the one actually lit up, "was on our ship at the Battle of Lepanto. I'm not sure about the others. You'll have to ask my father."

Now that we were standing still, I had some time to look around. I saw that the ceiling over the first third or so of the androne was half the height of the rest. An apartment had been created up above the entrance to the hall. It was one of the mezzanines that Davis had mentioned in his book. Its interior wall was a double curve into which two windows had been cut. Between these windows, which neither gave out nor let in daylight, hung an old, crimson flag.

"That banner flew at Lepanto," Gaia said as we all stared up at the relic.

Like the lantern, it had to be more than four hundred years old. Lepanto, one of the most famous battles in Venetian history, was fought in 1571. There the Serenissima, together with the French, succeeded in defeating the Turks.

We were standing in the center of the androne. The glassed-in lobby was behind us. The door to the Fondamenta Nuove was straight ahead. On our left, the floor sloped down between two of the gondolas until it reached a thick, wide wooden door, the watergate. Once this had been the principal entrance to Ca' Donà. When opened, boats inside the androne could slide down the ramp straight into the Canal dei Gesuiti.

Directly opposite the watergate was the only visible staircase. It was wide and made of stone. We could see daylight at the top as we followed Gaia who had started climbing.

At the first landing there was a wall of floor-to-ceiling windows. Looking out we could see the part of Ca' Donà's garden that had been hidden from sight before. The back of the stonemason's workshop was visible between the ancient trees and, to the left, we could see the rear of Algiubagiò. Over the roof of the caffè was the lagoon crowded with boats.

There were doors on the left and right of the landing but Gaia ignored them and, turning, headed up the next flight of stairs.

Straight ahead was a row of paneled, wooden doors perhaps twenty feet high. When we reached the landing, I saw that they had been decorated in the graceful, lyrical style of the eighteenth century. Against a gray background, fantastical animals and swooping garlands were painted in a steely blue.

Pretty good.

"My father lives here," said Gaia. "But he is in Milan most of the time."

The doors, which stretched the width of the landing, were the entrance to the piano nobile. Behind them was Ca' Donà's grandest apartment. And its biggest. It covered the entire floor of this gigantic building.

When James Davis was writing his book, Ca' Donà belonged to Gaia's grandfather. He and his wife had lived in the piano nobile. But Conte Lorenzo Donà dalle Rose and his wife had since died and Ca' Donà now belonged to Gaia's father, Conte Nicolò. The piano nobile was his apartment—when he came to Venice.

Fancy having the entire floor of a vast Venetian palace as a pied-à-terre.

A brown wooden bench was on the wall to the left. It had a narrow seat with a high, scalloped back. On it was painted a family crest. There were three red roses on a diagonal of gold, and it took no effort to conclude that this was the Donà coat of arms.

Maybe the bench was intended for people who were waiting to see il conte. Maybe it was there to give climbers a rest. Already I felt I needed one and there were still more stone steps ahead.

It was only fitting, of course, that the piano nobile should have higher ceilings than the mystery apartments below. But that meant we had to climb two long flights before we came to the next floor. I was finding it hard going, but I realized I'd better get used to it. Clearly we were going to be living at the top of this house. Gaia mentioned that she herself lived upstairs and I now understood why she had been slow to come down when we had trouble with the gate.

Even without knowing how many stairs there were between me and our destination, I had decided to leave my big, heavy suitcase in the androne. But that didn't keep me from huffing and puffing. Henry, far fitter than I am, had his suitcase and his computer with him and was keeping pace with Gaia. I crept along behind. Because I was advancing so slowly, I had time to notice the handrails. Like practically everything else in this house, they were fantastical.

Admittedly, the part of the rail I held on to was nothing special. A tube of brass ran the length of the staircase more or less at elbow level. However, the rail was held in place by a series of human hands. These were not the hefty paws of a giant but the narrow, elegant hands of a long-fingered woman—delicate but, being made of brass, also strong.

Every eighteen inches or so, one of the exquisite mitts curled around the hollow rail, its truncated slim wrists screwed firmly to the wall.

We were at the top floor. Even Gaia and Henry welcomed the respite, though I was the only one to show it.

The landing at which we'd arrived was small. On either side were metal doors painted an institutional maroon. Fire retarders, I assumed. Straight ahead was a set of double doors of the same material and color. In each of them there was a small round window at eye level. It was the sort of thing you might find in a hotel dining room. Those doors that allow the chef to peep out without being seen by the guests.

I sidled up to have a look.

DRIFTING
AND
DREAMING

7

Coming Up Roses

Through the portholes I saw a hall that was about twenty-five feet square. There was a door in each of its far corners and another in the middle of the wall on the left. To the right was an extraordinary object, an enormous, finely made cutaway wooden villa. I reckoned it was about five feet tall and somewhat longer, but shallow; maybe only a foot and a half deep.

Was this the kind of doll's house they have in palaces? Or was it an architectural model of their country house? I never found out. However, not every mystery about Ca' Donà was equally impenetrable.

"Giovanni and I are restoring that apartment," said Gaia indicating the door in the right corner. It alone was open wide. "We've been working on it for a year. It will be finished soon."

Until it was ready, she and her boyfriend were living with her brother.

"Francesco's apartment is over there," she reported, nodding toward the door opposite the doll's house.

There was no Francesco on the family tree I'd seen in James Davis's book. Francesco, the baby of the family, was now a student at the University of Venice, his sister said.

The three of us standing out on the landing had recovered from our alpine expedition by now and Gaia began fiddling with a key, trying to unlock the door to our left.

She pulled it toward her. Inside a second set of doors stood open. They were a smaller version of the ones we'd seen at the entrance to the piano nobile. Here the gray wood panels were charmingly painted with blue flowers, garlands and mythical creatures.

"Remember," Gaia warned as we followed her inside, "you must never close them. They lock automatically, and we don't have the keys anymore. We would have to break them down."

I noticed that a wooden wedge kept the rare painted panels ajar. It's the sort of thing you're quick to observe if you are a worrier who was born clumsy.

We found ourselves in the foyer. Immediately on the left was a staircase. Holding up the banister were posts cut from wide flat pieces of wood, stained the same dark brown as the stairs. Ducking my head, I peered upstairs and saw several small deer heads propped on a low chest of drawers. Above them was a ceiling of wooden beams. All that was missing was a cuckoo clock. The place looked like a miniature Swiss hunting lodge. Surely this couldn't have been what Vivian meant when she said the apartment was "very Venetian."

Gaia made no move to go upstairs. The chalet was obviously not what we'd rented.

The foyer was oblong, narrow and windowless. A bit of light leaked down from the attic. There was a gilded console table along the wall opposite and above it was a tall gilded mirror. A small sailboat rested on the marble tabletop. The wall to which the table was attached prevented it from capsizing.

To our right, and partly blocked by the never-to-be-closed wooden doors, was an amazing item: a banner that must have been eight feet wide by ten or twelve feet tall. The cloth was red and much of its surface was embroidered with stiff gold thread, long ago gone dull. The banner, which was obviously incredibly heavy, hung from thick loops threaded through a fat, red velvet–covered pole.

What was it? When had it been used, or where? Gaia didn't know.

"When my father shows you around the piano nobile, you must ask him," she said.

Imagine, one day we were going to be taken around this house by its owner.

All of this was exciting, delightful, curious and interesting, but for now at least I'd had enough. I wanted to get on with it; to see where we were going to live.

Another set of gray-paneled, blue-painted eighteenth-century doors faced us. Gaia opened them and led us into a room that was as charming as it was grand and as grand as it was large. Whoever lived here had a terrific sense of style. It was richly extravagant, even ornate, yet it was also homey.

Gaia stopped. The three of us stood in this marvelous room. We seemed to be waiting.

Nothing happened. We weren't moving. I got restless. Then irritated. Wonderful as this place was, I'd come a long way and what I wanted more than anything was to see the apartment I'd rented.

What in the world was she waiting for?

Then I got it.

We were not on the way to our apartment. We were in it.

Everything—from the monumental red and golden banner in the entrance and the hunting lodge upstairs, to this sumptuous yet sympathetic room—all of it was ours.

And there was more. Oh there was much more.

IN ITALIAN, *salotto* means living room (or drawing room, if you are so inclined). *Salone* describes a space used for holding receptions. While size did contribute to the impact of the salone, bigness wasn't its main attraction.

I'd been in ex–printing plants and fabric warehouses, now turned into living lofts. One friend of mine lived in what had once been an apartment house ballroom, recently turned into apartments. These places may have been as large as the salone but none of them came close to having its poetry. How could they? Here the fanciful blue-painted doors were, in their picturesque way, only a visual hors d'oeuvre.

Two hundred years before, a master craftsman had been at work in this room. Clearly he had been a man with a light touch and an inclination to make inert materials dance. With plain plaster of Paris he had created elegant, even enchanting, decorations. The Italian for plaster is *stucco;* its plural, of which here there was much evidence, is *stucchi.* There was so much of it in fact that the family distinguished this apartment from others in the house by calling it "the stucchi."

The enormous salone was wider than it was long. But the expanse of straight white walls and their right-angle corners was merely the simple setting for a lyrical display of delicately executed curves and swirls.

A series of panels within panels, all framed by thick lines of plaster with curling feathers at each corner, enlivened the walls. The gap between each set of borders was painted a dusty yellow. The center of the inner borders dipped down and at the lowest point of the curve a white plaster bow had been placed. A wall light of clear, Murano glass was placed on the knot of these bows as if it hung from them rather than from nails. This created the illusion that the weight of the lights, rather than the plasterer's craft, pulled the borders toward the floor.

The lights were handblown in the eighteenth century. Each had three branches which, like so many languid tulips, first lifted and then dropped and then lifted again. Now electrified, every branch was topped by a white cylinder pretending to be a candle. Small pleated yellow silk shades hid the bulbs.

Floor-to-ceiling, heavy, pale blue drapes, held back by stiff-fringed swaths of the same silk, hung from the two big windows in the wall to our left. Between them was the fireplace.

"No," Gaia told me. "It cannot be used. It's been blocked up." Open fires, if not outlawed in densely packed Venice, were much discouraged, she explained. Well, this was June; I wasn't too concerned.

The mottled-brown marble fireplace came forward into the room on two convex wings. The broad chimney above it held the most ambitious plasterwork in the salone. It was the width of the mantel at its base, narrowing slightly but decidedly as it reached the ceiling.

Here, too, were embellished plaster borders within borders. Again the space between was painted yellow, though this time the borders were fashioned to seem like folds of thick, stiff ribbon. At the top, the two borders were joined by a wide and floppy white stucco bow. These elaborate decorations framed a flat central panel painted a faded pistachio on which the maestro had carried out his best performance. For here perched a large and handsome, if also aloof, fat white bird. How satisfied with himself this plump king of his castle seemed as he craned his plaster head over his shoulder.

To the left of the salone's entrance were a pair of gilded console tables with scalloped pink marble tops. Eight mahogany dining chairs, their tall backs carved with curving interlocking loops, were placed around the long, dark wood dining table more or less in the center of the room. Between the "dining room" and all that was to its right, there was a vast open space covered by an old, faded Turkish carpet. Several other dining chairs were grouped in twos against the right-hand wall and between them was a simple low bed. It was covered with a pale green, antique silk cloth on the top of which were tossed four large pillows covered in shades of palest peach or violet.

There was a long sofa facing the fireplace and a pair of plushy club chairs perpendicular to it. I was amused by this elegant echo of the "conversation groups" popular in my childhood. And I was appreciative, too, because these pieces of furniture were upholstered in thick, bottle green velvet and finished at the bottom with a good six inches of silk fringe. Across from the chairs was a chaise longue covered in red silk damask, its wood frame carved with flowers. This was just the thing to recline on while eating violet-scented bonbons or, and far more likely, for watching the TV, at which it was pointing.

Bunches of pink silk roses were stuffed into the blue-and-white Chinese vases on the console tables. Big cushions covered in a yellow fabric strewn with bright red roses were plumped up against the back of the chaise. With a light touch, these were reminders that the Donà of the roses lived here. Or did.

Gaia noticed me devouring it all and started talking about the apartment's recent history.

"My parents used to live in the stucchi, when my grandparents lived downstairs," she said. "But my father left my mother when the four of us were little," she went on. "My mother stayed on for another year but after that she took us with her back to Paris."

I can't recall if Gaia only implied it or said so directly, but it became clear that there was another woman to whom her father was now married.

"I don't speak to her," Gaia said. "When she comes to Ca' Donà, I go away."

So sweet Gaia could be Gaia the unforgiving. I would not like to be on the wrong side of her.

All of this was really too much to absorb. The family story, the look of the place. But I was trying.

The finest piece of furniture in the room stood between the console tables. It was an eighteenth-century fruitwood secretary. It must be Venetian, I thought. There was none of the crispness or the austerity one might find in English or American furniture of the same period. This secretary was curvaceous, a word that may belong more to a 1940s description of a buxom blonde but in fact suits this secretary even better. This secretary undulated. Its top held a silvery mirror set in a curved frame that was, in fact, a door. Inside were many discreet small compartments and below were drawers. The secretary flared out at the hips, so to speak, and then narrowed at the ankles as if it were wearing a gathered, hobbled skirt.

With all this, the salone was not what the English call "over the top." It was so big that there were plenty of unoccupied places for the eye to rest. Indeed, the long wall opposite the foyer was filled, right to left, by floor-to-ceiling, straight-fronted, built-in closets. They dated from the 1950s, Gaia said. Opening one, she showed us the shelves for linens, china and blankets. And the area between the dining table and the daybed was so large and bare that I came to think of it as the Empty Quarter.

The wall of closets didn't go all the way across the salone. At its center there was an open arch which you had to climb into in order to pass through. The step, like the walls of the arch, was almost two feet deep.

The arch was bracketed by two fellows cut from flat pieces of wood. Nearly life size, these jaunty young men were mirror images of each other. They looked as if they were guarding the entrance, yet at the same time they seemed to be saying, "Can we help you? Do come through." Both figures had one hand upheld, palm opened, on which rested a fluted silver tray with a spike at its center. This was to secure the candles that would light our way.

We thought of them as boys because they were so clearly youthful. They belonged to the period of the stucco master; when Venice was still the Most Serene Republic and the life of the town was feverish with fêtes and parties. Each of them wore a painted costume of knee-length breeches, white hose and a billowing shirt. Each had a knotted bandanna around his head. As servants to the rich in eighteenth-century Venice sometimes were, these chaps were blackamoors.

If Vivian, when she'd phoned me in London, had said that the apartment was theatrical, I might have balked. Theatrical was not my sort of thing. Yet here I was in this place so very like an eighteenth-century stage set, relishing every flamboyant morsel of it.

The salone was created as the backdrop for someone else's play, no question about it. And someone whose life was unrecognizably different from my own. Yet I felt not only dazzled and charmed; most surprisingly, I felt at home.

There was nothing I hankered to hide away in the salone's closets. I didn't yearn to move the furniture around. The evidence of wear and tear was fine with me, too; the faded fabrics, the strips of paint that curled down from the yellow-painted ceiling beams.

The sofa and the easy chairs were squishy; the standing lamps at each end were there to give out light for reading. The oriental rugs, though large, were neither ancient nor rare. The round tables next to the couch were covered with lovely faded cloths that fell to the ground. When I nosily looked under those skirts I saw that they did not have pretty legs.

The floor was mottled brown, "pastellon." Gaia explained this was an old Venetian technique, the recipe for which calls for many applications of pulverized marble, terra-cotta, linseed oil, muscle and patience. She and Giovanni were going to build up a floor of this kind in their new apartment. I saw that in places there were chunks missing from this one. After a couple of hundred years, pastellon becomes brittle, she said.

The salone, although grand, was not overwhelmingly so, as I suspected I might find the state rooms of a piano nobile. In fact I was sure the formality of a piano nobile would make me twitchy, as if demands on me were being made that I couldn't and wouldn't want to meet. It was glamour on a human scale that I found in the stucchi. I loved it.

But there was more to this apartment than its foyer, its attic, and the salone. Much more.

Just as Gaia was about to climb the step-into arch, she waved her arm toward a door cut in the wall to our right.

"Francesco's apartment is through there," she told us. "I will get you the key and you can keep the stucchi locked from your side." When her parents had lived here, I wondered, were both apartments one?

The wide step onto which we now climbed, Gaia said, had been built to box in pipes. The deep walls of the arch were covered with blue-on-blue, old Fortuny silk. A set of double doors could be closed to shut off the salone. They were painted gray and within their gilded panels, figures of men and women in rustic eighteenth-century dress were outlined in blue.

We stepped down into the study.

THIS ROOM WAS PROBABLY little more than half the width and a third the depth of the salone. But it was not minuscule. And while more modest in its decoration, it couldn't be called plain.

On top of the pastellon floor was an embroidered Aubusson rug. The pale green carpet was six-by-eight feet, or thereabouts. It was strewn with a pattern of roses and rosebuds, framed by a wide border of pink cabbage roses, flat petaled white daisies and yellow morning glories, set off by blue foliage. And tied around the whole of it was an embroidered ribbon border of blue with a gold outline. The wall immediately to the left of the arch was filled by a tall bookcase. Its curving glass doors had leaded panes. From what I could make out, it was packed with books on art, architecture and gardens.

A mellow, fruitwood kneehole desk was placed on a diagonal in the far left corner of the study. Beyond it was the room's only window. It was framed by long, blue silk drapes identical to the ones in the salone. On the wall to the right of the arch stood a walnut chest of drawers above which was a gilt mirror with a curlicue frame. On either side of it were wall lights from which china flowers hung.

Across from the bookcase were twin beds covered with silk-fringed spreads made from yet another old Venetian fabric. These had a blue-on-blue design featuring Neptune and the creatures of the sea. The white headboards were plain or so I thought until I looked closer and realized they were leather.

But the ceiling was the star of this room. Its entire white expanse had stucco decoration. Ribbons and roses danced around its edges making a rapturous frame for the butterflies, birds and insects that flitted about on the interior. Every bit of plasterwork was painted. The ribbons and roses were the color of blackberry juice, while the butterflies and birds were shades of yellow, orange and blue. Just below the ceiling, stucco foliage interspersed with roses trailed up and around the cornices. Again the roses were purply red, the foliage a deep dark green.

In the center of the ceiling was a Murano glass chandelier strung with chains of plump but delicate clear glass beads. Colorful carnations and daisies, their dense petals blown from opaque glass, peeped out near the top of the chandelier. Each flower stood alone on the end of a curving, clear glass stem.

Gaia was guiding us toward another set of double doors painted blue and gray, directly opposite the arch. The studio, as she called this room, could be completely closed off from the rest of the apartment should we wish.

By now I had a bewildered smile on my face. What could be coming next?

The bedroom, as it turned out.

I DID NOT BLURT OUT, "HOLY COW!" But we now stood in a room that was as wide from left to right as the salone, if not as deep. To me it seemed as long as a bowling alley.

Some bowling alley.

The master carver had been busy here too. Butterflies darted across the ceiling, while birds with outstretched wings chased tiny insects. The limits of this aerial world were marked by ribbons of chalky red. Not a bit of it seemed cloying. As in the study, the cornices were looped with dark green branches and leaves interspersed with roses.

The walls of the bedroom were covered in pale, creamy silk. A double bed, its headboard covered in a deeper and more lustrous yellow silk, stood out from the center of the relatively narrow wall on the right. Above it hung portraits on glass of bearded men, each of whom was a Donà according to the labels on the simple gilded frames. A painting of the Madonna was directly above the center of the bed. It was a good thing my mother wasn't planning to visit us in Venice, she would be appalled.

On the long walls hung a set of wooden shelflettes. There were three of these delightful items. Each consisted of two thin, scalloped shelves made of the lightest wood and held apart by a row of uprights carved in the shape of four elongated ladies. All of this had been gessoed and gilded. The result was graceful, amusing and useless. Even a spool of thread would have seemed burdensome if it rested on one of them. Their only purpose was to give pleasure, and they did.

A six-foot-long library table occupied the middle of the enormous room. It was covered, almost to the floor, with a toffee-colored cloth, woven with spots of blood red, sea blue and apple green. As in the other rooms, the pastellon in the bedroom was pinky brown. But here, in mimicry of a rug, it had a wide, curving border of dusty green with a thin line of burnt orange separating the two.

Directly opposite the arch hung a mirror, six or seven feet tall. Its ornate frame, curved of course, was gilded and held a glass worn with age. Looking in it, I could see all the way back through the apartment to the silvery mirror of the buxom secretary in the salone. It was quite a vista.

On either side of the mirror, though closer to the ends of the room than to it, were two tall windows. A third window was in the wall on the left. I walked to the window near the bed.

Down below was the garden; to the right, I could see the path leading to the gate we'd struggled to open not very long before. For Venice, we were high up. Looking straight ahead, an expansive Cubist collage opened out before me.

Terra-cotta tiles became part of larger patches of squares and rectangles which abutted one another or overlapped. Rooftop followed rooftop all the way to San Marco. I could see the top of the campanile in the distance, its gilded lion facing in our direction. To the right was the bright white dome of the Church of Santa Maria della Salute across the Grand Canal. And above it all shone the sun, lighting up the Venetian blue sky.

It was a magnificent sight. What's more, I would be able to see it from my bed.

The view from the other window in that wall was not so good. The leafy branches of a tree came up to the shutters and pigeons had made themselves at home. There were pigeon droppings all over the sill.

"We can't prune the tree without the city's permission," Gaia explained. It seems they had applied but had yet to get the go-ahead.

At the far end of the room, the view was better. It was a version of what I'd seen on the first landing: The garden with its antique marbles all in a heap, the back wall of the mason's workshop and, looking left over the top of Algiubagiò, there was the great expanse of the lagoon.

Every window on that side of the house overlooked the lagoon provided you first turned slightly to the left.

The bedroom furniture was lovely and varied. Near the lagoon window was a small corner cabinet, painted bluish white and decorated with delicate garlands in carmine. On the same wall was another fruit-wood secretary, not quite as shapely as the one in the salone, but finely made and also eighteenth century. Near it was a big freestanding closet (an *armadio*) from the mountains of Italy or Switzerland that was painted with primitive folkloric designs in faded yellow, rose and blue.

Leaning against a wall in the corner near the armadio—and almost completely hidden by its shadow—I discovered an embroidered painting about three feet by two. I carried it into the light. It was one hundred years old or more and showed a single figure: He was a larger-than-life-sized standard white poodle with a round black nose. Facing straight ahead, seated on a high-backed blue velvet–upholstered chair behind which were luscious crimson drapes, was the spitting image of Zephyr.

From the time Vivian had called me in London with news of an apartment for rent and I'd learned it was in the pink palace on the Fondamenta Nuove, I had felt that it was somehow meant that I should live there. Now, standing in the bedroom looking at this portrait of one of Zephyr's ancestors, I felt even more certain that Ca' Donà was intended to be my Venetian home.

If you felt the need to bring things down to earth, you might at this

moment point out that the stucchi was just a glorified railroad flat. The
layout of one room opening into the next had been popular in New
York tenements because, without such a luxury as a connecting corridor
(and the privacy it offers), builders could cram in more units. I knew the
design intimately; in my early twenties I'd lived in such an apartment
up five flights on, as it happens, Manhattan's St. Mark's Place.

It turned out, however, that the stucchi only appeared to be a railroad
flat. I was about to discover its plan was more like an elongated horse-
shoe.

A set of double doors—wide and arched and cream-colored—was
near the bed on the inside wall. The top half was fitted with opalescent
material, shell most probably, which was crisscrossed by mock-Tudor
leading. The overall effect was like something out of a Noël Coward
play.

Gaia opened the doors. We followed her in. For the first time in my
life the sight of a bathroom made me burst out laughing.

THE WALLS WERE COVERED in pale grass cloth. The tub had been placed
longways against the wall to our left. Placed? It had been enthroned.

The bathtub sat inside a casing of mahogany. Two rectangular wicker
panels were set in its front. And the whole shebang was elevated. In
order to take a bath, you first had to climb up two shallow mahogany
steps, like a platform. They were even longer than the tub.

A scalloped arc of beaten brass, from which emerged the brass taps
and shower hose, served as the backsplash. There was a vast, square
gilt-framed mirror on the wall opposite.

The sink, set into a thick wooden top, had mirrored tiles on the wall
behind it and wore a floor-length skirt of tiered, somewhat exhausted,
ruffled tulle, as if it were a semi-retired ballerina.

"The sink can't be used," Gaia explained apologetically. "One of our
cousins was staying here just before you came. She dropped a ring and
couldn't open the trap. So she broke the pipe and didn't tell anybody.
But don't worry," Gaia sped on. "I've called the plumber. He'll fix it
tomorrow."

Although there was not a single window in the room, it was rich in doors. Besides Noël Coward's double ones, there were doors on both the right and the left of the big mirror. These opened into the study. To the right of the sink was a door which stood open. At its base was a deep wooden step, the continuation of the one between the salone and study.

Climbing up, we saw on our left a door to a little room with a toilet, bidet and another tutu-wearing sink. The landing created by the step was a miniature dressing room with a closet on either side. I opened one: It was outfitted with built-in, narrow drawers all beautifully crafted of dark wood. There were brass fittings for at least fifty neckties.

Walking on, Gaia opened yet another door and we stepped back down into the salone.

THE LAYOUT OF THE STUCCHI was perfect for a French farce complete with suspicious husbands, perspiring lovers, tittering mistresses all nipping in and out of its many doors and hiding in the closets. But it was a clever layout for other purposes as well.

You could walk from the salone or the studio or the bedroom directly to the bathroom without passing through any of the other principal rooms. And you could walk from the salone to the bedroom without going through the study, which offered some privacy to a guest—unless he or she was already in the bath with a glass of bubbly Prosecco.

COMING FROM THE DIRECTION OF THE STUDY, the kitchen was in the far-right-hand corner of the salone.

"My grandmother collected these," Gaia told us, waving toward the thick, white-glazed earthenware objects hanging on the walls. There were molds, tureen lids and plates. Along with the wooden countertops, cupboard doors and dresser, they gave a country kitchen feeling to the L-shaped room, its length running off to our left.

Facing us was a pine dresser with a marble worktop. Immediately on our right was a drop-down pine table and a pair of sturdy chairs set between the room's two square windows. To the left, along the far wall of the widest part of the kitchen were cabinets and the sink. Opposite them were the stove and refrigerator.

An arc of beaten brass, identical to the splashboard of the bath, was behind the sink. Here too, the spigots were big and fat and brassy. There was nothing else out of the ordinary in the room unless you count the "collectibles," otherwise known as the appliances.

There were two small, tinny stoves bundled together. The refrigerator beyond was tall and narrow with rounded-off corners. Once white, its enamel had turned a yellow which I am sorry to say reminded me of false teeth. It might have seemed a luxury item in an American apartment—circa 1950.

What was sensational about the kitchen was its view. The windows looked straight out onto the lagoon. Down below was the Fondamenta Nuove; to the right its vaporetto stop. Out over the water was the island of San Michele and beyond it, Murano.

Gaia walked left through the kitchen and opened a door. The big red and dull gold banner was facing us. We were in the foyer. The tour was almost over. All that remained was a visit to the heating apparatus.

UNDER THE STAIRS leading to the hunting lodge, behind a low wooden door was the dwelling place of the stucchi's hot water heater. Gaia pointed out its various dials. The setup looked simple; there wasn't even a timer. But it seemed this *caldaia* had to be watched over and fiddled with.

We were instructed that "the water temperature must never be allowed to get too high. The pipes are very old," she said. And made of lead. At least the heater itself looked almost brand new.

Gaia was about to leave. "The stucchi has been empty for five years," she told us. "I am glad you have come. It should be lived in."

Then she turned back toward the kitchen and motioned to the top of the marble counter. She had thoughtfully left supplies of coffee and butter, jam and rolls and a packet of spaghetti to get us started.

"Call me if there is any problem," Gaia said as she closed the metal door behind her.

8

Getting Connected

Alone in the stucchi, we roamed around opening windows letting in the warm summer air. Now, standing in the kitchen, I could hear the vaporettos grind their engines as they docked or pulled away. The rest of the apartment was so quiet we could have been in the country—although no country village would have so many different church bells banging away when they decided it was time to call the faithful.

We unpacked our clothes, with the surprises that invariably brings. This time I discovered I'd been unable to leave London without five pairs of shoes. But at least there was far more room for our things than we needed. In the bedroom alone there were two closets and two enormous matching chests of drawers—his and hers.

Since one of us did not want to eat out on our first night back in Venice, we walked to Standa, the small department store cum supermarket on the Strada Nova. The fresh food was never particularly attractive, but at least we knew where it was and that it would be open when we got there.

"I have been between heaven and earth since our arrival at Venice. . . . Never had I touched the skirts of so celestial a place . . . ," Elizabeth Barrett Browning wrote on her first visit to the city. I felt very much the same until I tried to use the stucchi's kitchen.

The stove had six burners only four of which worked. Each flame sent out a different degree of heat ranging from very hot (the better to get water boiling for spaghetti) to barely warm, for making French sauces, I suppose. This was not immediately apparent, of course. Instead I either burned what I was cooking or wondered why it was not getting done. (And I never could remember which burner did what.)

As I attempted to transform the food we'd bought into a meal, the refrigerator alongside the stove provided a quasi-musical accompaniment. The yellowed beast shuddered and banged so loudly, it rivaled the noise made by the vaporetto below.

No wonder the refrigerator trembled so noisily, it only had one speed, full tilt. Its only temperature was very cold. When I took out the salad greens I'd stowed there less than an hour before, they were glazed with ice. When they'd melted, their pertness had gone too. The freezing compartment, at best large enough for a single tub of ice cream, couldn't hold anything because it was packed with fuzz crystals. (Defrosting turned out to be a remarkably short-term solution.)

The cooked part of our first night's meal was a combination of burnt bits and mush. But at least the arugula, radicchio and tomato salad I'd made, if a bit on the limp side, was tasty.

We ate in the salone, seated at opposite ends of the long walnut dining table with what seemed like all the space in the world between and around us. Gilded furniture, velvets and silk embellished the periphery. On the table, inside their glass hurricane lamps, candle flames shimmied. But not only right in front of us, they pirouetted across to the secretary mirror. Multiplying as they danced, I could see them in the tall gilded glass of the bedroom, too.

I turned to look out the windows. It was dark, so I couldn't make out the lagoon but I could easily see a string of lights on one of the distant islands.

The two of us sat silently. We were too amazed and too tired to talk.

We had arrived in Venice, in this city I loved, and found ourselves in an apartment that matched dreams I didn't know I had.

Exhausted by the journey, the shopping, the misadventures in cooking, the unimagined glamour of the stucchi, as well as the long climb up, I fell onto the bed at 9:30. The mattress was lumpy—it too was an antique—but I was so exhausted it didn't matter.

* * *

SITTING UP IN BED our first morning at Ca' Donà, I looked to my right and saw the rooftops of Venice. Then, when I turned left, I realized that the geometry of the layout was such that if I looked through the open door into the study, I could easily see the lagoon through its window. I was in no hurry to get up. However . . .

I went into the kitchen and, since there was no toaster, I struck a match and went to light the oven. It didn't work. I tried the other one. With a ferocious whoosh it lit. But neither stove had a broiler. We would eat twice-baked bread. Henry now took over and handled the negotiations with the battery of burners. When the coffee was ready and the bread warm, we raised the pine table that hung from the wall between the kitchen windows and sat down to eat.

Both of us kept shifting our chairs because we wanted to see the lagoon. Whoever had planned this kitchen had placed the table so that it was impossible both to eat at it and see outside. This seemed preposterous, even wanton. But it confirmed a theory I'd been embroidering for a while—that Venetians are indifferent to views.

I do not mean Venetians don't care about the look of things. The whole of their city proves that the men of the Serenissima most certainly did. You need only approach the piazzetta in a boat to realize how impressed sailors and merchants must have been five hundred years ago when they first saw the Palazzo Ducale and San Marco beyond. The façades of the great houses were also created for effect. It's the view from the inside out that I am talking about.

The palaces of Venice are so tightly squashed together that many of them are dark and look onto calles so narrow you can't walk through them with an opened umbrella. As for the villas Palladio and other architects built for Venetians on their mainland farms, with a few exceptions, most of them seem to have been sited so that the nobles would have the shortest possible walk from their boats to their front doors, rather than to provide sweeping views from their windows. Vistas seem to have counted as little for them as they did for whoever set up the stucchi's kitchen.

We wanted to see outside.

With chairs pulled up to the window and coffee cups at arm's length, we were able to look out to the island of San Michele. On the right was a long thin strip of wooded land (Vignole, it turned out, though we didn't yet know its name). And there were other islands, too. Here the lagoon was busy with all sorts of rowboats as well as water taxis, vaporettos, barges filled with crates of vegetables or lengths of timber or piled high with furniture, Venetian moving vans.

"Let's try to find a small table we can put in front of the window," I said to Henry. He agreed. "I'll ask Gaia if she has one."

After breakfast I phoned Vivian, to thank her again for finding this apartment. I invited her round for a drink and said that afterward we'd like to take her to dinner.

She was of course pleased that I liked the stucchi so much and then she settled down to fill me in on the family in whose house we now lived. Much of what she passed on she'd learned from Gaia when she'd come to look over the apartment.

I already knew from the family tree that the first child of Nicolò Donà was Chiara, born in 1966. A boy, Giovanni, came along four years later. Then a year afterward there was Gaia. Only the day before we'd heard about the existence of the youngest, Francesco.

Vivian said that Giovanni had been groomed to inherit the position and responsibilities that would come with owning Ca' Donà. The pressures were considerable since it was now probably the only remaining palace in Venice continuously occupied by the family for whom it was built.

Why was Giovanni going to be the heir? I wondered. During the long life of the Serenissima, one son usually was chosen to inherit the family wealth. But in Italy now, an estate must pass to all offspring in equal shares.

I didn't question Vivian about this. It wasn't the time or place for further studies in the ways of Venetian inheritance. And anyway I now found out that, very sadly, indeed tragically, this was a moot point.

At the age of eighteen, Giovanni Donà had been killed in a diving accident while on vacation in Tunisia with his father. The catastrophic loss affected all the family, of course, and suddenly Francesco, a boy just entering his teens, was expected to take over as future heir of Ca' Donà.

Grand as the house is, and much as I was taken with it, I felt sorry for Francesco.

Vivian and I fixed a date for her to come over for Prosecco.

Now it was time for me to get to work, that is, to set up my computer, check my e-mail and stare into space while images of Leonardo da Vinci's inventions traveled across my computer screen.

So many people I knew said they envied me because I was going to live and work in Venice. I felt the same. I hadn't imagined I could be so lucky.

One thing that made it possible was that, in theory, I am able to work anywhere I can plug in my computer. I now unpacked it, along with the fiddly pieces of equipment I'd bought to make it usable in Italy. Next, I set out to look for an electrical outlet and a telephone jack for my modem. I required one of each, in close proximity.

I found a large number of telephone jacks in the stucchi. There was even one in the foyer near the table with the listing model sailboat. However, there was a little problem with electrical outlets. Where were they?

It seemed sensible to have a look in the salone behind the television set. I got down to crawl behind it and as I did I noticed for the first time what sort of table the TV rested on. It was low and had curved legs of gessoed, gilded wood. The top was a sheet of glass, cradled in a gilded wood frame under which was a tray filled with cotton wool. This was, in effect, a shallow display case in which nestled a collection of brilliantly colored butterflies and several pieces of pre-Colombian clay sculpture. Maybe some plainer base for the television would turn up and we could liberate this amazing item; move it to the other side of the dining table. It would be just right for the middle of the Empty Quarter, I thought.

As I'd suspected, there was an electric outlet behind the TV. However, it held a fully occupied four-way socket. (A crisscrossing superhighway of extension cords ran underneath the carpets.) Furthermore, there was no telephone connection nearby.

In fact, there seemed to be no place in the kitchen, bedroom or salone where electric and telephone outlets coexisted. Fortunately, I finally found just the duo I needed. This was on the study's far wall, hidden underneath a tiny corner cabinet near the window.

I put my laptop on the desk and saw that its plug would never reach the outlet. I shoved the heavy desk closer to the wall. This meant I would be sitting too near the window. I might want to see the lagoon when munching my toast, but it would be dangerously distracting to have it so accessible here. I shifted the desk again so it would be harder to stare out the window.

On my hands and knees I crawled to the electric outlet which was buried under the cupboard. I yanked out the plug already in it. Later I would go out and buy a multiple socket.

The plug I'd removed belonged to a handsome, old brass candlestick converted into a desk lamp. The wire also was antique, I now noticed—ancient, twisted, furry and in places worn through. If you were considering buying this lamp, you'd mentally add on the cost of its rewiring. It was a fire hazard. I got up and inspected the only other lamp in the room, the one on the table between the guest beds. It too had a fraying cord.

The stucchi had been modernized, of course. After all, Ca' Donà was begun in 1610. But when exactly was the last time this apartment had been rewired? Were any of the lamps safe? Would my computer be all right?

The various adapters I'd brought all seemed to do their different jobs. On came the computer's green light along with the familiar whirr as the machine booted up. The next step was to attach the modem.

The telephone connection was right next to the electric outlet. I was on all fours again as I crossed the green field of the rose-strewn carpet. I grabbed hold of the telephone plug and tugged. Out it came; fat, beige and Bakelite. Everything in this place was vintage.

I put my modem into its adapter and then into the plug. All was going well. Now I simply had to shove the whole business back in the wall.

In the dark I could make out the plug's general outline, but I couldn't match the configuration of its thick, round prongs with the holes of the socket. I stretched out flat and turned it right, then left and upside down. Eventually I succeeded.

For the first time, I sat down on the fine-looking desk chair covered in soft, caramel-colored leather. Folded underneath the seat was a step you could pull out. It was upholstered in matching leather. The chair was handsome and well suited to a library but it was extremely uncomfortable. Later I'd have to swap it with one of the others in the house. Now I was concentrating on the computer.

We were ready to go. I tapped in the dial-up number for Venice. The usual high-pitched tones followed. Then a screech. Like Pavlov's dog, I twitched with anticipation.

What was this?

A gray rectangle popped up on the computer screen.

"Not able to make connection."

I double-checked the access number. I backtracked and made sure I'd followed all the instructions technical support had given me before I'd left London. All was as it was supposed to be. Everything except the result.

And so it came about that on my first morning in Venice, my first morning in the house of my dreams, I was enmeshed in the obsessive activity of trying to connect to the Internet.

But why do I say "first morning"? I spent most of the next three days in the most beautiful city man has made, cooped up in a tiny, dark, and airless Internet shop in the Calle Lunga Santa Maria Formosa.

The one good thing about my computer troubles was that they led me to my neighbors.

NOT KNOWING WHERE ELSE TO GO FOR HELP, I telephoned Gaia. She was on the other side of the salone's connecting doors, in Francesco's apartment.

Gaia said she knew nothing about computers. Her brother who did was away in Rome.

"Let's ask Rachel," she said.

It had been wordlessly agreed that we would live as if there was no door between the apartments. So I went out onto the landing and through the double doors with their portholes.

Now I had my chance to get a good look at what seemed to be a cutaway, architectural model of a Palladian villa complete with a pediment, columns, a broad set of stairs leading up to the front door. The model just stood there, as much taken for granted as the nearby storage cupboard for suitcases.

I knocked at Francesco's door. Gaia, dressed for building work in blue overalls, her hair wrapped in a cotton scarf, answered. Behind her I could see a room that stretched all the way to two big windows facing the Campanile of San Marco. It was the length of our salone, studio and bedroom combined. And it was full of sofas, tables and paintings.

Gaia did not invite me in. We stood in the doorway talking. She explained that everything in her new apartment had to be redone, or done for the first time. The last person to inhabit it had been a woman in her nineties who for decades had camped in one corner of the vast semi-derelict space with only a single tiny heater to warm her in winter.

The old woman had moved someplace lower down and warmer, perhaps an old-age home, Gaia told me as she came out into the hall.

The hall, I now noticed, was covered with fine white plaster dust which must have drifted out from her apartment-to-be. The dust wasn't going to be content with resting here. Sometime later in the day, I felt sure, it would work its way into the stucchi. And it did. That afternoon, our kitchen looked as if someone had tossed an open sack of flour on the floor.

Rachel, who we were about to visit, lived in the apartment between Francesco's place and Gaia's future home. Gaia had phoned. She was expecting us.

THIN, SMALL-BONED AND TENSE, I took Rachel to be in her twenties. In fact, she was more than forty. Maybe it was her tiny size, her Betty Boop cheeriness and visual style that misled me. Rachel's hair was a stark (which is to say not God-given) black and bobbed in the manner of the silent movie vamp Louise Brooks. Though her smile was tight, she gave us an apparently carefree welcome.

Her apartment was small and plain. It had two rooms, a kitchenette and a bath. At the far end were a couple of large windows. A painful glare shot through them. Opposite, across the Canal dei Gesuiti, was the long whitewashed wall of a now disused convent.

The three of us were nearly shouting. It was a busy canal and Rachel explained that in spite of municipal regulations, many boatmen keep their radios blasting away. It had never occurred to me that there was a lawless, Wild West side to Venice, albeit waterborne.

Rachel, who spoke very fast, told me that she was English but had lived in Italy for ten years. She worked from home translating books and company reports into her native language. Her son, Tony, who was four, was off at school.

I assumed from what she didn't say as much as from what she did that Rachel was without a mate and that she had to earn a living for both herself and her little boy. Yet in spite of the pressures she must have been under—freelance translation is time consuming, highly pressured and poorly paid—she generously offered to help me.

Gaia went back to her building project and Rachel played around with the various settings on my machine. Nothing resulted in a connection. She then telephoned a man with whom she had bartered translation for Internet expertise in the past. He worked for a small Venetian server, or maybe he *was* the small Venetian server.

I couldn't follow her Italian as Rachel swiftly explained what was and wasn't happening. After she hung up she told me that if I still wasn't connected by the afternoon, I could go around with my computer and he would try to find out what was wrong. But first she had another idea.

"Let's try Michela. Maybe she can help."

Michela, Rachel explained, was a graphic designer who lived with her fiancé Daniele, a photographer, in the apartment directly across from the stucchi. With my computer back in its case, over we went.

Michela was around thirty, about five foot six, trim and muscular, with dark, thick, shoulder-length curly hair and tawny. Her smile was big; her walk as we followed her inside was bouncy. However, with Michela, the packaging had far less impact than the energy and confidence escaping from it. She is a woman who seems to embrace everything in her path.

When Michela opened the door she was warm and welcoming, but in a curious way there was something almost generic about it. She wasn't curious about her new neighbor. Nor was she trying to court or win my approval. She acted as if she already had it. And why not? The exceptional pleasure she took in being herself wasn't in the least irritating because it was at no one else's expense. Michela was confident, not competitive.

This apartment, though bigger than Rachel's, had a peculiar layout. Its front door opened into a sepulchral tunnel which ran the width of the place. The tunnel was lined with built-in desks on which half a dozen computers sat. A large rectangular window had been cut in the wall directly opposite the apartment's entrance. It let in a tiny bit of light. On the far right was the kitchen, with up-to-the-minute appliances, I noted. The bedroom, living room and Michela's office were beyond the tunnel on the lagoon side of Ca' Donà.

The great thing about this apartment was its views of the lagoon. Michela's office, at the front right corner of the house, had three windows and when I stood in the middle of the room, it was like being on a ship; there was water everywhere you looked.

Rachel busily translated as I laid out the problem. Through her Michela explained that none of the computers she had were IBM clones like mine. Her business was carried out on Macs. "Much better," she informed me. Also much different. She knew without even trying that she couldn't get me connected. But she immediately offered aid of other sorts. If, for instance, I needed to send or receive faxes, I could use her office and the same with deliveries by courier.

"Someone is always here," she said.

After this we were dismissed. Nicely but firmly. Michela had to get back to work.

I invited Rachel into the stucchi for a cup of coffee. And, as it turned out, a little gossip.

"WE'RE ALL FRIENDS," Rachel told me. "We're a computer commune," she said smiling. (Gaia, by her own account, was very nearly computer illiterate but I didn't quibble.) And Rachel was including me. We, the girls at the top of the house.

I smiled, too, but I knew that while their lives might be braided together, I was an outsider. Not only was I brand-new to Ca' Donà, I was older than the others—if not in Rachel's case by as much as I'd thought. And in two months I would be leaving. But I did not want to dwell on that.

Rachel told me she helped Michela when work in English had to be sorted out.

"Michela knows everybody in Venice," she said, practically gushing. "When we go out for a walk, everywhere we go, people say hello to her. Whatever bar we have coffee in, she always gets a big welcome."

I didn't disbelieve her but mentally I was squirming. Hero worship has that effect on me. But I kept my mouth shut. I had just moved in, after all.

I thanked Rachel again and as she left to go back to her work, I said I'd keep her up to date on my progress. Or lack of it.

Henry was out visiting churches. I was alone with my computer problems—and the stucchi.

I was besotted with the place, amazed at my good luck. As I looked around, everything made me smile. I couldn't get over those cut-out, breeches-wearing candle bearers. I couldn't get over any of it. The roses and swags, the marble and gilt, the velvet and Fortuny silk, the faded grandeur. But as I paddled around in the wonderfulness of my new home, I was being pulled by an undertow.

I felt I couldn't do anything until I got connected.

In the afternoon, I took out my map and plotted a route to the Internet shop. With my laptop back in its traveling case, I set out for the Calle Lunga Santa Maria Formosa. I'd been in the area before, when we'd lived at Antonella's. But starting from a different direction was almost like starting all over again. Everything was turned around.

During the next three days, I got to know the route between Ca' Donà and the Calle Lunga very well. Along the Fondamenta Nuove to the hospital, then right, following its canal, past the *pronto soccorso* (help in a hurry, i.e., the emergency room), and then into the square with Verrocchio's statue of the ferocious-looking Colleoni seated on a high-stepping horse—the Campo Ss. Giovanni e Paolo.

I scrapped the rule, "Never pass a church without going in." I was staying on course for the computer shop. I walked around the side of the Gothic church and across to the opposite side of the square. When I found an alley at the corner of the pasticceria Rosa Salva which looked like it wasn't a dead end, I took it. Up and over a bridge, jigging right and then left, I came face to face with a low house in the middle of the path. I went around it and a minute later I arrived at the Calle Lunga.

Now, was I supposed to turn right toward the church of Santa Maria Formosa or left toward I didn't know what? I took a chance and went right. I came to where the calle opens into the campo. I had not found the shop. Back I went. I arrived at the other end of the calle. Still no sign of it. I made this trek back and forth more than once. My computer case felt like it was stuffed with rocks. At last I made out the faded letters, Internet, on a storefront.

The shop had no ventilation and the only light came from the banks of computers that crowded the shelves on its walls. The program on every one of the monitors was written in English, not that anyone on duty spoke it.

As Rachel had instructed, I asked for Vittorio. He was in his twenties and full of goodwill. He also looked like he was a stranger to both daylight and food.

Since I couldn't articulate my problem, I tried to show him what was going wrong.

Vittorio was confident he could fix it. And he did. But as soon as he had, he'd lost the connection again. It was only briefly comforting that the reason for the problem wasn't my ineptitude.

Outside it was breezy and sunny. Outside was Venice, for pity's sake. Yet here I was cooped up in a dark room trying to get onto the Internet while practically every other new arrival in the city was gliding along the Grand Canal in a gondola.

I'D CHOSEN MY ISP for its ability to get me connected wherever I went. But they had no help line number for Italy. Their 800 numbers for Britain and the United States cannot be dialed from abroad. We couldn't get their expert technical advice, assuming they had any.

Vittorio kept plugging away. When he finally got discouraged, he suggested I come back the next day and he would try again. I did. The same thing happened. Which is to say nothing.

Three days was my limit. This was absurd. No doubt it was

Vittorio's limit too. He had other, one hoped, more productive work to get on with. Then, just as we both were giving up, in walked Marco.

Marco was in his forties and he had a way about him that made him seem like Vittorio's former boss, though his exact position in relation to this Internet setup was never clear. His relationship to the Internet, however, soon was obvious. Marco was a Web wizard. He immediately grasped the problem.

An exceedingly long string of numbers was then tapped into some dropdown—or do I mean pop-up?—display on my screen and—*Eccolo!* I was connected. Finally.

I thanked them all. No one would take any money.

The next afternoon I dropped by the shop again. I handed Vittorio a bottle of Prosecco and thanked him again. He was surprised and embarrassed.

Had I done the wrong thing?

But a bottle of Prosecco can't be the wrong thing, surely.

"Buon giorno," I said and was off.

I never needed to visit the Internet shop again. Though this wasn't the end of my troubles connecting to the Internet.

Often when my computer tried dialing, there was a busy signal making connection impossible. Why? Francesco had now come back from Rome. I would ask him.

Francesco Donà dalle Rose was in his early twenties, well over six feet tall, and strong. He didn't have a round baby face, yet he somehow looked like an overgrown boy. He appeared to have a sweet nature and he had lovely manners. He wanted to be helpful, I could see. But he didn't know why I got a busy signal so often.

"I have another question," I said to Francesco. "It's about the electricity. There don't seem to be many electrical outlets. And I am not sure which ones are safe to use."

"The house was completely rewired as was demanded by law in 1984," Francesco said as if reading from a prepared statement.

I probed gently to try to find out what precisely this might mean, since I hadn't seen any obvious evidence of rewiring in the stucchi.

Hadn't I noticed the series of black metal boxes down in the mail room, off the androne? I confessed I had not. Evidently those boxes contained a mechanism that greatly reduced the danger of the house catching fire. Whatever was in the boxes would shut down the electrical system if it was overtaxed.

Well that was nice. But I steered us back to my more local dilemma.

"There are only two points in the stucchi that can take a heavy draw on current," I was informed. "One is in the kitchen, for the iron. The other is where the television is plugged in."

So that is what rewiring a house meant to him.

As I absorbed this, Francesco told me a story.

"One day I was out and there was a big thunderstorm," he began. "My computer was downstairs in the amministrazione. When I came home, it was gone. Entirely burned out." He'd had to buy a new one.

Lightning had struck Ca' Donà and his computer had been fried. Along with everything on it. The *amministrazione,* the family's office, was a series of rooms off the androne. Heaven knows what else in the house had been ruined that day.

I wasn't going to pack up and move out, but I was going to do my best to remember to always unplug my computer when the weather looked uncertain. I did not yet know how very quickly the weather changes in Venice or how often. I did, however, grasp all too well that I would be taking a big risk plugging a printer, a computer and a desk lamp into a single extension of an electricity line not designed for heavy use. I had signed on for a sort of hi-tech Russian roulette.

There was another thing I wanted to ask Francesco. I had tried to open the glass doors to the study's bookcase but they all were locked. When he heard this, he walked off and came back with a paper carton big enough to hold a pair of knee-high boots. In it were hundreds of keys: ancient large ones, tiny ones with curlicues on top. One in every fifty or so had a small white paper tag attached, identifying its target.

We looked at one another and then at the keys. Francesco took the box back to where it had come from.

Later I tried the bookcase doors again. A little gentle prying with a nail file did the trick. The door hadn't been locked but, because there neither were knobs nor handles, I'd had nothing to grip. One of the books I found inside was Davis's account of the Donà's history.

These first few days in the stucchi, I often felt impatient. When would my longed-for life in Venice begin?

I didn't realize that I'd already had quite an introduction to Venetian life. I'd found out about the skittish undependability of the city's communications systems. This was not only a nuisance for me but, as I later found out, it had worrying implications for Venice's future vitality. I had met my neighbors—the ones at the top of the house, at least—among them two women who became my friends and one who was to become an enemy. And I had discovered that I had come to stay in a house where a long-divorced man and woman living far away had left two of their children engaged in an aristocratic version of Let's Play House. Which, as the summer went on, sometimes looked very like a game of hide-and-seek.

9

Our Doge

The enchantments of the big pink house I had brooded about on those early boat rides to Murano made me feel wonderfully light-headed. However I sobered up abruptly whenever I remembered that we only had the stucchi until the end of July. I did not want to go.

I certainly knew that this fairy-tale palace wasn't all butterflies and garlands of flowers. Besides the perilous electrical wiring and the ludicrous refrigerator and stove, there was the threat of cold. Ca' Donà was naturally air-conditioned, which was lovely in summer, but I worried about what it would be like the rest of the year.

And then there was money.

Henry was not in love with the stucchi. Worse yet, he positively disliked living in another man's castle. Though it was not to my advantage, I couldn't help being beguiled by this display of territorial instinct. I appreciated its animal nature, which no heart-to-heart talk would melt away.

H. was not going to be completely unreasonable, however. If I insisted on renting it for a longer spell, he would join me—at least part-time. But he would not contribute to something he didn't want to do. I would have to pay the bills.

Well then, let it be my folly. Somehow I would manage it. I must discuss it with Gaia.

Gaia and I often passed each other on the stairs. But no sooner was "Ciao" out of her mouth than she'd scurry away. No doubt she didn't relish being the acting landlady. This tenant might have something to report and indeed I did. For example, the plumber had not shown up to fix the bathroom sink. But when I did manage to get in a few words, I didn't complain. All I said was that I wanted us to get together soon, "to talk about the future."

Gaia would smile her radiant, open smile and nod. Sometimes, as if this had reminded her of her original promise, she'd add: "I will show you the piano nobile later in the week."

I was concerned but not alarmed. After all, Gaia had already told us that the stucchi had been empty for most of the last five years. The Donà family would be happy to hear I wanted to rent it for longer. Although Henry pressed me to nail down a date for our tour of the piano nobile, I didn't want to seem overbearing. Gaia said it would be soon.

FRANCESCO, GAIA AND I almost always spoke English, although the two languages in which they were entirely at home were Italian and French. Like many multilingual people, they stuck to a single language when they talked and that included all proper names—except their own. So when they introduced me to the family dogs, it was Jek and Alicia I met. But I understood that whenever we spoke in English they would be known as Jack and Alice.

Jack was a liver-and-white pointer, and Alice, a wire-haired terrier. At night they slept upstairs but they spent their days in a wooden doghouse, shaded by the old rosebushes in a corner of the garden near the path to the house. When we stayed at Antonella's, the campo's mynah bird would greet me most mornings. At Ca' Donà, it was the dogs.

If a dog can be opaque, Jack was that dog. He was also alarmingly skinny. Gaia said he was Francesco's and Francesco said he was Gaia's, which may explain his standoffishness with people and his slavish attachment to Alice. For him, her only rivals were birds. Jack was a hunter.

Gaia, when she first showed us around the stucchi, mentioned that Jack might bark a lot. "Just yell down and tell him to be quiet," she said, walking over to the bedroom window and shouting out a demonstration.

I said I wouldn't mind the barking, but I was wrong. It could go on and on and on. I took Gaia's advice and shouted. When told to shut up, it was Jack who didn't seem to mind or notice.

From our bedroom window, I could see him race across the garden. When he'd gone as far as he could—to the wall at the Fondamenta Nuove, say, he'd bark nonstop as if that would coax the birds down from their branches. When, eventually, he abandoned this effort, he raced as far as possible in the other direction—back to the garden gate. There he started barking at birds again.

Alice was more interested in people. Giovanni above all.

They were an odd couple—Jack, large and silky, and Alice, compact, tightly curled and domineering. Whenever they heard footsteps, Alice would jump up onto the low wall that separated the garden from the pergola-covered path. Then she'd stick her nose through the wire mesh fence. Amazingly, Jack, so very much bigger, managed to tuck himself in right behind her on the narrow ledge. There they would sit, expectantly.

It was a comfort to me, who'd had to leave my dog at home, to see them whenever I went in or out of the house. They weren't trying to adopt me, but I thought maybe I could adopt them. I bought packets of pungent, leathery strips from the pet shop and whenever I came back to the house, I slipped one through the mesh. I would give Alice her treat first—to keep her busy so she wouldn't try to grab Jack's.

In a way, I set about adopting the Donà family, too. Both Henry and I did. There was no reciprocity in this case. But none was required nor expected.

The conceit that the story of the Donà and their house, unlike histories of other families in Venice and their Venetian palaces, was "ours" soon became our private joke. We laughed at ourselves but at the same time we were serious. When, for instance, I read that there was a bust of Leonardo Donà in the church of San Giorgio Maggiore where he was buried, we took the vaporetto over to the island to have a look. On previous visits neither Henry nor I had noticed this carving perched over the church's door. But why was it important to see him now? What was all this about?

* * *

WHEN I FELL IN LOVE WITH VENICE, I became, in a way, like a girl who wants to see even the baby pictures of her new boyfriend. Everything about Venice's past had interest for me. But, as I've said, I'd had my difficulties with the study of history. Now, with the Donà to guide me, the history of the Most Serene Republic came alive.

As it turned out, we were not only lucky to find the stucchi, we were also fortunate to find the Donà. They were quite a tribe. Their archives date from the twelfth century and, in the centuries since, the family had produced some of almost everything—the very rich, a few who'd gone broke, pillars of the community, scoundrels and even the odd traitor. There were well-educated Donà, the passing literate, the fecund as well as the childless. Of merchant/sailors there were many, of heroic warriors a few. But it was one person in the long history of the family who stood out more than any other. He was Leonardo Donà, "our doge."

"LEONARDO," writes Alvise Zorzi, "was one of the greatest figures in Venetian history."

Born in 1536, this Donà was ambitious, determined, clever, financially astute and principled. "A wise and just man," his near contemporary Isaac Walton called him. But he could also be bold and even fierce when putting his beliefs into action and defending them.

In a letter written when he was in his thirties, Leonardo Donà revealed himself to be an early—and altogether Venetian—precursor of Patrick Henry when he wrote, "We would live with liberty and in the proud manner left to us 1,200 years ago by our ancestors . . . whereas without liberty and that way of life, to a man we should choose to die."

Venetians preferred their doges to be old and when Leonardo Donà was elected to the office he was seventy. It was then that he demonstrated how far he was prepared to go in defense of the liberty to which the Most Serene Republic was dedicated, because it was then that he took on the pope.

Leonardo Donà had vowed to remain chaste and by the time he became doge, his whole life had been devoted to serving the Republic. (I often wondered if such a vow meant no sex or only no marriage. I never found out.) Fortunately he had money enough (both inherited and as a result of his investments) to afford his career as statesman and diplomat. Many were financially ruined when they became ambassadors because they had to buy the sumptuous velvets, dazzling silver and whatever other folderol was needed to impress foreign courts with the splendor and power of the Serenissima.

Donà belonged to and then led the group of nobles called *"I giovani,"* the youths. Their name referred to their outlook rather than their ages. They were radicals who, for example, championed Galileo. Leonardo Donà, in fact, was both a supporter and friend of the great scientist. When Galileo first demonstrated his telescope at the top of the Campanile of San Marco, Doge Leonardo Donà was there. Indeed, Galileo dedicated the device to the doge.

The "giovani" engaged in many battles with more conservative politicians over urban renewal projects in Venice, influencing everything from the modernization of Piazza San Marco to the look of the Rialto Bridge; they backed da Ponte, whose design won. And it was the youths who wanted to see the northwest boundary of the city extended into the lagoon.

If you look at early maps of Venice, a big scoop seems to have been taken out of the shore facing Murano. In 1590, in order to improve drainage and increase the amount of land for housing, the scoop was filled in and the Fondamenta Nuove was built at the new border with the lagoon. It was on this site that Doge Leonardo Donà began to put up his house.

Jacob Burckhardt, historian of the Italian Renaissance, speaks of Venice's "compact splendor" in this period. Put more prosaically, the beautiful city was crowded. In 1575 as many as 190,000 people lived in Venice. Everyone's health suffered and thousands of lives were shortened as a result of the population being jammed together: In a period of only fifty years, two bouts of plague wiped out a third of the city's people. The first of these epidemics had already occurred when Leonardo Donà chose the location for his palace. Whatever his other motives may have been, Donà's decision to build on the Fondamenta Nuove was surely public-spirited. Perhaps he hoped to encourage others to do the same and by spreading out, all Venetians might have healthier, longer lives.

But crowded Venice was unquestionably also ebullient and gorgeous Venice. Not only the palaces but the people, too, looked fabulous. The women were practically swaddled in pearls. Shipments of sapphires and diamonds, rubies and pearls arrived in the city from the East. Much of this was intended to be sold elsewhere, but the women of Venice had a craving for pearls which they, their husbands and their lovers satisfied extravagantly. Too extravagantly the government began to think.

So many pearls decorated the necks, hair, wrists and clothing of Venetian women that laws were eventually passed to put a stop to it. In 1582, for instance, it was declared that no woman could wear pearls until she had been married for ten years. There were limits also on how many pearls a woman could possess. Everything in excess of that had to be handed over to the authorities. This, of course, could never succeed. Women had their lustrous, beautiful pearls copied and delivered the fakes to the authorities.

The "giovani" did not share this taste for extravagant display. On the contrary, aesthetically and ethically, they were against ostentation. This extended to architecture also. Buildings should not be covered with elaborate decorations. So it was that while Leonardo Donà's ambition and his stature led him to build big, his principles demanded that the house on the Fondamenta Nuove be plain.

The architectural historian Manfredo Tafuri writes: "Sober and laconic, the building . . . can be seen as a personality portrait of the doge."

Ca' Donà may not be pretty, fantastical or marble glorious but it stands as a self-portrait of a doge who had conviction and force of character enough to defy a pope.

IN 1606, when Leonardo Donà was elected doge, Venice was in the midst of a power struggle with Rome. The crisis could be described as an especially acute outbreak of a chronic condition. The Most Serene Republic had always been both reverent and independent. Her cathedral, for example, was at San Pietro in Castello, about as far from the center of town as you can go and still be in Venice. Magnificent San Marco was said to be merely her doge's chapel.

In the years just before Leonardo Donà became head of the govern-

ment, tolerant mercantile Venice was well known both for its grandeur
and for the free exchange of ideas allowed there. Humanists gathered
in the city where they were able to speak openly and have their views
published by the city's many famous presses. Indeed, the mood of independence was so strong in Venice that some people expected the
Serenissima to break away from the Church of Rome altogether and
join the Protestants.

Alarmed by what was going on, the Church, when it published its
index of "dangerous" books in 1596, demanded that Venice's booksellers stop trading in them and, in addition, that they immediately
swear allegiance to Rome.

The booksellers were no more compliant than were their pearl-
draped wives. Their refusal in itself did not lead directly to a showdown
with the pope but it contributed to the one that came.

In 1605, Paul V was elected pope and Venice did two things that
drove him to act against her. First, for all the free talk in the city, many
Venetians were devout Roman Catholics and left legacies to the Church,
often in the form of property on the mainland. When this land went to
the Church, Venice saw her tax base shrink. Therefore the Republic
ruled that the writer of a will must have its approval before leaving land
to the Church, approval it was unlikely to grant. Following this, Venice
arrested a pair of law-breaking clergymen and prepared to try them.

The pope demanded that Venice revoke its new property law and
that the arrested clergymen be turned over to the Church for trial. If the
Serenissima did not capitulate, he would issue an interdict and the
Republic's churchmen would be forbidden to perform their duties.
Venetians would be denied even last rites.

This was the situation when Leonardo Donà became doge. Devoted
to liberty and to the Republic, he would not yield. The pope made good
his threat.

Leonardo Donà's response was to ignore the interdict and insist that
everyone else do the same. Any copy of it that appeared in the city was
to be handed to the government at once, on penalty of death. All
churches were to remain open for worship; and they did. Gary Wills, in
Venice: Lion City, writes that church attendance during this time actually went up. In a way, the Venetians were saying to the pope that in the

Republic the churches were theirs not his. They were devout and stead-fastly behind their doge.

Donà appointed the brilliant intellectual Fra Paolo Sarpi to lead a campaign to influence international opinion and encourage leaders else-where to support him rather than the pope. The King of England, James I, was among those who did.

The power struggle between Venice and Rome lasted for a year. The papal bull was at last rescinded. Leonardo Donà had seen Venice through one of its most difficult battles with Rome. He had stood up to the pope and he had won. The independence of the Serenissima was safeguarded, even strengthened. It is for this that he is judged to be a great man in the history of the Republic.

IN 1612, Leonardo Donà died. His brother seems to have managed what the pope did not. The doge died of apoplexy and some said it was brought on by the endless, volatile arguments he'd been having with his brother, Nicolò. Their dispute wasn't about religion or politics; it was about the layout of Ca' Donà.

In all Venetian palaces, the plan of the piano nobile is much the same: There is a central hall known as the *portego,* with rooms opening from it on both sides. The portego, often richly decorated with tapestries and mirrors, chandeliers and gilded furniture, runs the entire length of the piano nobile from watergate to the land door. (The androne, below, fol lows the same course.)

At Ca' Donà, however, the portego and androne do not cut across the building from the watergate but are at right angles to it, running from the garden entrance to the land door on the Fondamenta Nuove. Of course, no one knows with certainty whether the fights about the house's design in fact triggered Leonardo Donà's death. But arguments between the brothers certainly were bitter. All the more poignant then was the doge's will.

The bachelor Leonardo left his palace on the Fondamenta Nuove to the sons of his brother Nicolò, saying: "I beg my nephews to stand united and live together . . . This is the most precious memento I can leave them."

To live *in fraterna*—brothers, their children and wives, all in one building—was a sensible way to reduce expenses. There would be one common roof to mend, one warehouse to maintain and one set of servants to support. For generations this system helped the Venetian nobility hold on to its wealth.

I had wanted to learn about the beginnings of the house in which I was living, to which I felt so attached. But things were turning eerie as the present and past strangely merged. Because now, hundreds of years after the doge's death, there was another nasty feud between Donà brothers going on. This time more than the layout of the house was at stake. The future of Ca' Donà itself might be in jeopardy.

The dispute between counts Luigi and Nicolò Donà was being fought out in Italy's law courts. The saga was ugly and disturbing because the opponents were brothers. It was compelling for the same reason. Because they were a noble family and a fortune was involved, this was a succulent meal for Venetian gossips. There were even stories about the fight between the Donà dalle Rose boys in the local paper.

Late one morning I ran into Michela and Daniele at our vaporetto stop.

Daniele, tall and muscular, with a square jaw and blue eyes, was in his forties. He's a rower and a rugby player and a Communist with a terrific sense of humor. Our communication was limited because, beside Italian, his languages are French and, his preference, Venetian.

"Bondì," good day, was all the Venetian I knew. It was enough that I was trying to learn Italian. Yet curiously, provided that neither of us was too exhausted or preoccupied to make the effort, we managed to have some sort of exchange.

Daniele asked if I'd seen the *Gazzetino* yet. I hadn't. He told me there was a story in it about the fight between the brothers Donà.

Back upstairs, with the newspaper in my hands and the unabridged dictionary in my lap, I sat on the green velvet sofa and worked my way through what the reporter described as the "interminable saga of brotherly dispute."

The latest installment was this: Luigi Donà dalle Rose was being accused of having removed a painting by Palma il Giovane from Ca' Donà. It was protected by Venice's Soprintendenza ai Bene Storici e

Artistici, the government agency responsible for looking after the historic and artistic heritage. And not only had he taken the painting from the house where it was supposed to be kept, he was being accused of trying to sell it.

According to Luigi Donà's lawyer, the painting had become his property after an agreement made with his brother Nicolò a few years before. And in any case, Luigi had not tried to sell the painting. Certainly not. He'd left it with the auction house merely for safekeeping. He was intending to convey this fact to the superintendency but hadn't done it yet.

The article went on to give the background to the fight between these "protagonisti."

The two brothers had not only been good friends, they had been business partners in a construction company based in Milan. Together their company created Porto Rotunda, "il paradiso per vip" on Sardinia. The Aga Khan later built his luxury resort nearby on the Costa Smerelda. In time, he bought out the Donà, although the family continues to have some property there.

In 1992 the partnership broke up. Nicolò thereafter brought a civil action against Luigi, and one of his partners, claiming that in the settlement of their affairs, he'd been swindled out of 30 percent of his share of the company. Dispute followed dispute. The two of them had even gotten into a public fistfight at the Porto Rotunda Yacht Club.

The battle went to arbitration and Nicolò Donà had won. His brother Luigi was directed to consign his share of Ca' Donà to Nicolò and to pay numerous thousands for various goods. Luigi, claiming new evidence, had taken the judgment to an appeal tribunal in Milan. No ruling had been made yet.

Millions of dollars were at stake. So was the ownership of Ca' Donà. In the meantime, very often the cash didn't flow in the palace on the Fondamenta Nuove. This last fact I did not learn from the *Gazzetino*. I heard it from my neighbor.

"Sometimes Gaia comes for my rent," Rachel had told me, "and she says, 'Please, we need it. We don't have any money.'"

*   *   *

TO HAVE A CASH FLOW PROBLEM does not mean you are in big money trouble. But I too sensed that my rent often came in very handy, very fast. I was benefiting from this of course. If they'd been feeling richer, the Donà might not have rented out the stucchi. Gaia's mother could have used it when she came from Paris, instead of camping out with her son.

"The money is going to the house," Gaia had told me, when she thanked me for agreeing to the rent, as if that made the transaction somehow cleaner. As if she, a noblewoman, wouldn't otherwise be engaged in the sordid business of dealing with tenants.

If in a way I was the beneficiary of their money troubles, I was also inheriting their hardships. The Donà family didn't spend enough on the house. Our kitchen appliances were only one example. Every few days I was discovering others. The children didn't know how to run a house of this size and scale, a fact they understandably kept from their parents. No one was willing—or perhaps able—to employ a professional manager for the palace and it needed one. With the goodwill of its inhabitants Ca' Donà often seemed to be running itself. If only just.

THE DONÀ WEREN'T THE ONLY INHABITANTS of the palace with a family drama, as it turned out. Rachel was having her own legal troubles. And they were very messy. She told me she was involved in a difficult custody dispute with the father of her child, which was disturbing her greatly.

But everyone in the house seemed to have settled on a strategy of trying to ignore the mess they were in. The atmosphere wasn't at all heavy. And very soon it was positively buoyant: Michela and Daniele were going to get married.

The wedding was to be on the eve of the Festa del Redentore in mid-July. The party would be at Ca' Donà. And we were invited.

I was excited. A Venetian wedding. In our house. And Henry and I would be going.

THERE WERE MORE PEOPLE living at Ca' Donà than those of us at the top of the house, although I never worked out exactly how many. I was never sure if the people I passed in the androne or on the stairs were guests or residents or Michela's employees. Francesco said there was one apartment (in a mezzanine) that none of the living members of the family had ever been inside. The wary tenant was taking no chances. But it was rumored that it, too, had stucco decorations. I came to know only one other tenant, Titti.

Titti, smartly turned out, with carefully coiffed red blond hair, was, as she soon explained to me, a refugee from Albania. She had come to Venice with her husband and daughter. In Albania they had been middle-class people and she had worked as a dental technician. Now she was Ca' Donà's housekeeper. Titti was relieved to have a job and with it a nice place to live. She and her family had an apartment tucked up in a mezzanine. Though, of course, she didn't enjoy the change in her position.

Valiant, sympathetic and philosophical, Titti was both worked hard by the family and a hard worker. I imagined that she was not well paid for her labors and that the family probably thought they were being overly generous. She was clear-eyed but not bitter. If being a servant was her new job, it did not mean she would be servile.

In my broken Italian, I asked Titti if she would work for us. She agreed, though she clearly found it puzzling that someone living in such a grand apartment should speak so poorly. Well, I thought to myself, that will improve soon. I was about to start school.

I was not relaxed about Italian studies. There was no doubt in my mind that every day I would be humiliated by my lack of facility, tormented by my lack of aptitude and my surplus of that troublemaking twosome: shyness and pride. But if I was going to live in Venice and get closer to this city I loved, I had to learn to speak its language. It had to be done.

10

The House of Good Neighbors

I knew that the University of Venice's Language Institute at Ca' Bonvicini was near Campo San Polo. But after two failed attempts to find it, I asked Henry, who was much more adept at tracking, for help. He said we should take the vaporetto from Ca' d'Oro across the Grand Canal to San Stae, which is exactly what I had done with no success. Henry, however, had no trouble at all. After a few minutes' walk he led me into a short, narrow calle and Ca' Bonvicini's door.

The office was upstairs in the corner of the high-ceilinged portego of the palace's piano nobile. The room was decorated with naive frescoes of country scenes and below these views of leafy trees and pale blue hills, a procession of electric green, molded plastic chairs stood against the walls. A big wood table was in the middle of the room. On it were scattered brochures for the various intensive language courses being given in the summer school.

Classes in "Italian for strangers" would meet every weekday morning. Those who wished to attend were asked to register the day before school started. On the appointed day I set off, alone this time, since now I knew where I was going. I climbed the steep flight of marble steps to the piano nobile and approached the secretary's desk. There followed my introduction to Italian bureaucracy.

First I was asked to fill out registration forms. Next, I was told to go

up another flight of even steeper stairs to take a test which would deter-
mine my level. I waited for the results and when they came I was proud
to find out I was in the intermediate group. Then I was handed yet
another form.

"You must take this to the main post office near the Rialto Bridge.
That is where you pay for the course. They will stamp the paper when
you have given them the money."

It was too late to get to the post office before it closed but they made
it clear that I would not be allowed to attend class until the stamped
document was returned.

Early the next morning I went to the post office. I was nervous. I
didn't want to be late on the first day of school. But where was the window I needed? It turned out to be upstairs. I hadn't even known the
place had another floor. I gave the clerk the paper and my cash, since
credit cards were not accepted. I was anxious to get going. But the
woman behind the counter refused to stamp the thing. Instead she kept
repeating some words I didn't understand. Then I got it. She wanted
more money.

But I'd already handed her almost three hundred dollars, the published fee.

"Si, si, ma. . . ." The "but" was that I would have to pay more.

Though the figure sounded vast, in fact it was a tiny sum, really, a
tax. I had to give the post office a sort of handling charge for stamping
the paper. Shaking my head, I paid and dashed over to school. I did not
then know how many similar charges await a person wanting to live in
Venice. The bank, for example, charged me simply for opening an
account.

I got to school on time. Lessons began and almost immediately so did
my recollections of Jenny. I hadn't thought of her since the end of fourth
grade.

Jenny was blonde with a wide brow and large, barely blue eyes. She
sat two rows ahead of me. Not long before, my family had moved from
the Bronx to the suburbs. The town we now lived in was on the south
shore of Long Island. We lived inland but Jenny lived "down in the
harbor."

More than once, Jen invited me out on her father's boat. Apart from ferries, I had never been on a boat before and I liked it. But it wasn't because I was now living in a city surrounded by water that I began remembering Jenny with such painful clarity.

Bluntly put, I thought Jen was thick. She rarely knew the answer when the teacher called on her. She tried. From my desk I could practically hear her brain stripping its gears.

Now in this hot classroom at Ca' Bonvicini, decades after I had lost track of her completely, decades in which I had never once thought about her, I was feeling a kinship with Jenny for the first time.

We students came from all over the world. There were a man and wife from China who were teachers of Chinese at this very institute. A svelte blonde from Vienna was spending the summer working at a hotel on the Lido because she'd fallen in love with Venice and hoped that, if she became fluent in Italian, she would be able to find a permanent job. There were students from Mexico, Israel and Germany. Some were men but most were female and came equipped with various love stories in which an Italian usually figured. The flamboyant, ambitious South African singer I sat next to, however, was in Venice to study bel canto opera.

Class was in Italian and not a word in any other language was permitted. Ca' Bonvicini means the house of good neighbors and, in fact, a fragile camaraderie developed among us as we struggled. It was obvious from the start that most of the other students were more advanced than me and therefore a little more relaxed. (The Mexican was positively jolly. All she did was put an Italian ending on her Spanish words. When, rarely, that didn't work, she smiled and, Latinly, shrugged.) Usually classes included a spell of working together, during which we would make up little speeches about something in the news, say. For this we worked in teams of two and Adele, the opera student, because she sat next to me, was my partner. She was practically fluent, but she was patient with me. That, however, didn't last very long. I was touchy about this shift in attitude but I couldn't really blame her. A woman who is sure she is on her way to perform at the Metropolitan Opera House can't be expected to enjoy working with a person who has linguistic lead weights tied to her tongue.

The Chinese professors and I were about twice the age of everybody else, not that anyone minded. The two of them were like Jack and Mrs. Sprat. He knew Italian very well and was full of confidence when he spoke—but no one could understand a word he said because his Chinese accent or inflection was so pronounced. His wife's Italian diction was wonderfully clear but her vocabulary was limited and her delivery tentative. Though look who's talking.

When I was called on by Ivana, our newly married, well turned out, and good-hearted teacher, I would open my mouth determined to speak. Most of the time what I produced was garbled Groucho Marx Italian. Henry, who knows several languages and had previously acquired some Italian, suggested that I try to make what I needed to communicate match up with what I was able to say. I just couldn't get myself to follow this sound advice. I wasn't going to speak in sentences suited to a six year old. I wanted to speak fluently and I couldn't or wouldn't ditch my pride, although I realized it was holding me back.

Class met from ten until one. By then we were all drooping from the heat. There was no air-conditioning. Except for the fanciest boutiques, hotels and restaurants, almost no place in Venice is air-conditioned. Ca' Bonvicini did not offer afternoon classes in summer because the teachers, like their students, wouldn't have been able to cope. Even in the morning we wilted quickly. We campaigned for a fan and got one but it didn't make much difference. Sometimes I felt that going to school didn't either. I decided I'd better try to find a private conversation teacher.

Vivian told me about Silvia. I telephoned. Silvia lived in the north of Cannaregio while I was on the Fondamenta Nuove, so we made a date to meet more or less halfway between at a caffè in Campo Santi Apostoli.

I took to Silvia on sight. She was tall and thin and gangly. Her hair was dyed a color between orange and magenta. Born and raised in Venice, her long, black dress and platform shoes betrayed an atypical awareness that such a thing as fashion exists. Most Venetian women dress with great care and taste, in a mode that might best be called timeless. It was nice to have a little sartorial entertainment.

A literature graduate of the university, Silvia knew English pretty well. But we agreed to stick to Italian. It transpired that neither of us knew how a conversation class ought to be structured. And with my vocabulary, our exchanges didn't have great range. Silvia suggested we find a single topic and see how far we could go with it. Books were proposed. No good. That would become too frustrating too quickly.

"What about shopping?" I piped up.

We were off.

I was already secure with the use of *basta così*. That's how I let the fruit and vegetable man know I'd finished my order. "Basta" alone would have done. But after years in London where it is impossible to say please and thank you too often, a naked "basta" sounded too abrupt.

In the department of shopping I had many questions. For example, I had noticed there are at least two ways to say "a slice" of something. But which should be used when?

I learned to say *una fetta* when what I wanted was a slice from something flat and round like a pizza but to ask for *una trancia* when the cut was being made in a loaf, say, a terrine. But there were subtleties. I should say *mi tagli un etto di salame tagliato . . . fine* when I wanted cuts to be thin and *spesso* when I preferred them thick. In a flash I memorized *aspetti un attimo*. More or less it means "Wait a minute." Very handy when trying to figure out the next phrase.

I wouldn't claim I became confident, but at least I was a little less flustered when I went shopping. And through Silvia, I found my way to food heaven: Sandro e Nives.

I'd asked if Silvia knew anywhere to buy already cooked foods—roast chicken or maybe lasagna.

"There is a shop near where I live," she told me. "My mother goes there often."

She didn't know its name. But she told me it was in a calle near the San Leonardo market, just outside the ghetto.

What a find. While the ambitiously wrought productions of a French *traiteur* are wonderful, this was the glorified home cooking I could have every day. Though it wasn't only the food that made me enjoy my expeditions to Sandro e Nives.

Eventually I worked out that the broad woman behind the counter with the wide, clear face and an angel's smile—when she felt like smiling—was Nives. The other woman, thinner and prettier with clear blue eyes, was Paola. Maybe Sandro was the cook. It was a busy place but they were not short with me as I stuttered out my requests.

The shop's atmosphere was homey without being strangulating. To Nives, many of her customers were *cara* or *tesoro*. One day as I waited to pay, she introduced me to the man whose turn was next.

"The greatest glassblower in Murano," Nives announced. Another day I met a *dottore* to whom she was positively deferential.

Was he a doctor of philosophy or a treater of the sick? I didn't find out. In Venice, it could be either. From engineers to chemists, everybody in Italy who can scrape one up is addressed by a title. *Geometra* was my favorite. It means land surveyor.

At Sandro e Nives, no one was ever going to be introduced to me. I was not going to be Nives's "treasure," but we made a kind of contact. And if banter was almost out of the question, ordering wasn't very hard. *Un mezzo pollo*, a golden and succulent chicken fresh from the spit. *Tre cento grammi di pasticcio*. (Though it was three hundred grams of lasagna I wanted, Venetians use the word pasticcio instead.) I'd order *due cento grammi di baccalà mantecato*, or *venti olive ascolane*, when someone was coming over for a drink. Their baccalà was excellent; the cod mixture had just the right degree of both creaminess and salt. But it was the stuffed olives that were outstanding; the best I ever tasted and I fast become quite a comparison snacker.

As far as I could work it out, olive ascolane are made by taking a large pitted green olive, stuffing it with a mixture of such mild minced meats as chicken and veal to which herbs and maybe Parmesan cheese have been added, then smoothing another layer of the same mixture over the stuffed olive, rolling it in bread crumbs and giving the whole business a plunge in the deep fryer. As you bite into one of these oval tidbits, layer upon layer of tastes and textures are revealed, pleasure and calorie count rising together toward the sky. But how dangerous could this be? Italy has a very low rate of death from heart disease. I gave Sandro e Nives an order for two dozen of these delectable treats as we prepared for our first dinner party in the stucchi.

We had been at Ca' Donà a little more than a month. I was more edgy than I would have been at home about having guests, what with the game-playing stove and the refrigerator that was all too literally an icebox. Also, we didn't know the people we'd invited very well. How could we? We didn't have old or intimate friends in Venice.

Rosella Mamoli Zorzi and her husband Marino, both Venetians, were coming. To our great good fortune, Tamara in London had given me an introduction to Rosella; both women are Henry James scholars. The Zorzis had already had us over for a meal at their house near Campo Santa Maria Formosa. Rosella is a fine cook and the dinner she prepared included both pasta and meat courses, as well as antipasto, of course, and dessert. I felt I would never be able to equal the standard.

Like a great many people in Italy, a country where eyeglasses are desirable fashion accessories rather than evidence of an imperfection needing repair, both Rosella and Marino wore them. Hers were deep blue with a white keystone over the bridge while his were unembellished tortoiseshell. Rosella, about my age, wore her long straight hair pulled back from her face. It had been brown when we first met but became blonde soon after. Marino has short wavy brown hair and a kind smile. They are as they look: intelligent, cultivated and reserved. Marino, for example, would never have told us that he himself is a count. This we learned from their friend Faith, an American living in Venice, to whom Rosella had introduced us. Faith, who first met the Zorzis when the youngest of her three children was a tot, would be coming to our dinner party also—as was that infant, now a stunning twenty-seven year old who seesaws between Paris and New York, when she isn't in Venice living at her mother's handsome house near the Salute.

Rosella teaches American literature at the University of Venice. Marino, a historian and much younger brother of Alvise (who has written so many books about Venice), is director of the Biblioteca Marciana, the great library of Venice that faces the Palazzo Ducale across the piazzetta.

Heart, head and genes, Marino is heir to the men who made the Most Serene Republic. For him, Venice is the center of his world and, I suspect, the true center of the whole world. Rosella, by contrast, is a robust internationalist. If she weren't, we never would have met. The four of us, two mixed pairs of the outgoing and the self-contained, seemed to get on.

The stucchi came supplied with a china service for twelve, so we were all right for dishes. Of wine glasses there were scores. And we had the necessary number of knives and forks, although they were of the flimsy, tinny kind that could have come from an Italian Woolworths. I didn't like eating with them, never mind using them for guests. But they would have to do.

We wanted to serve fish for our main course. School was only five minutes from the Rialto market, once you knew the way. It would have been easy for me to do the shopping en route but there was no place at Ca' Bonvicini to keep food cold. The fish would have rotted before I got it home. As for shopping afterward, by the time class was over the fish and vegetable markets were shut.

On the morning of our dinner party, H. and I walked to the Rialto market. We had thick slices cut from a nice piece of rosy, moist tuna. Then came arugula, which was a staple of my diet by this time. Radicchio and fennel, which I would sauté together, went into the shopping bag, followed by an assortment of fruits. In the poultry shop across from the stall selling organic honey, where the dark-haired woman behind the counter always spoke with considerate slowness, we bought quail's eggs. They were put loose into a brown paper bag.

Henry took everything back to Ca' Donà; I went on to the study of Italian verbs and pronouns.

MOST AFTERNOONS AFTER SCHOOL, I went straight back to the house to get down to my homework. Either I would go to San Stae, take the vaporetto one stop across the Grand Canal and walk to the Fondamenta Nuove or I'd trek across the Rialto Bridge and do the whole trip on foot. It took twenty minutes either way. On the day our guests were expected, I chose the latter route because I wanted to pick up tarts at Didovich on the way home. But when I got to the house, I did not sit down with my homework. I went straight to the refrigerator and got busy with preparations for dinner. Henry, I noticed, had already seen to the first course.

Two rows of three, blue-rimmed medium-sized white china plates were now set out on the marble counter opposite the stove. On each dish there was a clutch of hard-boiled quail's eggs, halved and topped with mounds of black fish eggs. Carrot sticks and green olives kept them colorful company.

I set about marinating the tuna. Just as I finished and was putting it to one side, I became aware that it had turned peculiarly dark outside. When I'd first taken the tuna out of the refrigerator, I had seen sunshine and tranquil water from the kitchen windows. Now, gray clouds filled the sky and whitecaps were crashing against the fondamenta. There was something unnerving about the speed with which the storm had rolled down from the mountains.

Lightning turned the sky white. Thunder crackled over the lagoon. It started raining. The rain was not falling. It was hurling itself straight at us.

"Come here," Henry shouted. I raced into the salone.

A lake had formed in front of the fireplace. The enormous pool of water that had so swiftly appeared had already soaked through the rug in front of the sofa. Its red border was running into its beige background; its flowers had been given a green halo by the dye normally confined to its leaves.

I looked up. Water was running down the walls on both sides of the fireplace. I ran to get a dish towel. I must try to stop the precious plasterwork from being ruined.

In the midst of all this the doorbell rang. I sped across the apartment to see who it was.

GAIA STOOD IN THE DOORWAY, her arms full of thick towels. She ran into the salone and flung them onto the lake. I tried rolling back the rug. With all the water it had absorbed it was tremendously heavy, of course. Gaia rushed out and returned with yet more towels. A short, thin fellow wearing a dark red uniform with brass buttons down the front materialized holding a mop.

I grabbed something to prop up the rug and keep it off the pastellon. I hoped this would prevent the rug from getting wetter. Then with fresh dish towels from the stack in the kitchen, I went back to patting the walls on either side of the fireplace, trying to dry them before the water coming down could spread to the decorative eighteenth-century stucco.

The indoor waterfall finally stopped. The storm had blown itself out, or anyway it had passed over us. If rain was now bashing against houses in some other sestiere, my mind wasn't occupied with their fate. I was only relieved that water was no longer pouring into our salone.

The lake had been drained even if the rug still was drenched. The fellow with the mop went away to wherever else it was in the palace he had been working.

Gaia now walked into the kitchen. She noticed the dishes Henry had set out on the counter. "You are having guests?" she asked, concerned.

"Yes," I said. "They'll be here at 7:30."

There hadn't been time to think about our dinner party or to wonder how we were going to entertain with so much of the salone damp-to-sodden. Yet all of a sudden, and apropos of nothing that had been going on, as if I were on automatic pilot, I asked, "By any chance, do you have any knives and forks I could borrow until tomorrow? We don't have enough cutlery."

"Oh you must use the silver," Gaia said.

Ten minutes later she was climbing up from the piano nobile carrying a large, tall and very heavy wooden box. It was a canteen of sterling silver knives and forks and spoons belonging to her father.

The sun came out. We opened all the windows. The dark yellow patches on the wall began fading. The floor, too, was beginning to dry out. When our guests came to dinner, no one appeared to notice that, when they walked across the carpet, it squished.

The quail's eggs were a hit. Faith even complimented us on our cutlery. Turning over a fork to inspect its hallmarks, she said, "Oh I bought the very same silver when I married."

Only later, when everyone had gone home, and we were clearing up and talking about the food, the people, the storm and mess that followed it, only then did I get a funny feeling. If Gaia and her pile of towels had arrived at our door almost simultaneously with the tempesta, then very likely this was not the first time the stucchi had been flooded.

11

Social Dancing

Henry and I, no longer jealous of our time alone with Venice, were ready to branch out in our exploration of the town. Our timing turned out to be rather good. It was the high season for art world partying.

With only a little encouragement from me, H. telephoned Jane Rylands and introduced himself. When his mother had visited Venice during the last decade of her life, she and Jane had become friends. We were immediately invited to lunch. Jane's husband Philip runs the Peggy Guggenheim Collection and we were to meet at its restaurant.

The eighteenth-century Palazzo Venier dei Leoni, which Peggy Guggenheim bought when she moved to Venice in 1947, remained her home until she died more than thirty years later. It is on the Grand Canal in Dorsoduro. The palace was never finished and has no upstairs but this low-slung, white stone building gives no impression of lacking a thing.

Almost every building along the Grand Canal rises straight up from the water, but not the Palazzo Venier dei Leoni. A broad terrace at the water's edge leads up a set of low marble steps to the double glass doors of the house. Between the building and the water, clearly visible from any passing vaporetto, is Marino Marini's bronze nude on horseback, his arms thrown wide. In order not to shock certain visitors, Marini made the rider's penis detachable. But the penis kept getting lost or stolen and one was eventually made that was welded into place.

In an exceptionally simple will, Peggy Guggenheim bequeathed her palace and all its contents—art, furniture, the works—to her late uncle Solomon's New York foundation. The only constraint she placed on her generous gift was that the paintings must remain in Venice. If the city should sink, the art must be moved to the mainland—nearby. The Solomon R. Guggenheim Foundation (SRGF), with its headquarters on Fifth Avenue in Frank Lloyd Wright's glorious if not art-friendly snail, made the house a museum soon after her death in 1979.

Jane Rylands had been a friend and confidante of Peggy's during the heiress's last years. And, what with one thing and another, Jane's husband Philip was chosen to run the museum when Peggy died.

Philip Rylands, an art historian, has been the deputy director of the Peggy Guggenheim collection (hereafter called the PGC, as they do) ever since. Being perpetually titled "deputy" I suppose reminds everyone there is only one director in the Guggenheim empire: the head of the SRGF in New York.

If you enter the Palazzo Venier dei Leoni from the land side, you come into a large, lush garden which runs the length of the rangy place. In the days before Peggy Guggenheim lived here, Marchesa Luisa Casati, an even more flamboyant exhibitionist, was in residence. Her leopards paced under the broad canopies of its many old trees. Peggy Guggenheim kept smaller, fluffier creatures: mop-like Lhasa apsos. They are buried at the far end of the garden; her grave is next to theirs.

On the calle side of the property, parallel to the Grand Canal, are houses that have now been turned into additional exhibition space, a shop and a restaurant with a garden-facing terrace where we went to meet Jane Rylands.

We'd seen a snapshot of Jane sitting at the side of the Grand Canal with Henry's mother on a sunny day. The women looked happy and relaxed, clearly enjoying each other's company. But when we showed up at the terrace restaurant lots of people were having lunch and it took a while for us to find our hostess. Then we noticed a small creature hovering over one of the round tables near the back.

Jane Rylands, in her late fifties I guessed, had a birdlike, about-to-fly-off nervousness. As we came closer, I saw that she had sharp blue eyes and deep creases in her face—as if she were a heavy smoker or a champion sunbather. Her coat was tightly belted, fitted and beige. Not a wisp of her hair escaped from under her very large, brown and white hat, a sort of turban. Her sense of style was either idiosyncratic or absent, I never worked out which.

A hostess with a firm if not always well placed hand, one-two-three Jane had welcomed us, given us a big smile, told us where to sit and introduced us to the young couple already there. He, a fellow with the largest Adam's apple I'd ever seen, was a theater director. And she, his wife and leading lady, was charming. They were open, talkative, in love with one another and Venice, which they were seeing for the first time. It was one of those encounters that are perfectly pleasant, entirely empty and a little too much like work. But as we said thank you and goodbye, Jane invited us to a party in the museum's garden a few nights later. I, in turn, said I hoped she and her husband could come to dinner at Ca' Donà.

A few nights later we were back for the party. Now, long tables covered with white cloths were set out at each end of the garden. Another table occupied the center of the terrace restaurant. Serving men and women were ladling out drinks from punch bowls. These were filled with something called "a Guggenheim," Jane told us as she darted into view. This was strawberry juice and Prosecco, the PGC version of a Bellini, she amplified. After a room-spinning introduction to daiquiris at the age of sixteen, I have avoided sweet mixed drinks. I took my Prosecco neat.

Big round silver trays with canapés were placed on the tables between the glasses and drinks. There were miniature pizzas and olive ascolane, to which I had become addicted.

Jane introduced us to her husband. Like her, Philip is short. He looked like an English public schoolboy who has grown older without having aged. This further exaggerated the difference between them, which was five or even ten years.

Philip, in a lightweight blue suit, shirt and tie, gave us a smiling hello and then rushed on. In a few minutes we heard his voice over the public address system. I looked around and saw that he was up on the restaurant terrace.

The deputy director welcomed us all to the Peggy Guggenheim Collection. He spoke in Italian. Though a private museum owned by an American foundation and the former home of a famous American heiress, the PGC did not want to be seen as an American colonial outpost. Not only did Dr. Rylands speak in Italian, he had invited large numbers of Italian people to the party.

Unlike the English, Italians do not queue. As Dr. Rylands finished his speech, the general movement toward the tables was a forward lunge. But these predators in pursuit of Prosecco and pizzas had a glamorous, gala look.

Almost every man, in fact I can think of only one exception, wore a jacket and a tie. The high-collared, high-fashion look of Armani—out of Nehru—was absent here. All-black Prada did not make an appearance either. Such getups evidently were only seen during a Biennale. The women wore cocktail dresses or dressy suits with nipped-in jackets and short tight skirts. Most of the suits were silk and brightly colored, some in splashy prints. Gold jewelry dominated. And I mean dominated. Earrings were big, bracelets chunky, necklaces like scaled-down motorcycle chains. There was a scattering of women dressed like rich bohemians, in luxurious versions of the billowing caftan. I couldn't get near enough to discover their country of origin. I only noticed a single couple—short and middle-aged—who wore what looked to me like fine quality outfits intended for playing tennis or going to the gym. They were, of course, countrymen. And it soon turned out they were friends of a friend.

I slowly walked through the crowds, pivoting my shoulders in my effort to penetrate the blockade of bodies near the tables. It was an advantage to be tall—and practiced. The English patiently wait in line but if they are journalists nothing interferes with their move to the goal line. I helped myself to a few olive ascolane and another Prosecco and as I passed the group in which the sportif couple stood, I heard somebody say, "Carole Rifkind."

Ms. Rifkind, an architectural historian by training, was a friend of my garden-designing friend Deborah Nevins. If I remembered right, Debby had been a student of Carole's at Columbia University. Carole and her husband Dick, a distinguished doctor and administrator, live in Manhattan. But Debby had told me they also own a house in Venice. I'd heard that Dr. Rifkind was on the board of the Solomon R. Guggenheim Foundation.

"Is Carole Rifkind here?" I asked, aiming my question at no one particular in the group.

The short woman in a first-class tracksuit smiled. "That's me," she said.

I explained who I was, or rather whom we both knew. Carole was immediately warm and friendly. Bubbly even. And I was quickly introduced to her husband. She was just giving me her telephone number when a hefty fellow in his early twenties approached.

"You must meet Paolo and his wife," he started saying to Carole in Italian.

Carole finished writing down her number. I gave her ours. We said we'd get in touch. Then the chubby boy barged in again. "They are dying to meet the Rifkinds," he told her. "They'll do anything to meet you."

With a messenger like this one, the supplicants would have been better off with a carrier pigeon. That's what I thought. But Carole didn't appear to mind. The rich, like models and actors, must get used to effusive fawners, to being approached and petitioned rather than doing the approaching themselves. And while we're on the subject, just what was I up to? I am the one who went out of my way to say hello. What was I after?

A social life is part of the answer, but only a smallish one. I'd had an interest in Peggy Guggenheim and her house for a very long time. This was a chance to pursue it. Dick Rifkind is not only a trustee of the foundation in New York which owns the palace, he is also a member of the PGC's advisory board.

The palace, the garden, the gold jewels and the silk, the Grand Canal, the olive ascolane and Prosecco—it all gave the party added glamour.

I TOOK JANE RYLANDS TO LUNCH partly because I wanted to hear her Peggy Guggenheim stories. This was not a great success. She turned out to be better at volunteering than responding. And one of the things she volunteered as we sat out in Campo San Samuele was an invitation to her house.

"You must come and meet the Hollises," she said. "He's a new member of the PGC's board. You'll like them. We're having some other people over too."

I accepted of course. And, since by now I had begun to grasp that what I think of as dressing up is what women in Venice do whenever they leave the house, I paid special attention to what I would wear to this gathering at the Rylands'. I settled on a beautifully cut wide tunic and trousers made of thin white linen. I didn't wear this outfit often because I liked it so much and feared I would ruin it by spilling something, anything, down the front.

It was warm on the night of the party. I didn't need a jacket or shawl. Henry and I walked slowly to Palazzo Caotorta. As we approached the entrance and were about to ring the Rylands' bell, another couple appeared. They were rather older and grayer. Dignified. The buzzer sounded to let us in. We followed the path lit by candles in shallow little bowls placed on every step up to the first floor.

"Meet Prince and Princess Clary," Philip said when we got to the top, gesturing toward the couple with whom, by chance, we'd entered.

The prince and princess live on the very top of a palace that bears their name. It is on the Zattere in Dorsoduro. "We live at Ca' Donà," I said. This was not the start of a lively exchange or even a dull one.

Men in white jackets held trays of champagne flutes filled with Prosecco. Waiters wearing gloves circulated handing out the canapés. There were at least 150 people. Oh why hadn't Jane warned me? The perfumed women were bejeweled and wearing colorful silks. I felt like a giant albino radish.

WE DIDN'T KNOW ANYONE apart from the hostess. I went around eavesdropping where I could. I wondered, was it possible to just sidle up and join a conversation or was a person supposed to wait to be introduced, as in England?

Just then Jane appeared and pointed out a woman: blonde, middle-aged, chunky. She was standing alone and looked, not lost, but isolated. I didn't know what I made of her face.

"That's Patricia Curtis," Jane told me. "She lives in Palazzo Barbaro, where Henry James used to stay with her grandparents."

Feeling that this was an introduction of a kind, I went over.

I said hello to Patricia Curtis and asked, "Do you feel haunted by Henry James?"

This was not a brilliant opening gambit, but you've got to start somewhere.

Or maybe you don't.

There was no reply. Not a word.

With my tail between my legs, I slunk away. (It was a long time later that I was invited to her house where she was warm and forthcoming and filled with pride when she talked about the past.)

Back I went to stand next to Henry. Seeing that we were not enmeshed in the life of her party, Jane reappeared and led us over to meet the Hollises, the couple whom she'd alleged were the reason for this event. She dropped us—two mice at the feet of Tom and Kitty Cat—and went back to her other guests.

Bill was in his mid-sixties and Andrea considerably—say twenty years—younger. He was a chubby, gray-haired, pink-faced Southerner. She was slim, toned, with straight brown hair cut in pixie style. Both of them wore glasses. And both were polite. He was the outgoing one. Warm. Amusing. She, it was immediately obvious, was very intelligent and quick but cool and extremely careful.

Bill wore a navy blue blazer with gold buttons, Andrea had on a wonderfully cut, deceptively simple columnar dress. On her finger, she wore a noticeably large, without being vulgar, emerald-cut diamond. The four of us chatted about Venice and I don't know what all. We made some kind of contact. I took their phone number and said we'd get in touch.

In London this would have been an example of my overstepping the invisible but steel solid boundaries of social tact. "Acting like a puppy dog," Henry had called it when, new to England, I had made my first efforts to show what I took to be normal friendly interest. Well, whatever sort of animal I'd been performing like hardly matters. The result did. It hadn't worked.

But this wasn't London. Venice, as I had suspected, was my kind of kennel.

THE HOLLISES CAME TO CA' DONÀ for drinks on the Fourth of July. He was still catching his breath from the climb when I realized that neither of them liked the stucchi. Apart from Bill remarking that the chaise might be better kept out of sight or out of the house, their disapproval was not stated in so many words. Instead they just assumed we were having to make do with this apartment until we could find someplace better.

Better? I'd never considered that somebody might not love the stucchi. But I'd done time in the suburbs and I could see that, from their point of view, the salone was shabby—what with the curls of paint twisting down from one of the ceiling beams and the faded fabric on the daybed. Then, too, it was up so many stairs and in the wrong part of town. They lived in San Marco on the Grand Canal. We hadn't seen it yet but I was positive not a hair would be out of place.

I wasn't offended. Though of course I'd liked it better when Rosella, having first made sure we didn't mind, dashed across the salone to stretch out on the chaise, striking a Grande Dame pose.

Still, Bill was as warm and chatty as he had been when we first met. He was not, however, the easygoing, jolly fellow he had seemed. Andrea, though, remained the same: faultlessly well mannered and guarded.

The four of us, with the quickness to intimacy of people thousands of miles from our voting addresses, began to talk about our lives now and before. Though in fact it was Bill who did most of the talking.

He'd inherited his money not so many years before. It was the result of a miscalculation on his father's part. The old fellow who had built quite a chain of supermarkets had not wanted to make any of his children rich. But the privately held stocks he'd given them went up and up and the company was eventually forced into paying dividends. When it did, Bill retired from teaching. Also, whether or not coincidentally, he left his wife, the mother of his girls.

"I'm a poet," he said. And he'd brought us one of his books. (When they left I opened it and saw he was both publisher and author.)

Andrea, he told us, had been top of her class at Vassar. (Bill was an energetic booster of them both.) She longed to be a flautist, but to please her parents had gone to medical school and become an anesthetist. After her marriage to Bill, she too retired and now she was a photographer. The same firm that brought out her husband's poems published her books. Bill boasted that every day, without fail, Andrea practices the flute for an hour. Indeed when they'd been looking for an apartment in Venice they used to stay at the Gritti but only after the hotel agreed to provide her a practice space.

Andrea practices; she does not perform even privately. But neither of them seemed aware that her behavior might be thought obsessive or a little wacky. As they saw it, she was simply a top musician diligently practicing her craft.

I was bemused. I didn't know whether to admire their chutzpah or laugh at their pretensions. But this flute business aside, I respected Andrea because alone among the women I'd met who are rich because they've married someone with money, she didn't act like a bossy know-it-all. Bill I found sympathetic. I sensed that in spite of having chosen it, he was as lonely in his house outside Philadelphia as I was in London. In Venice he had found hugs, as he described it. It cheered him up.

They said they would have us over to their place soon.

PLENTY WENT ON IN THE CITY for which no special connections or invitations were needed. In fact, I was discovering that in Venice most of the time all you need to do is keep your eyes open.

Along some calles whole walls are covered with posters advertising coming events. Some of them are graphically powerful—what you might expect from Italian design—bold, colorful and spare. But as far as I was concerned, the main virtue of the posters was what they announced. Whenever I saw something that appealed to me I tried to write down the where and when information on the spot. You could never be certain that you'd see another such poster anywhere else in town. And after a rainstorm, many posters would slide off the walls into a wet heap on the pavement.

The whole system was on the medieval side. It was like living in a place with a town crier. "Hear ye hear ye, next week at the Ateneo Veneto . . ." Old fashioned and effective, too.

Thanks to the posters of Venice we found our way to art exhibitions, concerts, dance performances, the lectures which became our evening Italian lessons, operas and all sorts of special events including an imaginative *spettacolo teatrale* out in the lagoon at Fort Sant' Andrea, which normally is not open to the public, and a wildly funny and imaginative, if also difficult to follow, performance of the extraordinary fabulist Marco Paolini at the Goldoni Theater. Anything that caught my attention, I tried to follow up.

One day I saw a poster announcing Venezia Suona, a day of music all around the city, part of the Festa Europea della Musica, evidently. Brochures listing all the events could be picked up at the railway station.

Something like four thousand people were to perform in Venezia Suona. There were to be dozens of events, some on bridges, some in campos, some along the fondamentas—the Bluesy Duo, for instance, was to appear along the Fondamenta della Sensa. The festival would start in the afternoon and carry on through the evening.

With the program in my pocketbook, I set off into the streets of Venice. My first stop was Campo Santi Apostoli, not far from where we lived. Gospel e Danze Antiche was scheduled to begin at two.

It was a gray, cloudy day. Not at all warm for early summer. When I got to the square there was no one performing or getting ready to. Obviously something had delayed the troupe. I walked on.

That day I patrolled most of the city searching for Venezia Suona. I had the date right. I double-checked. Once in a while I noticed a couple of other people drifting around in a campo as if they too were looking for this musical ghost.

Niente.

When I had crossed and recrossed the Grand Canal and found myself in an empty Campo San Samuele, I decided I'd had enough. I was going home.

A tanned blond, curly-haired fellow of say twenty-eight walked into the square. He was carrying a bright blue clipboard. When he got near, I saw that he wore a badge printed with the Chagall-like design used on the festival's brochure.

"Dov'è la musica?" I asked him.

"È in ritardo," he replied.

"Quando comincierà?" I inquired.

"Maybe at seven." He shrugged.

I knew what that meant. The music scheduled to be performed in this campo might begin at seven, or maybe ten, or possibly next year.

"But . . ." then I showed him the brochure. We both agreed it was plainly written that the Scuola Musica Antica was to have been performing now in the very place we were standing.

"C'è musica a Campo Manin," he told me, as he walked on in the opposite direction.

At least that was on my way home.

It was colder and grayer by now. In Campo Manin, four or five people were sitting on the steps of the Cassa di Risparmio, the savings bank. This rare example of twentieth-century architecture in the center of Venice is deservedly reviled. Any conservative wanting to pooh-pooh the idea of more modern buildings in the city need only mention it and discussion stops.

On the right side of the large, empty square stood an electric piano. A row of schoolroom chairs was lined up facing it. To complete the surreal scene there was the pianist.

She sat at the piano, a woman with long black curls wearing a bright pink dress. The dress was very short, revealing legs which were also short and perhaps not her most marvelous feature. For shoes, she had chosen high-heeled silver sandals. Her shoulders, like her toes, were bare.

On she played, this vision in Day-Glo and goose bumps. Tune after tune, out came the sort of music you might hear in the bar of a run-down hotel. It swooped across the campo, to no one's evident interest including her own. Then she switched to something more elevated: "Für Elise." I knew it well, having worked over it for a year during my stint as a pupil of the piano. I had no more gift for that than I was now showing for Italian.

In the charcoal light of the chilly, almost deserted square with a hulking bank for a backdrop, the sound of tinny piano music being played so earnestly and so mechanically made for a melancholy mood. I had set off to find a festival, I returned home sad.

That night, a work specially commissioned for this jamboree that never happened was scheduled for 10:15. Its onset was to be signaled by sirens and bells. Following this, a searchlight would be beamed onto the Campanile of San Marco. The program instructed that wherever we should happen to be in the city we were to sing the note dictated by the color of the beam. When it was white, sing "do." Magenta was to unleash "re"; green "fa"; blue "sol." The piece was to take about seven minutes, *senza interruzione.*

At quarter past ten, Henry and I stood at the bedroom window. Bells were ringing and the light show began. The beam was so powerful that it not only lit up the campanile. Our bedroom, too, turned red, then green and blue. It was a little spooky but compelling. As for the singing, I did not join in. I felt I'd already done my bit for Venezia Suona trying to find it. Besides, I can't carry a tune.

12

Beginnings and Endings

Rosella telephoned. "Are you going to be in Venice for Redentore?" she asked.

The Feast of the Redeemer, the celebration of Mass giving thanks for Venice's deliverance from plague in 1576, takes place on the third Sunday in July. The night before there are many parties and a spectacular, hour-long show of fireworks in the bacino.

"Yes, we are," I told Rosella.

She and Marino wanted us to come and watch the display from his office at the Marciana Library. It faces directly on the waterfront, she told me. He was opening it for a few friends. The door would be locked and there was no bell so we should be downstairs at the entrance at ten o'clock, promptly. At the appointed time, someone would let us in.

This was an unexpected privilege. Henry and I were delighted.

What a day to look forward to. In the afternoon we would be going to Michela and Daniele's wedding party at Ca' Donà. Then, at night, we would go to the piazzetta and join the intimate gathering at the Marciana.

THE WEATHER WAS EVEN HOTTER NOW. The streets were empty of everyone but tourists when I walked back from school. In the afternoons, I sat next to the open kitchen window and did my lessons. How could I get myself to remember such slippery items as the second person plural of common verbs? In the evenings there were lectures or plays or restaurants where we could try dishes that were new to us, like *cannochie*—a sort of floppy, albino crustacean with wonderfully sweet flesh that is native to this part of the world. And I felt more and more at home in the stucchi.

Giovanni and Gaia had disappeared. For that matter so had Alice. Now, whenever I returned, it was Jack only who came to get his treat.

Gaia had told me earlier that she and Giovanni had spent years restoring a wonderful old wooden sailing boat and now it was finished. Maybe they'd taken off in it and Alice was with them. Well, whatever they were doing, wherever they were, Jack was unhappy. In fact, Jack was bereft. He took to chasing birds and barking almost nonstop. The neighbors must be really fed up, I thought. I was. Then, one afternoon, I heard Jack crying. It was a penetrating, awful sound and I couldn't ignore it.

I looked down into the garden. Jack was draped over the top of the wire mesh fence. He hung there, unable to go back into the garden or forward onto the path. He hung there and he wailed.

I rushed downstairs, went into the garden, grabbed his body from the back and managed to lift him off.

"Would you like to come upstairs?" I asked. Jack followed behind as I climbed to the stucchi. I left a message on Francesco's answering machine telling him where he could find the dog.

This was the first of many times I went to the rescue of an impaled, loudly whimpering Jack. One day I had to ask Daniele to help. Henry wasn't home and when I'd gone downstairs I hadn't been able to lift Jack free. He cried and cried but he was stuck on the bending wire mesh in such a way I couldn't release him. It was heartbreaking.

I worried that during one of his escape attempts he might hurt himself badly. And I hated hearing his cries. I would have much preferred keeping Jack in the stucchi all the time. But he wasn't my dog, and Francesco didn't seem bothered about what was happening. In fact I wasn't sure he even got my messages. Francesco, like his sister, also came and went. His fiancée lived in Rome.

One afternoon I was doing my homework with Jack under the table next to the couch in the salone. Hidden by the floor-length cloth, he had chosen this as his stucchi doghouse. I was very hot and got up to get some juice. Out in the hall I heard Gaia's voice. Ah, they were back from their holiday.

Gaia sounded agitated. I opened the door to see what was wrong.

Titti, behind her on the stairs, looked troubled.

"Jack is missing," Gaia said in a panic.

"No, he's not," I assured her. "He is in here."

She was not pleased to hear that I'd had Jack while she'd been terrified he'd run away. Then I explained about the fence, his attempted escapes and the reason I had him with me. She recovered her charm as Jack trotted out to greet her. Taking advantage of having her attention, I said, "Let's fix a time to talk."

Gaia now made good on her earlier promise. She suggested that at two o'clock the following afternoon we should meet at her father's apartment. Following that, she and I would have our talk.

At almost two o'clock precisely, Gaia pulled open the tall, gray and blue doors and she and Henry and I walked into the portego of the piano nobile.

Ca' Donà is big and the portego ran the entire length of it. The whole wide, long sweep of the room was decorated with paneled plasterwork done by the hand of the same eighteenth-century master craftsman who had worked in the stucchi. Here, panels of raspberry pink and pistachio were set against a background of cream.

"I must wash all this," Gaia said as much to herself as to us. "The paint is very dirty."

Gilded console tables were set against the long, side walls of the portego. Tall mirrors rose above them. In between, the tables were straight-backed gilded chairs. At the far end of the portego was a wall of floor-to-ceiling windows. They overlooked the lagoon. Reflected light shimmered into the grand room. Directly in front of the windows was a large glass case in which stood a venerable model of an ancient Donà boat sent sailing by the rippling light.

In the dining room an enormous Murano chandelier hung above a large round table. We saw the salotto on the other side of the portego, with its many historically important papers and maps. Gaia told us that the family had its own small chapel, but we couldn't look in because the door was locked and she couldn't find the key. Our visit took us to all the state rooms but none of the private ones—apart from the kitchen.

"There used to be many more of these," Gaia told us pointing to the thick white earthenware jars and plates and tureens on the kitchen walls. They were like the ones upstairs. "My uncle took them away."

No one said a word about the court battle between her father and his brother.

We thanked Gaia. Then Henry went off into Venice and she and I went up to the stucchi.

Boom! There it was. A blow straight to the heart.

People from Milan had already made arrangements with her mother. They wanted to buy a place in Venice and Ca' Donà would be their base as they searched for one.

I tried to look composed. I concentrated hard to keep my tears from tumbling. But I couldn't hide my distress.

"I give you my *parola d'onore* that you can have the stucchi as soon as they leave," Gaia promised.

I thanked her.

"If you want to stay in Venice for a few days before you are back here, you can stay with us in the piano nobile," she added.

I appreciated the kind offer, though we both knew I would never take her up on it. Gaia left. And I walked downstairs stunned. We would have to wait months before we could live here again.

For two days I cried. I cried when I went to bed and cried in the morning. I didn't feel like going to school but I went. I could barely pay attention. My brain, never altogether functional during Italian classes, was now out of order entirely. I was a body in a chair but my spirit, on crutches, was limping around the rooms of the stucchi.

I was angry with Henry, unreasonable though that was. He wasn't gloating but he wasn't dishonest either. He didn't want to spend as much time in Venice as I did. He wasn't keen about living in Ca' Donà. I knew he had to welcome the very news that had made me feel inconsolably miserable. And I resented it. This made me feel even more miserable.

The stucchi where my mind and spirit or soul or whatever it should be called, would be able to drift and dream, to fly about with the butterflies and birdies, the stucchi was being taken from me.

I was told that Gaia's mother, la contessa Françoise, as Titti referred to her, would be arriving on the eve of Redentore. I was expected to meet her. I wanted to meet her. Maybe she and I could work something out.

The next morning I ran into Francesco. We made an appointment. I would meet with his mother at 10:30 on Sunday, the morning of Redentore, the day after the wedding, after the fireworks, the day after tomorrow.

Daniele and Michaela were to be married at the registry office on the Grand Canal at around eleven in the morning. But what time was the reception in the androne?

I asked Rachel.

"Anything you do will be fine," she said. "They are casual people." As an answer, this satisfied Rachel but it was no help to us. So at about 12:15, Henry and I took turns sticking our heads out the bedroom window, looking for a sign of the newlyweds or their guests at the garden gate. At 12:30, we saw a dozen people heading for the house.

The sound of voices was bouncing off the walls of the stairwell as we walked down. When we got to the androne it was a roar. A string trio was playing but no one could hear them. Michela and Daniele, who had arrived by taxi, were already there. Daniele was wearing a suit—the first time I'd ever seen him in one. Michaela was wearing dark trousers and a pale silk sweater. They looked radiant—and stunned.

A drinks table had been set up between the watergate and the stairs. There was no sign of Rachel nor of any of the Donà family. Rachel turned out to be in the newlyweds' apartment helping Titti set out the food and drink. No Donà ever appeared.

I was puzzled. In England, the owner of a great house surely would come to toast the young couple who were his tenants, to wish them well. Nicolò Donà was not in Venice, but Gaia and Francesco were. And as we'd watched over the calle we'd seen Giovanni arrive in his boat.

"They were invited," Rachel later told me. She too was surprised they hadn't turned up.

Francesco and Gaia were titled members of an old family and aware of it, certainly. But neither of them seemed actively snobbish. Giovanni, I suspected, was a different story.

Gaia had told me that Giovanni came from an aristocratic Genovese family; that their palace had been requisitioned during the war and never returned. He had a hugely long title, I later learned.

Occasionally I'd meet Giovanni on the stairs in the morning as he came down with Alice and Jack. Invariably he wore sunglasses, a jacket would be slung over his shoulders and his stance as the hunting dog and wirehaired terrier advanced before him on their long leashes was that of a 1930s, chocolate-box, aristocrat leading a couple of wolfhounds.

Giovanni seemed intelligent, wide awake and proud. I had a hunch he might feel he was too grand to be seen mixing with mere tenants. I was making all this up, of course. I had no idea why no one in the family had come. And if I thought them mean-spirited, the party certainly didn't suffer from it.

Everyone was talking and toasting, happy for the bride and groom. Many of the guests acted as if they had never before been inside Ca' Donà and probably they hadn't. They were impressed, and why not? And they were curious. Some were so curious, in fact, that they went up to the first landing trying the doors to see if they get into the mezzanine apartments.

After about half an hour, we all went upstairs. Titti was serving food. Much of the furniture had been put in the bedroom. The office and living room were lined with tables—all of them covered with platters of food and bottles of wine. There were whole salmons, filo dough parcels with mushroom filling, scrumptious *crepelli*—thin pancakes—wrapped around a mixture of *melanzane* (eggplant) and béchamel sauce. There were olives and cheeses, meat and fish pies and baccalà spread on toast. There were many other dishes, too, along with lots of Prosecco and dry white wine.

I approached several people and tried to make conversation. My Italian was so limited this was not rewarding, least of all for the others. Then I met Manuel who works part-time for Michela in her graphics business but who more often works as a tour leader and courier.

Manuel's English is perfect and zippy. He had trained as a lawyer, he told me, but didn't care for that world, so now he did special courier work with visiting individuals and groups. He loved telling stories about his job and I was loving hearing them.

One day Manuel was leading a group of well-off Americans around the Veneto to visit the villas of Palladio. They had started by boat, traveling along the Brenta Canal, and then went inland by minicoach. One of the women was from Texas.

"Tell me," she said buttonholing Manuel, "can you give me the phone number of this Palladio. I'd like him to do a villa for me."

Manuel didn't say how he broke the news that Palladio had been dead for more than four hundred years.

I chatted with Titti and her daughter, an art student with a sense of humor. And I met a woman who lived in Palazzo Pisani Moretti on the Grand Canal. Famous for the eighteen enormous glass chandeliers still lit by candles in its piano mobile, the Pisani Moretti is often hired for gala balls and parties. More than once I'd seen a Japanese bride in a long white gown being rowed in a gondola to its pontile for her wedding reception.

After Henry and I said goodbye to the bride and groom, we went back to the stucchi and took a nap.

"Let's go to the Zattere and watch the Redentore boat races," I suggested when we woke up.

We did but there wasn't any regatta. I had muddled up the dates when I'd seen the announcement on a poster. It wasn't the first time I'd done such a thing and it wasn't the last. If I didn't write down the details immediately on reading them, they often mutated before I got to my desk. The boat races were to take place on the following day, Sunday, the Festa del Redentore.

We strolled along the Zattere and watched the army finishing its construction of the bridge of boats across the Giudecca Canal leading to Palladio's church of Il Redentore. Between 1575 and 1576, fifty thousand Venetian men, women and children died of the plague. Each year on this holiday, thousands of Venetians walk across this temporary bridge to attend mass at Palladio's church built by the Serenissima to give thanks for deliverance from that calamity.

All sorts of craft were arriving. There were rowboats, others with motors and big cargo barges. But in every case, pleasure not commerce was the business of the coming evening. Even the biggest boats were decorated with strings of colored paper lanterns and fairy lights. Baskets filled with food and casks of wine were packed in between the people. They were all getting into position for the feasting and fire-works later on that night.

We went home and, a little before ten o'clock, we left again—this time for the Marciana Library in the piazzetta.

CROWDS WERE GATHERING IN THE SQUARE. The fireworks were going to be set off from boats in the bacino. Crowds were also filling up the Zattere and the fondamenta across on the Giudecca. People with the muscle to commandeer such spaces had set out tables on the pavements where they were going to have late night supper parties and watch the *fuochi artificiali* (fireworks).

We went to the main door of the library. Several other people were already there. We all stood patiently but only for a minute or two. Then Rosella appeared from inside and we followed her upstairs.

The director's office was formed by two rooms that opened onto each other. A table with pastries, Prosecco and mineral water had been set out in the first of them. Both rooms were lined with books and the second one we entered also had a series of portraits above the book-shelves—they were previous directors of the library. Henry asked Marino if he was going to have his portrait painted to join his predeces-sors. Marino smiled.

The office had two enormous windows facing the water. To the left we could see the illuminated island church of San Giorgio Maggiore. The bacino was almost completely filled with boats now. Michela and Daniele, Rachel and Tony were out there in one of them. We'd seen them leave from Ca' Donà in a barge as we set out.

Rosella joined us as we looked out the window.

"Afterwards everyone goes in their boats to the Lido for a swim," Rosella told us. It would be morning before many of these boats returned home.

We felt no envy for the people out on the water. We were delighted to be here in this historic library, with our front row view. Soon about twenty of us had gathered, among them Rosella's agreeable and lively sister and her husband. Henry was speaking French with an elegant woman with whom we had been waiting downstairs. I could only smile. I didn't dare inflict my Italian on such a dignified soul.

With astonishing promptness the fireworks started at eleven. They went on and on . . . a thundering, multicolored, hour-long display crashing across the black sky. Stars became circles, squiggles gave birth to many squiggle offspring, arcing flares pretended to expire only to be reborn—and all of it was not only in the sky but also on the water.

Some people in the room chatted nonstop throughout the whole splendid bombardment. Truly this was a very Venetian evening. But the two of us were silent as we watched, shifting our feet in order to get a better view as the women who had pushed in front of us shifted theirs.

As soon as the fireworks were over, the party was too. We went back into the piazzetta.

It was like Times Square on New Year's Eve. But however many people in the packed crowd may have been drunk, nobody was threatening. We walked slowly toward the basilica. Once San Marco was behind us, so were the mobs. The streets of Venice were quiet and empty as we approached the Fondamenta Nuove.

AT 10:45 ON SUNDAY MORNING, the feast of the Redeemer, I telephoned Francesco. A woman answered and I explained, as best I could in Italian, that I hoped to see Francesco's mother. We had an appointment. The woman told me, in English, that she was Francesco's mother. She would come to the stucchi in ten minutes.

Françoise Donà Marsot, as she introduced herself, was close to my age. She had a youthful air and indeed she was young looking. As might be expected of an upper-middle-class Frenchwoman, which she was by birth and upbringing, Françoise Donà Marsot dressed casually but with sophistication. Yet I wouldn't have called her chic. She took care and had an eye, but she didn't appear to be concerned with fashion.

Nor was she a coquette. She didn't wear makeup and wasn't trying to impress. She was a good-looking woman and I imagined that when she was young she quite possibly had been a beauty in the Ingrid Bergman department.

Françoise is not a snob. I very soon was calling her by her first name, as she too called me Paula. But she was a businesswoman, as Gaia said. She set to work with her sales pitch.

"Did you know there is a boat directly for the Lido leaving from downstairs?" she asked me, as if I needed to hear that this apartment had transportation advantages.

In fact I hadn't known and I was glad to find out about it. But I told her that I didn't need convincing.

"I love this apartment," I said.

I knew this wasn't tactically clever. But I felt my passion for the place was what I had to offer as a tenant. Someone else could pay a higher rent, but it wouldn't be easy to find another person as love-struck as me and therefore with such protective feelings toward the stucchi.

I was not so gaga about the apartment, however, that I failed to point out that the refrigerator was a menace.

"Oh I know," Françoise laughed. "It's an antique. I wanted to replace it, but Gaia is so fond of it."

Maybe Gaia would like it for the apartment she and Giovanni were decorating, I found myself thinking.

"The people from Milan who have rented the stucchi are friends of my husband's," Françoise now explained. "They will only be coming here once or twice a month. I will speak to them. Maybe if they are not going to be using the apartment, they will let you come."

I was relieved, but not greatly. If these people had money enough to rent the apartment for very occasional use, they would have no incentive to bother sharing it. Besides, I wanted a nest not a perch.

"The family and I would like you to have it when they leave," Françoise told me. "I am not retiring for another four or five years. I will not come back to the stucchi until after that."

We would be able to return. And to stay on. It was only a question of when.

Françoise and I would keep in touch. As soon as the Milanese had found a place to buy, she would let me know. Henry and I could move in again.

We would come back. It was arranged. Even if the details were vague.

THE NEXT DAY I asked Gaia if we could keep a few boxes up in the hunting lodge.

"Yes of course," she said.

It was convenient not to have to cart everything back. Guidebooks, for instance. Michela's sister had illustrated one for children, called "VivaVenezia!" which I loved. Not only was it useful, but I could understand every word. And then there was a vase I'd bought because the apartment lacked one, candles we hadn't yet used, exhibition catalogues we'd acquired. Also, of course, it was a way of saying we would be returning.

Now it was very close to our departure. This was Monday. Our flight to London was on Thursday. The Italian class end-of-term test was tomorrow. Afterward we were all going out to lunch. One of the students had booked the restaurant, a pizzeria in Campo Santa Margherita. There was so much to do.

Going downstairs to buy a paper, I heard Titti talking to someone in the androne. When I entered the hall I saw a man coming out of the amministrazione. He was dark-haired and had a soft, slightly rounded face. He wore a pale yellow cashmere sweater and beige trousers and at his feet were two alert-looking, white Scotties.

"Buona sera," said the man. "Nicolò Donà dalle Rose."

Instinctively I reached out to shake his hand.

Il conte Donà dalle Rose took my hand in his, raised it toward his mouth and bowed. When my hand was inches from his lips he lowered and released it, returning himself to the perpendicular.

This was my introduction to the man who owns Ca' Donà and to the hand-kissing-that-isn't-quite, which is the Venetian noble style.

I felt flustered. But not so rattled that I bolted.

We stood in the androne and talked. Something about Nicolò Donà made him seem like a man in a dream, a lovely dream. All his edges appeared curved and smooth. There was an atmosphere of ease about him; a gentle somewhere-elseness. In his company it was not possible to think of lawsuits, fraternal warfare, money troubles. It seemed wrong even to imagine such things existing in his vicinity.

"You are not seeing the stucchi at its best," Nicolò Donà said, apologetically. "Four large paintings are in Padua being restored. But," he added, "when you come back, they will be here."

I did not leap up and down. I am a little old to act on it when I feel like a hysterically happy five year old.

Everyone knew, everyone had agreed, we would be coming back to Ca' Donà to live.

I wanted to show him that I, too, was friendly.

"We have a big white poodle exactly like the one in the embroidery painting in the stucchi," I said. (There was another motive for my mentioning this. I wanted it. You never could tell, one day he might think of deaccessioning. After all it had been propped up in a corner behind a closet as if no one cared about it.)

Nicolò Donà now told me a story. The family, he said, had a villa in the Veneto. But a few years before, there had been a big fire. The house had been destroyed. Everything in it had burned. There was nothing left of the villa but a shell—and the needlework portrait of the white poodle. He would never give it up. It was all that remained of that country house.

Count Donà might look like he was dream walking but he'd heard what I'd said and had grasped what was behind it. With a mixture of directness and delicacy, he'd turned me down. I was a bit disappointed but I was also charmed.

Both of us were smiling as we said goodbye.

Feeling dazed, I glided out into the toasty Venetian sunshine.

A VERY
VENETIAN
STORY

13

Peggy Guggenheim and I

When Henry and I were back in London I couldn't settle down. I had no idea how long it would be before we could return to the stucchi. Everything depended on what happened with the Milanese. I didn't want to feel I was living my life in a railway station waiting room.

"Let's go to New York," I said.

He agreed. Soon I arranged to write some pieces for the *New Statesman* while we were there. And I made appointments with people in New York to talk about articles I might later write in Venice. Above all, I wanted to see my friends, among them Clover. It was when I first got to know Clover that I came into Peggy Guggenheim's orbit, or she came into mine. I was fifteen.

During the decades that followed, Peggy Guggenheim and her palace had a complicated attraction for me. Though for years this had been half-buried, it resurfaced when Henry and I went to live in Venice. It was what led me to prompt Henry to contact Jane Rylands. It was why I'd approached the Rifkinds at the PGC party.

Like all unfinished business, my feelings about Peggy Guggenheim and her palace tugged at me. Tidying up was wanted, but I didn't know what that meant. The story which began when I was a teenager hadn't found its resolution yet.

*   *   *

A MOST WONDERFUL THING had happened to me by the time I'd met
Clover. My parents had given me an extraordinary gift: They had sent
me to boarding school. They, as it happened, did not see this as an astonishing present but rather as a desperate, oh my god what are we going
to do, solution to a problem: me.

After we had left the Bronx, I'd found myself plunked down into a
world of cheerleaders and baton twirlers and football players. Not only
did these boys and girls prize athletics more than anything else, they
loathed reading and readers. I only knew one person who read books—
Gert Soderstrom, the mother of six who lived next door in a white clap-
board house set in a yard surrounded by a white picket fence, just like
in the movies. I spent a lot of time over at Gert's in her very uncine-
matic, book-filled, dusty living room where the ashtrays were piled
high with butts.

At school, I was excluded on all counts. Not cute, not bouncy, a physical coward, a klutz who read. I did not go to church. Leaving aside the
anti-Semitism this might, and sometimes did, provoke, it meant that
while all the rest of my classmates had friends from Sunday School, I
did not. I was painfully isolated from everything around me and, Gert
apart, from everyone.

When I got to junior high, the situation deteriorated. I had to act. I
asked the guidance counselor to help me work out a program so that by
studying summer and winter I would finish school as soon as the law
allowed.

When everything was settled, I told my parents.

They balked. Nice Jewish girls of the middle class into which we had
risen did not leave school at sixteen.

Without my knowing it (they could work in secret also), my parents
talked to their friends and relatives. It was my good fortune that one or
two of them had difficult offspring and therefore knew about a few private schools.

I chose the Cherry Lawn School on a rambling former estate in
Connecticut where there were boys as well as girls, and blue jeans were
allowed. It is to my father's great credit, since he had to pay the sub-

stantial bills, that he agreed to let me go. Few places could have seemed
more foreign to him.

As it turned out, it was weirder than either of my parents was aware.
But wacky as a lot of them were, the place was full of intelligent, imaginative people, students as well as teachers. Altogether it was the best
school I'd known or ever would know.

Clover and I were in the same year. She was one of the few students
who did not board. Her mother and stepfather lived in Rowayton, a
town about twenty minutes away. Both of us were close friends of Lucy,
whose family lived in a richer and more Jewish town on Long Island
and who was one of my roommates. It was through Lucy that Clover
and I got to know one another.

Her name was not the only thing that made Clover different from
anyone I'd met before. She spoke with a French accent, for one thing,
and while many of us had faces that were putty-soft waiting for exposure to the world to do its modeling, Clover already had finely carved
features. I felt she'd been born that way.

Thin, with short brown straight hair bobbed below her ears, Clover
wore a beret slapped on her head. It never came off. The rest of her uniform was a T-shirt and jeans. (This was not in fashion at the time. My
mother had studied the subject and I arrived at school outfitted with a
gray blazer and various Bermuda shorts.) Where I hid behind my long
hair and stooped in a further effort to be less visible, Clover had a
stance. She leaned backward slightly and seemed to be studying every
angle of a situation before giving an opinion. I found her unimaginably
sophisticated. And then there was her family.

Both her parents had more than one mate and each of them had children from more than one of these liaisons. Clover had a stupendous collection of steps and halves as well as wholes. I think there must have
been a dozen brothers and sisters of one degree or another. Most of
them were living abroad. Nor was she the only one among them with a
rare name. One of her sisters was called Apple, one of her brothers
Sindbad.

Her stepfather, a dark, aloof fellow, was called the Baron von
Frankenstein. He was teaching at yet another small school in
Connecticut, which, I think, is why they'd all come to live nearby. Her

mother, Kay Boyle, was a well-known novelist and writer of short stories—a woman even more extraordinary looking than Clover. The von
Frankensteins' daughter Faith looked like Tenniel's Alice and Ian did
too, though he wasn't as fair.

Kay Boyle was all profile, like a Borzoi. Seen from the front, her face
was exceptionally narrow but from the side a good deal of territory was
covered between ear and nose. She had a high brow, beautifully bony
nose and sculpted jaw. Her hair was wavy and fairly short and she wore
it swept back from her face. She wasn't pretty but that seemed irrelevant to her. With my upbringing, this was astonishing. Kay Boyle made
not the slightest attempt to soften her features or conceal them as my
mother would have advised. On the contrary. She was stunning, she
knew it and she made the most of it by heightening her looks rather
than by selective camouflage.

Their house on the rocky coast of Long Island Sound was as extraordinary as they were. It looked like a castle. Kay Boyle wrote in a room
at the top of a tower approached via spiraling stairs. The whole thing
was stupefyingly exotic. I didn't mind in the least that Clover's mother
was polite rather than warm or interested. I felt I wouldn't have known
how to talk to her or to the Baron, so it was just as well it wasn't
required. It was enough, more than enough, for me to be there.

Clover was an artist. She was one of the stars of our school. She was
always drawing or painting in her notebooks as well as in our art
classes. She did many illustrations for *The Cherry Pit,* our yearbook.
And in her family's house, her mother had let her cover the dining-
room walls with rolls of what looked like brown wrapping paper.
From floor to ceiling, Clover was at work in the dining room on
paintings of very highly stylized, elongated people.

But this wasn't all.

Clover Vail's father, Laurence, was an American artist who had been
born in Paris to wealthy expatriates and, apart from a period during the
war, he had made his home in France. "The King of Bohemia," some
people called him. He, too, was extraordinary looking in the photographs I'd seen; a handsome man with another sensational profile. Kay
Boyle had been his second wife. His first had been Peggy Guggenheim.

Laurence Vail and Peggy Guggenheim had two children: Sindbad and Pegeen. She didn't have more. By the time I met Clover, those children were grown and starting families of their own. Though both Laurence and Peggy had other love affairs and marriages, they continued to be friends. Clover's father often visited the Palazzo Venier dei Leoni alongside the Grand Canal. And in the summers when she went to stay with him, he took her along when he went to see Peggy Guggenheim.

As my first year at Cherry Lawn was coming to an end, I was invited by Clover to come with her to Europe to stay with her and her father in France. Lucy would be coming too. At some point we would go on to Venice and stay with Peggy.

I had longed to go to Paris since I was a little girl. Now, finally, I would. And I'd get to Venice, besides. We were going to stay with the famous Peggy Guggenheim! It was all so unbelievably, incredibly glamorous. I could not believe such a fantastic thing was about to happen to me.

It didn't.

"You are too young," my parents said.

I would never forgive them.

Lucy and Clover went to France. I spent that summer "volunteering" at a day camp intended to help children suffering from cerebral palsy, which was my mother's idea. It was to keep me busy and teach me the virtues of good works.

A week or so after we were all back at Cherry Lawn, Lucy and I sneaked off campus to get ice cream sundaes at Howard Johnson's. As we came to the far side of the lake and began walking through the woods toward the main road Lucy said, "I'm pregnant."

We had been sheltered, sexual innocents when summer started. I was overwhelmed.

Lucy told me that among the people staying at Peggy's palace was a writer named Alexander Trocchi who lived in Paris. It was his baby that Lucy was carrying, though he didn't know it. She was not going to tell him, nor was she going to have it. Abortion was illegal and dangerous. I promised to go with her once she'd found a doctor and the money.

My parents had been right. I was too young to have gone to Peggy Guggenheim's.

It's not that I thought that I would have had an affair or returned home pregnant if I'd gone. I had no idea about that but I was sure that I would have been in way over my head. The more exciting life there was, the more scared I would have been. Yet I was also aware that this would not always be true.

From that time on, Palazzo Venier dei Leoni shone out like a beacon on the faraway coast of a silver-streaked sea, where one day I would go sailing. I just knew it. I would get to that glamorous shore.

CLOVER AND I lost contact with one another after Cherry Lawn. But we'd run into each other a few years earlier and, for both of us I think, it was an unexpected but welcome reunion. In a way we were getting to know one another for the first time, yet we still shared a corner of the past.

A few days after Henry and I got to New York, Clover and I met for a snack just off Union Square. Though we had been in contact by e-mail while I was in Venice and London, there was a lot of catching up to do. She told me that one of her nieces, Sindbad Vail's older daughter Karole, was now living in the city. Although Sindbad had been allergic to the art world, perhaps feeling his mother had paid more attention to it than to him, Karole was now working with the family firm, the Solomon R. Guggenheim Foundation. Indeed she was planning an exhibition to honor the hundredth anniversary of her grandmother's birth.

Immediately I felt that I wanted to write about this show, about Peggy Guggenheim and what she had done. I asked Clover if she would mind if I did. Not at all, she said. But she made it clear that she had not been in the least bit fond of her father's first wife.

"Peggy was terrible with children," Clover said looking stern.

Clover gave me Karole's number and I rang her up. We met at the open-plan SoHo offices of the SRGF. Although she had grown up in Paris, she had lived just outside Florence for many years with her Italian pianist husband. After they split up, she'd come to New York.

Now she had chosen to hitch her ambitions to the art world Guggenheims. The exhibition to honor the centenary of Peggy

Guggenheim was her introduction to curating. She was not yet on the foundation's permanent payroll.

Karole was exceedingly chic, very much in the high-styled Italian mode. Her short black hair was oiled and, worn slicked back, tucked behind her ears. Her body was toned, her skin tawnily tanned and her clothes figure-hugging. She was forty or so.

Karole told me that the exhibition would open in New York and then move on to the palace in Venice. She and her sister Julia had inherited their grandmother's guest books and although Julia had been reluctant at first, she at last had agreed and for the first time the books would be on public display. The list of Peggy's guests provided a social record of the time of course but the interest of these books was not only anthropological. Peggy Guggenheim's many famous guests left notes, even poems in them and there were drawings too.

Jean Cocteau, Truman Capote, Man Ray, Saul Steinberg, Paul Bowles and Alberto Giacometti are only some of the celebrated figures who had visited the palace during the period when I might have been staying there myself. By that time, as Karole observed, Peggy Guggenheim had become a legend and "everybody" who turned up in Venice wanted to see her.

Besides the guest books, there would be other artifacts in the exhibition. Furniture, for example, that had been especially designed for Peggy Guggenheim's now famous New York gallery, Art of This Century, which opened in 1942. Karole had not been able to track down the Poiret gown in which her grandmother had been photographed by Man Ray during her marriage to Laurence Vail. And Jane Rylands was refusing to lend Peggy's Fortuny gown. Mrs. Rylands seemed antagonistic to the idea of this show. Karole did not wish to dwell on it.

Though Karole Vail was friendly—personable is the word that comes to mind—she was plainly guarded. It was as if she expected that any moment someone would rush from behind a tree and attack. Eventually I discovered that the Guggenheim/Vail forest was thick with family who were not necessarily any cozier than Grandma Peggy had been.

*   *   *

I SET OUT TO WRITE an article about Peggy Guggenheim and her grand-daughter's show for *Town & Country* magazine. As part of my research, I got in touch with the Rifkinds. I'd heard rumors that Peggy Guggenheim's collection in Venice was going to be swallowed up as part of one great, interchangeable, global Guggenheim which certainly had not been its benefactor's wish. I hoped Dick Rifkind could fill me in.

It was his wife who answered the phone and she who generously invited me over to chat in spite of the fact that she was in the midst of preparing to move. When I got there, their apartment on Sutton Place was more than half empty. Much of what remained was stacked, waiting to be packed. We sat at a table in what had been their library. To begin, we talked of Venice.

She asked me how I was getting on. I told her I was becoming even more interested in the city and I wanted to write about its problems and their solution.

"Are you meeting enough people?" she asked.

Not wanting to miss an opportunity, I said, "Not really."

"We are in charge of a foundation," she went on, quickly adding, "It's not our money." Nothing more was said about whose money it was or how they came to be handing out grants from the Norman and Rosita Winston Foundation, as I later learned it's called. But she did tell me that one of the things they were spending the money on was setting up and backing Guggenheim Public (GP).

The Rifkinds' house in Venice is near Campo Santa Margherita. Several times a year they arrive for ten days or two weeks. With Dick on the board of the Peggy Guggenheim Collection they'd had a close look at how it works. Most Venetians, they'd observed, don't think that the museum has much to do with them or their city. The intention of Guggenheim Public was to bring Venice and the PGC closer.

GP was an intellectual salon, she told me. Every Wednesday evening, local writers, artists and philosophers gathered at the PGC. First there was dinner. "We subsidize that, too," I was told. Afterward somebody might make a presentation. "There have been some rather eminent people," Carole said. Usually the discussions were in Italian.

"You won't be able to participate, but you might learn something," she said.

I hoped she was referring to the shortcomings of my very wobbly Italian and not my assembled brain cells. I didn't probe.

GP was run by Anita Sieff. She planned the programs and was the moderator/introducer. I learned that this Anita had once worked with Michelangelo Antonioni. Since I had much admired Antonioni's films and once had a fantasy about working with him myself, I naturally thought Anita Sieff must be alright.

"When Dick and I go back to Venice, I will be giving a paper on architecture at Guggenheim Public," Carole told me. "If you are going to be in Venice, why don't you come along with us and I will introduce you to Anita."

"Thank you," I said. "I would like that."

I admired the Rifkinds for their attempt to build a bridge between Venice and the PGC. And of course I wanted to go to the meetings of Guggenheim Public. I was intrigued. But when we began talking about the museum itself, the mood was not so good.

"With the exception of Guggenheim Public, I don't have anything to do with the PGC," Carole Rifkind told me. I grasped that this had to do with her feelings about Jane Rylands.

"But Jane can be very funny," I said.

Carole's face was stony. I felt as if I'd said that Hitler had a cute mustache.

Well, this wasn't the first time I'd met someone who was allergic to Jane Rylands. A number of Ezra Pound's old pals in Venice still are furious about what they see as her meddlesome relationship with his "widow," Olga Rudge, and what they considered to be her questionable handling of the poet's estate. An otherwise mild-mannered New Englander had shaken with rage when she gave me her version of the story.

The subject was dropped.

I SOON DISCOVERED that I was going to be able to accept the invitation to hear Carole Rifkind give her paper at Guggenheim Public. Françoise Donà had sent a fax. To my relief and enormous pleasure, our year in the stucchi would begin September first.

Then, just as my article in *Town & Country* was going to press, I learned that something crucial had been left out of what I'd been told about Karole Vail's exhibition. The paintings collected by her grandmother would not be included in the show.

If the evidence of Peggy Guggenheim's gifts as a collector and patron of the art of her time, above all if her early and therefore crucial backing of Jackson Pollock, was not going to be illustrated by the paintings she had bought, then what was going to be celebrated? Without the art, the popular image of Peggy as a well-heeled, sex-crazed dimwit in slinky silk, a trivial if glittering figure, would only be given new life. She might not have had an admirable character, but Peggy Guggenheim had spent her money in ways that benefited the artists of her time and influenced them. The evidence is there in the pictures, sculptures, Joseph Cornell boxes. Astonishingly, that evidence was not going to be on view. Not in New York and, worse yet, not even in Venice, where most of the time those works lived. It had been decided to send them on tour.

I immediately proposed writing an article questioning the foundation's way of honoring her centenary. But my main purpose would be to look again at Peggy Guggenheim's reputation. I wanted to explain why it should be polished up rather than polished off. The Sunday *New York Times* gave me the go-ahead to write the piece.

Of course I was pleased. I was also blinkered. I didn't see the trouble that was coming.

14

A Merchant Ivory Production

September looked as if it was going to be one long party. And we planned to plunge right into it. What a perfect way to start our Venetian year.

Already I had learned that an awful lot in Venice seems exciting and rewarding simply because it happens in such a splendid town. Even lectures I knew I would find boring in London engaged me because they were in Italian and took place in amazing rooms. So, when I heard that the Venice Film Festival had been moved from August to the first week of September, I sent off for my press pass. Never mind that I, a former two-double-feature-a-day girl, had become a woman who often only watches movies on airplanes.

I was looking forward to seeing all those movie stars, producers, critics and heaven knows who else traipsing around the Lido, zipping across the water in their taxis or sitting on the terrace of the Gritti—a field of baseball caps, a fondamenta of running shoes.

There were also going to be art openings. Besides the Peggy Guggenheim "Celebration," a major show was being launched at Palazzo Grassi, the Fiat-owned museum on the Grand Canal. The Grassi has one blockbuster exhibition every year. This one was on the Maya.

The Grassi gives a lot of attention to the display of objects and to promotion. Quite a few art journalists were being flown to Venice to cover the opening. I was not among the junketeers, but I arranged to join them at one or two of their dinners as a sort of satellite. I was curious to see how this kind of operation works and I thought it might be fun.

As soon as I made our plane reservations for September first, I faxed Francesco, giving him the time our flight was due to arrive.

Having decided to ship some things on ahead, I roamed the shops near our house with a tape measure. When I had three cartons as near as I could find to the maximum postable size, I stopped accumulating and started filling. One box was packed with books and papers; the others held the silverplate knives and forks and spoons I'd picked up at Covent Garden's Monday antique market, a hooked rug from the Lake District with jolly pink circles to replace the wan, thin scatter rug next to the bed, my Italian textbooks and my sturdy green Wellington boots, in case there was a flood.

Only a couple of days after I'd shipped off my parcels, I came home to find an ominous message on the answering machine. The voice of Françoise Donà reported that something had come up. They wanted to talk to me about our starting date. She left the number of her mobile phone.

Unfortunately Françoise Donà didn't tell me what country she was calling from. Nothing I tried worked.

I was rattled by what I could make out from the message on my machine. I wanted so much to be back in the stucchi and had been fearful that something might go wrong. Now it looked as if something had. I lost patience trying to reach Françoise and phoned Gaia in Venice to ask how I could contact her mother.

Giovanni answered. Gaia was out. Françoise was in Paris.

"Okay, I'll call her office," I said.

Then, just as I was going to hang up, Giovanni added, "They would like you to come later."

"But I've already booked our flight," I said. "The tickets can't be changed or refunded."

The Donà clearly had considered that possibility because Giovanni then added: "They thought you could stay in the apartment downstairs for ten days."

Did they really?

I said goodbye and immediately punched in Françoise's number at work. She was in the middle of a meeting, she said, but would call me back soon.

IT TURNED OUT that Merchant Ivory Productions was introducing its new movie at the Venice Film Festival. They had arranged to rent the piano nobile where they would stay for the first ten days of September.

I listened but since none of this had anything to do with me, it was with a jumpy heart that I silently waited.

The agreement between Merchant Ivory and the Donà family was for a party of ten. Later the movie people decided there would be fourteen after all. With no space in the piano nobile for the extra four, the family would need the stucchi, too.

But I already had rented the apartment from September first. I had waited patiently for it and we had agreed on the date of our return. The apartment was not free to be rented out to someone else. It had been rented by me.

I could understand why the Donà family were asking me if we would mind staying somewhere else in the house for ten days. It would be very convenient for them and financially rewarding, no doubt. But Henry and I had already seen the alternative apartment they were proposing and we didn't like it.

Earlier, Titti had told us a mezzanine apartment in the house was probably for rent. Thinking it might be a place we could stay until we went back to the stucchi, I'd asked Francesco if we could see it.

The apartment was up a flight of stairs behind one of the doors leading off the androne. Gaia had only just finished redecorating it. While there were some fine furnishings, the place lacked charm. And certainly beauty. There was no stuccowork, no painted and paneled doors. As for a view, the apartment overlooked the glaring white wall of the church of the Gesuiti across the canal. The only part of it I'd taken to was the roomy kitchen. But I hadn't liked it that much. We hadn't wanted it then; we certainly didn't want it now.

"Why not put the other people in the apartment downstairs?" I asked Françoise.

"They are very important people," she replied.

I thought it better not to reply.

After a long pause, Françoise said: "You will not have to pay rent for those days, you will be our guest."

Their *guest*?

From the time I'd heard Françoise's message on my answering machine, I'd been nervous. Once Giovanni had told me what they wanted, I was alarmed. Now I was getting angry.

"I don't think I want to do that," I told her. "If this had come at some other time I might consider it. But it is the very beginning of our stay in the house."

As soon as the words were out of my mouth, I realized they must sound nonsensical to her. We had lived in the stucchi for two months already and we were about to live there again for much longer. Why should moving in a few days later make any difference to me? But it did.

If we were forced to live downstairs in a place we didn't like while "very important people" were sleeping above our heads, sitting in our chairs, writing postcards at my desk . . . Well, Goldilocks would have understood, even if Françoise did not. It wasn't a question of being inconvenienced. I felt that if our stay at Ca' Donà didn't start right, it wouldn't go right.

Since it would be pointless to mention any of this to Françoise, I produced an objection that would sound purely practical: "There are two exhibitions opening during the first week in September," I told her. "I have to write about them. It would be too disturbing to keep moving around. Besides," I added, hoping this would close the subject, "I've already started giving people the telephone number of the stucchi and it is essential that I can be reached."

"Ah, that is no problem," Françoise replied. "We can switch the telephones."

It took a little while for me to grasp what this meant. Our telephone line, our telephone number, could be plugged into from other apartments in Ca' Donà. Presumably, the surplus jacks in the stucchi connected to numbers used by other people elsewhere in the house. I could call out, or pick up calls, on their lines—they could do likewise on ours.

Maybe this is why I'd had so much trouble connecting to the Internet. Well, well, well.

I remained silent.

"We could have lied to you," la contessa now bluntly pointed out.

Involuntarily I smiled and shook my head.

"Ummm. I know," I acknowledged curtly.

This was getting absurd. Was I supposed to feel grateful that they hadn't?

Let's say the Donà had told me that one of the ceilings had collapsed; or that there was a gas leak that needed to be repaired and, therefore, we would not be able to occupy the apartment until the middle of the month. Did they think I wouldn't find out what really had been going on when we did come? Did they suppose that Titti or Michela or Rachel would forget to mention that strangers had been occupying the stucchi during the period the Donà had said it was uninhabitable?

I loved the stucchi. I had made that plain. It was an apartment full of their family's possessions—books, fabrics, even stacks of notebooks with thin, blue lines in which the children had written their homework lessons. Could the family be so foolish as to willfully turn us from friends of their house who had concern for its contents into mistrustful, resentful adversaries? Did they have no imagination?

After a pause, Françoise asked with some warmth in her voice, "How have you been?"

"Very well," I replied. "I hope things are good with you."

Then, wanting to end the conversation, I repeated that I did not wish to arrive from London and move into the apartment downstairs. Françoise said she would tell Gaia about our exchange.

"You will hear from Gaia tomorrow," she said before hanging up.

"You won't hear from her," was Henry's comment when I reported the above conversation. To my relief, he was right.

Good. Let this Merchant Ivory business turn into an anecdote, a story I could laugh about with friends as we drank Prosecco in the stucchi. I was glad I wouldn't have to argue anymore with the Donà family about our date of arrival or where we would stay when we got there.

Henry, who had no interest in a Venetian life, Henry, who wanted to remain in his house, had budged. He was coming with me to the stucchi, though later he would commute. But he would not live in that mez-zanine apartment. Well that was no problem, neither would I.

There were only two weeks until we left for Venice again. It seemed an impossibly short time for me to do all that still had to be done. The usual business of getting the house in order, taking care of bills, giving people our new address and our apparently universal phone number.

At 8:30 on a Friday evening, just as H. and I were about to go out to dinner, the telephone rang.

"Hello," I said, lunging across my desk to pick it up before the answering machine did.

"Hello, it's Gaia," said the voice on the other end of the line.

Half an hour later, with Henry standing in the hallway waiting for us to leave, Gaia and I were still talking.

Gaia had hurled herself into a speech about James Ivory. It was an elaboration of what I'd heard from her mother.

At first there were to be only ten people in the group. There are five double bedrooms in the piano nobile so that was just right. Then after the agreement was made, they changed it.

"I didn't know this would happen," Gaia insisted.

In fact she had waited so long to talk to me about it because she'd hoped they'd change their minds again.

"But you see now why we need the stucchi," she said.

There was no point in repeating my earlier suggestion that this four-some stay in the mezzanine apartment. I'd already heard it was not suf-ficiently grand. Instead I asked, "Why don't you give them your place?"

Gaia and Giovanni had finished their apartment. They'd made a beautiful home for themselves overlooking the lagoon and the mountains to the north. They'd installed an enormous medieval stone fireplace; their bed was overhung by a hoop which let down a drift of mosquito netting; the kitchen was charming; the bathroom was lined with tiny turquoise tiles. She'd showed it to me just before I left.

A brief pause followed while she recovered from the shock of my unexpected suggestion.

"There is only one bed," she finally replied.

"You can borrow two from the stucchi," I offered. "We won't be hav-ing guests right away."

I will not claim that this was a generous offer on my part, but it was at least an attempt to find a solution.

No, that would not work either. "The bathroom is too small," she said. Adding conclusively, "You can hear everything."

"What about Francesco's place?" I then piped up.

"But he lives there!" she bleated.

What could be plainer? However "important" these movie people might be, they were not as important as the family.

Even Gaia noticed that as an explanation, hers wasn't all that it might be.

What followed was an account of the peeling paint in Francesco's apartment, rain that comes in through the roof and the damp in the bathroom.

At this point Gaia offered us her own apartment. She and Giovanni would move back into Francesco's and the foursome from Hollywood or London, or who knows where, would have the stucchi. I could have the first month at Ca' Donà free.

Now it was I who was surprised. I was aware that she was being more generous than she'd imagined she would have to be.

I said "No, thank you." I really did not want to be camping out. And what was more important, I felt sure that Henry would reject the idea.

Gaia now was pleading with me. She explained that this was the first time in the history of Ca' Donà that the piano nobile was to be rented to strangers. The roof of the house needed redoing. The palace was so expensive to keep up. They were going to get more in rent from James Ivory for his ten days in the piano nobile than they were getting from me for the entire year. She was working all day, every day, to get the piano nobile ready. Everything had to be cleaned.

"It has to be all or nothing," Gaia said. "If they can't have the stucchi, too, they won't come."

"Don't you think you are being hard on me?" I asked. "Is it fair to have promised them what I have every right to? And now to make me feel guilty if I refuse?"

"But if they can't have the stucchi, they won't come," she said, her voice high and constricted.

My heart was pounding but I did my best to keep my voice calm. And I said no all over again.

"I will have to phone my mother," Gaia told me.

"Why?" I asked, my voice now getting louder. "Are you suggesting you are thinking of breaking our contract? What else is there to say . . . ?"

"I have to go," Gaia said.

I was shaking.

Henry of course had heard everything I'd said. He complimented me on how reasonable I'd sounded. We went out to dinner.

In the restaurant, I filled him in on Gaia's side of the exchange.

"I wouldn't object to staying at Gaia and Giovanni's, you know," he said. "They would be making a sacrifice too."

How could I have guessed?

That night, in the long intervals between bouts of sleep, the whole thing turned and turned again in my head. I was sorry for the family, but I felt they'd been unfair to me. I had rights. I could appreciate their problems. But they shouldn't be throwing their aristocratic weight around. All I'd wanted was peace of mind, to feel at home. Instead, there was this jangling around.

Early in the morning, exhausted, I telephoned Françoise. She was not in Paris. I phoned Ca' Donà. Again it was Giovanni who answered.

"Françoise is in Sardinia," he told me. I think I laughed. Hardship certainly is relative. Then Giovanni added, "Gaia is engaged in finding another solution to the problem."

"You mean there is one?" I asked incredulous. "It isn't a matter of the deal being off if I don't agree?"

"No," Giovanni answered.

He went on to say that probably it had been a language problem; Gaia was only trying to be direct and friendly.

"Good," I said. I was not going to say "baloney." Then I said, twice, to make sure it got across, "If it really is the stucchi or nothing with these movie people, I will work out a compromise with Gaia."

"Thank you for being flexible," Giovanni replied. I had no idea if he was being sarcastic.

"I will see you in September," I replied.

"We are looking forward to it," Giovanni told me.

"So am I."

"Ciao."

"Goodbye."

TWO DAYS LATER a fax came from Gaia. "I see I must apologize," it read.

And I could see that she'd typed those words with one arm twisted behind her back.

I was sure that Gaia would never forgive me.

She never did.

15

Revisions

At 8:50 A.M. on the twenty-seventh of August, four days before we were due to leave for Venice, la contessa Françoise Donà Marsot telephoned. I give her full title because she was about to give me the full treatment.

"I am sorry, but I will not be in Venice when you arrive," she said. She would be going to Venice that very evening but would have to be back in Paris for work on Monday. "I will see you September sixth."

Okay so far. Cool, but polite.

"I look forward to it," I said using the formula I'd picked up from Giovanni.

Now to what was really on her mind.

"Francesco will explain to you that it is necessary to have a contract," she announced.

I noted that she did not say a "new contract." I did not remind her we'd already agreed on terms; we already had a contract.

Françoise and I had talked in Venice. When I'd gone to Paris on a short visit, I'd met with her again in the Café Marly at the Louvre to discuss further details of our agreement. The last time I'd seen her was at Waterloo Station in London, when she came to town on the Channel train for business. Finally she felt we'd talked enough and told me to mail my check to Francesco. He got it and faxed me confirmation of its receipt and the terms of our agreement, albeit in the briefest possible prose.

I mentioned none of this to Françoise now. What would have been the point? She knew it too. But I was also keeping quiet because I'd been caught off guard. I hadn't expected the aggression in her voice.

Françoise had further instructions.

"You must pay the cost of insuring, via Lloyds of London, the paintings by Alessandro Longhi," she said, "and certain *mobile.*" (That meant furniture.)

She might have said, "I am afraid I forgot to mention . . ." Or, "I hope you will not mind, Paula, but . . ." She didn't. Forget kindness; there wasn't even the suggestion that this might be an exchange, the beginning of a conversation. As far as Françoise was concerned, I was a mere foot soldier. It was for her, the general, to give orders.

I had not seen the paintings by Alessandro Longhi, but I knew their size: four simple plaster moldings had been set into the walls of the salone especially to hold them. This had been done in the eighteenth century when the stucchi decorations had been made. I'd seen a reproduction of one of the pictures in James Davis's book.

The painting showed a man in a powdered ponytail with rows of curls above his ears. He was wearing a frock coat, deeply cuffed in silk brocade, and was accompanied by his whippet who looked up at him inquisitively. Davis suggests that this might be the portrait of the senator Leonardo Donà whose dates were 1750–1822. Presumably the stucchi had been his home in the family palace.

Historically, and aesthetically too, the return of family paintings to the walls for which they were intended was good news. But given what I was hearing this morning, it wasn't going to be a good thing for me.

"I have an apartment in New York," I told Françoise who already knew this, "and when I sublet it, I pay the insurance charges. I do not demand the money from my tenants." I did not add that if I'd ever considered asking for such a fee, I wouldn't wait until after we'd struck a deal and I'd taken their money before raising the subject.

Ignoring me, my landlady, as I started thinking of her, now fired off another demand.

"The contract requires you to pay two months' security deposit. It's the law," she said.

The law? What law? I didn't ask.

The agreement we'd made, first verbally and then confirmed by a fax, all twenty-five words of it, was legally binding or so I supposed. I'd already given them one month's rent and the same amount as a security deposit. They had accepted it. What was all this talk about?

"I will need some time to transfer the money," I said, at least having the wit to stall.

"That is all right—as long as you pay before the tenth of the month," she replied, curtly.

More than once in the months that followed as I hunted for Francesco in order to give him the rent, I would remember this exchange and laugh. But I wasn't laughing now.

What prompted me, I do not know, but the next words out of my mouth were:

"I assume the refrigerator is there?"

"Yes," she answered.

"The new one?" I persevered. By now I'd sensed that nothing should be taken for granted when dealing with these people.

"No," she said firmly. "The bathroom has been completely renewed. We can't do everything at once. That will be done in September."

Her tone made it plain that I was being unreasonable.

Unless you're trained to it, it's impossible not to take some things for granted. Only later did it occur to me that I should have asked: "September—which year?"

We'd made the agreement, the contract was done, and now they wanted to change it. Wanted to? They intended to. As for their promises to me, like our "contract," these had vanished because it suited them.

I didn't care for any of this; not at all. And, as if it would help, I began making up an explanation for what must have gone on.

This was the first time the piano nobile had ever been rented out to tenants. Had Nicolò Donà agreed to it now only to please his daughter Gaia? And, as a precondition, had he insisted that first everything must be fully insured? Then had Françoise, handling the "business side," asked her insurance broker to come up with a package rate—for the

piano nobile and the stucchi? Ivory would pay part; I would pay the
rest. At no cost to themselves, the family would have their most treasured possessions covered.

I tried not to dwell on this. There was so much to do before we left
London.

AS SOON AS HENRY AND I collected our bags from the luggage carousel
at Marco Polo Airport, we began the trek across the floor of the terminal building. The airport seemed peculiarly crowded. There were an
unusually large number of men in dark suits holding up signs with the
names of the passengers they'd come to collect. And what a lot of
immaculately turned-out men and women were milling about. It
looked as if a convention of Milanese boutique owners had just flown
into town.

Oh, of course . . . The Venice Film Festival was about to start.

As we neared the automatic glass doors opening onto the pavement, I
saw a deeply tanned fellow with pomaded dark hair approach an expen-
sively dressed twosome, manicured from top to bottom. "Paramount
Pictures," he said by way of introduction. Mr. Pictures went on to report
that there was a little transportation problem. As a result, they would not
be going straight to the Excelsior by boat but would drive to Venice and
take a boat to the ritzy hotel on the Lido from there. The lagoon was
closed to all traffic, he explained. There had been an accident the night
before. The police were dredging for the body.

A murder in Venice? The lagoon *closed* to all traffic? This was
extraordinary, terrible.

The next morning I learned that there was no murder, though there
had been a death. It seems that a man had gone out fishing illegally
and, therefore, without lights on his boat. He was rammed by a boatman who couldn't see him and had fallen overboard. He had yet to be
found.

Because of this unhappy incident, instead of taking a water bus across
the lagoon to the Fondamenta Nuove, we would have to go by land to
Piazzale Roma. From there we'd have to schlepp to the vaporetto, and
after another half-hour ride, we would get to Ca' Donà.

The terminal's automatic doors slid open. We walked out into a soft damp cushion of heat.

WE HAD KEPT A SET OF KEYS to the garden gate and to the stucchi. They were a kind of talisman, I suppose. But we did not let on that we had them. I rang Francesco's bell.

Francesco smiled and welcomed us as if there'd been no difficulty between me and his sister or his mother. It is quite possible that he didn't know.

Jack and Alice were there on the brick ledge of the garden wall as we passed under the pergola. Then the sunshine of the calle was gone. We entered the by now familiar but always magical androne. This time the ship's lanterns on both sides of the staircase were lit. And the place shone. The chessboard floor had been washed and polished. The stairs swept. It was impressive.

All this must be for the benefit of Merchant and Ivory. I wondered if they'd moved in yet.

Francesco, strong and strapping, hoisted my enormous suitcase up onto his shoulder.

"It's very heavy," I'd warned him.

"I have to keep in shape," he said, almost apologetically, as if I were doing him a favor.

Francesco let us into the stucchi.

"Would you like to read the meters together?" he asked.

"That's okay," I told him. "You go ahead. I'll do the telephone."

This was the system: You dial 1717. A computer-generated voice recites a figure. It is the number of *scatti* (units) that have accumulated since the previous phone bill. This becomes your baseline. When you want to calculate how much you owe, you dial 1717 again. Subtracting the original figure from the new one, you have the number of scatti you've used. Reckoning the cost of each unit as the price of a call from a public booth, it's easy to work out how much you owe the landlord. There are other, more complicated, systems for arriving at the bill but this is the one we had agreed on.

Francesco and I kept copies of the starting number of scatti as well as the readings of the gas and electric meters. While all this practical business was taking place, H. and I were looking around the stucchi.

Henry quickly noticed that the base of one of the page boys had a big crack in it. He pointed this out to Francesco so that later on they wouldn't think we'd broken it.

"I'll mend it," Henry said.

"That is my job," Francesco replied firmly. "I have special glue. I will take it to my apartment and bring it back when it's done."

Lifting up the wooden figure, Francesco went off. Within two minutes Gaia turned up. She was markedly polite as she handed us two sets of keys and two bars of soap. Half under her breath she muttered that her mother had given her a list of things to get for the stucchi in advance of our arrival but this was all she'd had time for.

I fished out the bottle of perfume I'd bought for her in a London shop. I'd bought it simply because it was called Gaia. And I had bought it before our problems flared up. It was ridiculous to be giving it to her now.

"Do you know what *gaia* means?" she asked me, taking the gift.

"Yes," I said. "It means Earth."

But in Italian, *gaia* means gay. I didn't know it, and she didn't say.

THE STUCCHI had been given a fantastically thorough cleaning—even the dingle-dangles on the Murano glass sconces were sparkling. This was a pleasant surprise. But the next surprise was not. Since our last stay, somebody had been busy taking things away. The stucchi was a great deal emptier.

Where was the silk-covered chaise? The little velvet side chairs? And what about the enormous, almost flat, handblown Murano translucent glass plates, one of which had been placed on top of each of the round tables flanking the sofa? Before there had been a pair of tall glass hurricane lampshades covering the candlesticks on the dining table. The glass shades and the candlesticks had vanished, too. So had the silk-covered daybed. In its place, a ghastly, if doubtless genuinely Venetian, humpbacked sofa now stood against the far wall. It was upholstered in a deeply carved velvet print featuring garish orange and green flowers. Thank goodness I hadn't been able to resist a bargain when I came across meters of natural-colored linen in the street market near our house in London. I'd used it to wrap things in the cartons I'd shipped to Venice. I would throw the lot of it over this monstrosity.

However, the portraits by Longhi had been fitted back into their eighteenth-century moldings. Each picture was about four feet by three. Here was Leonardo Donà dalle Rose, the senator born a hundred years or more after the doge. The others must be his children. All the pictures had an awkward, almost naive, quality. Heads didn't sit quite naturally on necks; arms didn't connect with, shall we say, anatomical accuracy to shoulders at one end, or hands at the other. Yet the result was somehow winning. And, in spite of there now being four Donà in residence and only two of us, their presence wasn't overpowering.

Henry, it soon transpired, could recall every work of art that had been in the stucchi the last time. When we were alone he described to me every one of the many that had been removed. The painting of the Madonna that had been over our bed, for instance, had been replaced by a much newer and cruder one which, previously, had been tacked up on one of the kitchen walls.

I was going to miss stretching out on the high-backed, red chaise as I watched the TV news every night. And, with the little velvet chairs gone, if we had more than a couple of people over for drinks, they'd have to sit on the dining room chairs. Still, there were a dozen of them.

During my negotiations with Françoise Donà, it had never occurred to me to double-check that everything in the apartment would be as it had been. I didn't like what I found. But I had to unpack. I got busy, hanging up those clothes in most urgent need of uncreasing. When I finished, I had another look around.

"You know," I said to Henry, "I think the stucchi looks better with less in it."

And it did.

We went out to buy some food, feeling tired but cheerful. After dinner we finished unpacking and then we slept and slept.

In the morning, before we managed to get out of bed, we heard singing. The voice was pure and high. "Non so più, cosa son, cosa faccio." It was Cherubino's song from *The Marriage of Figaro*. The singing was coming from the piano nobile. This wasn't a recording, somebody was rehearsing.

Merchant, Ivory and company must be in residence. Was the singer the girlfriend of one of the troupe? Or was she a performer who was going to entertain at the party they were bound to give during the festival? These film people, who however unwittingly had been a source of aggravation and worse, were giving us quite a welcome. What a grand way to begin the first day of our return to Ca' Donà.

AFTER BREAKFAST I went out to buy the paper. When I got to the landing of the piano nobile, its big, very heavy door was open—a crack. I peeked in and from what I could see of the portego, it had been spruced up even more than the stucchi. Its pink- and pistachio-painted walls had been washed, probably for the first time in ten or twenty years.

Down in the androne I saw Gaia. Overnight she had grown several inches.

In the towering rope wedgies she was wearing, she had become almost as tall as me. And, for the first time, I saw her long hair hanging loose. Gaia was wearing a skimpy, sleeveless knitted top and a sarong tied low on her hips. Her midriff was bare. Even her face had changed. A scrubbed, unembellished, lovely patrician had been replaced by a tough, if pretty, girl on the make.

Well, what do you know, could it be that Gaia was hoping to be "discovered"?

I walked over to Campo Santa Marina. Raffaelo the newspaper seller recognized me. We exchanged buon giornos as if I hadn't been away. Now I bought the *Gazzetino* as well as the *International Herald Tribune*. It would take me a long time to read even the Venice section of the paper but it was time to make the effort. When I got back to the stucchi I picked up the phone and started calling friends and neighbors. Rachel almost immediately came over to say hello.

Quite the opposite of Gaia, Rachel, I am sorry to say, seemed to have shrunk. She was thinner and more tense than when we'd left. Her eyes had dark patches underneath. She looked as if she had not been eating or sleeping. The custody dispute with the father of her child had worn her out.

I suggested we go for a coffee.

We found a shady corner on the terrace of Algiubagiò, Ca' Donà's caffè, as I'd come to think of it. The sky was blue, golden circlets of sunlight skipped along the surface of the lagoon. Seagulls lazily stood watch on the rooftops. It was a beautiful and languorous afternoon, but I was hearing an upsetting tale.

Rachel was moving to Vicenza. She described this as a new beginning but she sounded like a woman hounded. And not only was she leaving Venice, she said she didn't feel able to go on looking after Tony.

I tried not to show how shocking I found this.

Gaia and her family had been giving her a good deal of comfort since she'd made these choices, Rachel told me. But Michela was a different story. Once she'd heard about Tony, Michela would have nothing more to do with Rachel.

"This has hurt me badly," she said.

The computer commune had come to a miserable end. Gaia had not only stood by Rachel, she'd decided that Michela was morally wrong for turning her back on a friend. Michela, not surprisingly, took offense. The two women were no longer friendly. In fact they weren't speaking.

A boat had already come to take away most of what Rachel was sending on to Vicenza. She would be leaving the next day.

For comic relief, I began telling her about my misadventures with Gaia. And about the so-called contract and the attitude of Françoise Donà.

Rachel, otherwise occupied, hadn't even known James Ivory and his entourage were moving in. Nor was she interested now. But she did have definite views about my dealings with Gaia's mother.

"You must have a contract," she told me.

I explained that I wasn't interested in having anything more elaborate than the one we had already. And as we talked about it, I discovered that although she had been living in the house for two years, Rachel herself had never had one. It would have seemed cruel to laugh.

I wished her well. What else could I say?

I couldn't share her manic enthusiasm about the new life she was starting. And I felt so very sad for Tony.

I was feeling a little sorry for myself, also. The only other native English speaker in the house was leaving. She had been a friendly neighbor and a computer helper, too.

Rachel and I agreed to keep in touch. We both wanted to. Yet we were also aware that contact would be so much more contrived the next time we met. Fixing dates in advance, consulting train schedules, spending long hours together rather than having a chat and a cup of coffee at Algiubagiò . . . It was hard to think our friendship could sustain all that. But we would try.

As the two of us climbed the stairs, I realized that it wasn't only the ersatz computer commune that had broken up. Before, we the women living at the top of Ca' Donà had formed a loose, unself-conscious confederation; we had an easy goodwill toward one another. Now that had vanished too.

16

Hares and Tortoises

I said goodbye to Rachel and went back to the stucchi. I sat down at the desk, got out my list of telephone numbers. The first person I called was Beate. Beate Barner, the PGC's press officer, was intense, ambitious and endlessly hardworking. At the same time she seemed always to feel that she wasn't doing enough. Beate must have been an ideal employee. She was also kind, thoughtful and warm—a lovely friend.

"We're back," I said. "Why don't you come around for a drink?"

I told her we were living at Ca' Donà.

"But that's where Michela lives!" she said.

One of Michela's clients, I now learned, was the PGC.

Having lived in Manhattan, where anonymity is both normal and prized, and then in London, which in certain ways felt like being washed ashore on a damp desert island, I was always surprised by the number of people in Venice I met who knew other people I knew and the number of people I recognized.

Already it was an unusual day when I walked around the calles or rode the vaporettos and didn't pass at least one person I'd seen at a lecture, a party or a book launch. And in Cannaregio, near its boundary with Castello, I had already identified a familiar cast of local characters. Take, for example, the tortoise and the hare, as Henry began to call them.

The hare was Frederick. Tall and fair with spectacles, he did not look like a picture-book bunny. It was his swiftness that made for the comparison. I never saw Frederick walk. He darted. He was perpetually speeding through Cannaregio twice as fast as anyone else. And he talked three times faster than even a rapid-fire Italian, whether he was speaking in his own language, English, or the local one. We knew his name and indeed we knew him slightly because we'd met him at the Rylands'.

An American in Venice, Frederick was at work on his doctoral dissertation. His subject was Tintoretto. But if he was fast and fleet in motion and speech, he was King Molasses when it came to writing. Year after year, he was about to finish his dissertation. Well who could blame him for hanging on to his excuse to stay in Venice?

The tortoise was a Venetian we knew only by sight. She was small and elderly and leaned on a cane. Probably two out of three times when I was approaching the bridge leading to Santi Apostoli I would see her already standing on it, leaning on the parapet with one hand while with the other she slowly tapped her way up or down its steps. No one ever helped her. And she, completely occupied with her efforts, sent out no message that assistance was desired.

One day during our summer in the stucchi, Henry had come into the house and said, "I've just seen the tortoise on the Strada Nova. She's not blind."

What did he mean? She walked with a stick. She tapped.

No, he insisted. Now he was sure there wasn't anything wrong with her sight. The ailment she suffered from was one of those obsessive, tap-tap disorders. This creeping about, hitting every surface with her stick as she passed along, was not her way of finding her route; it was a compulsion in which she was trapped.

In time I was to learn that, in spite of its being a small town where everyone seemed to know everybody else, Venice is also the cosmopolitan home to a great many scenes that do not necessarily overlap. Paintings, music, architecture, theater, film—each area has its players, headquarters, programs, stars and cliques. Then there's the world of the Venetian nobility, of expatriates, of professionals, of working people, of rowers, of craftsmen and of professors. Not to mention the foreign charities, government bureaucracies, political parties—and museums.

Beate now was inviting us to yet another do they were having at the Peggy Guggenheim Collection. "It is a small party on the roof in honor of Beverly Pepper," she said. "It starts at six, tomorrow. Would you like to come?"

"Oh yes," I said. "We'll see you there."

During our last stay in Venice, riding the vaporetto in the evening I would sometimes pass the Palazzo Venier dei Leoni and see a party up on its roof. In summer there seemed to be quite a few. I'd watched as men and women, all dolled up, strolled around where Peggy Guggenheim—often naked, people say—used to stretch out and sun-bathe. There was a whiff of F. Scott Fitzgerald about those parties. I suspected that the guests enjoyed knowing that they were being ogled by passersby like me. Well very soon Henry and I were going to be transformed from being onlookers to being among the looked at.

I supposed that the party was one of the entertainments the museum provides for the fifty or so members of its advisory board; the quid pro quo for their financial contributions. Bill Hollis had told me each of them was expected to give $10,000 as a kind of joining fee and pledge another $3,000 every year thereafter. For Americans, these sums are tax deductible since they are contributions to the SRGF in New York. The advisors have no say in how things are run but in return for their dona-tions, they are petted and lavishly entertained.

Never before had I seen or rubbed up against so many very rich peo-ple as in Venice. They come from all over the Western world to acquire a trophy palace, an apartment or a small house. Many of these elabo-rately plumed, gold-beaked, migratory birdies seem to spend the year flying around the globe looking for diversions. And one way some of them made sure they'd find them when they descended on Venice was to join a board—of a restoration charity, perhaps, or the PGC. In the case of the latter, neither an interest in art nor knowledge of it was required. At first I was shocked by this but by now I almost took it for granted.

September is one of the months when this flock alights in Venice. They stay for only a few days or perhaps a few weeks. There are so many other places for them to set down before they begin their circum-navigation again. And this September even I was getting caught up in the draft created by their social flapping about.

* * *

ON OUR SECOND MORNING IN VENICE, we again woke to the music of Mozart coming through our bedroom window. Never mind that the singer had only one song; it was a honey.

Gaia had not left us a "starter pack" of coffee, bread and jam this time, of course. And her mother must have given Titti orders to clear out everything in the kitchen. From salt to aluminum foil and paper towels, there was niente. With parties coming up, the film festival, the opening at Palazzo Grassi, our first week in Venice was going to be so busy that I thought I'd better stock up now while I had the chance. I didn't want to leave Venice for the mainland having only just arrived. And I liked shopping in the town's mom-and-pop stores, which, in Venice as in all of Italy, have not been wiped out by big chains. But Panorama in Marghera was the most sensible place to get all the essentials we needed right away.

Panorama is one of those colossal hangars where, besides food, you can buy garden supplies, stereos, bicycles, underwear, car batteries and telephones. This *ipermercato* is set in the midst of acres of asphalt-covered parking lots.

Every half hour, a free shuttle bus leaves for Panorama from Piazzale Roma. The store is at the edge of the run-down petrochemical port that, along with Mestre, which you pass through on the way, is part of the municipality of Venice.

Marghera is bleak, hideous in fact, if you're not in the mood for industrial blight. Once we took a boat tour of its port, where mountains of rusting machinery and heaps of scrap metal line the water's edge. It was poetic in a grisly way. The bus approaches Marghera via the highway, a route absent of even that perverse charm.

At the end of the Second World War, Mestre was still a small town built around a simple, charming square. The square remains, overwhelmed by miles of apartment houses and concrete villas. In 1951 something like 175,000 people lived in the historic center while 96,000 lived in mainland Venice. Now 175,000 people are living in Mestre and Marghera. The population of the historic center is less than 70,000 and falling. Many of the waiters, office workers and even the gondoliers of Venice commute to work in la bella città from the not-so-lovely terra firma. And it is the mainland that supplies most of Panorama's customers, of course. Nevertheless, the bus from Piazzale Roma over the causeway, through Mestre to Marghera, was packed whenever I took it.

Panorama offers more choice to more shoppers, more cheaply than any emporium in Venice. However, its range, while wide, is limited: fine and fancy goods are not its specialities and the bus that takes you there is a textbook case of "you get what you pay for." It is dilapidated and it rattles. The orange, pebbly curtains, which block out the sun, are stained. The windows seem permanently fogged up, though it is possible to make out the landscape as you ride along. Flat and forlorn, the randomly placed warehouses and garages do nothing to cheer things up.

As the bus pulled in, Panorama's parking lot was busy with satisfied customers stowing cases of mineral water into the trunks of their cars. I envied them the ease with which they could keep themselves supplied. Schlepping *acqua minerale* to the stucchi was a tiresome and tiring job. Mineral water, too, was less expensive here but it wasn't on my list. I wouldn't have had the room or strength to carry anything else.

Once off the bus, I marched briskly to one of the large, clear plastic hutches nearby. In these sheds were the supermarket trolleys which, like circus elephants, are kept nose to tail and chained together. Inserting a coin, I liberated one of these hardworking beasts and my shopping blitz was ready to begin. Like everyone else on the bus, I wanted to get through the checkout in time to catch a bus back to Venice without having to hang around in the parking lot. The return buses also depart every half hour.

Visions of Venice, with its marble palaces reflected on the ripples of the Grand Canal, sights I had been enjoying only twenty minutes before, were replaced now by platoons of rubber boots, tables covered with placemats and bottles of shampoo, whole salmon looking up, beady-eyed, from a bed of gray chipped ice, cabinets piled with slabs of taleggio and special offers on parmigiano—but only if you wanted to buy at least a kilo. It made me blue, but this was no time for moods. I was here to shop.

Mind you, Panorama could have been a great deal worse. Its fruits and vegetables, for instance, are abundant and fresh. The store is brightly lit, clean, and well organized. It has a deli counter where big rounds of hard mountain cheeses are cut to order. There are plastic tubs filled with fresh ricotta or roasted eggplant and a counter selling pizza by the slice, three steps from which are plastic tables and benches at which to eat it. Not even at Panorama would a shopper munch and walk at the same time.

At the checkout counter, I filled my lime green string shopping bag and slung it over my shoulder. Next I stuffed my other shopping bag, a big satchel made of strong, brightly striped canvas, with the heavy things like olive oil and rice. I then gathered up a couple of plastic bags supplied by the store and filled them, too. I would hold the dozen rolls of shrink-wrapped toilet paper by its pink plastic handle. I'd ended up with more than I could easily manage. It would be a struggle to get it back to the stucchi. But when everything was in the cabinets or the cranky refrigerator, I would feel pleased that I'd done it. I would not need to shop again for a while.

After paying with my credit card, I pushed the shopping trolley back to its plastic garage. I trudged over and boarded a bus with a broken air conditioner. Only a single vent in the roof was open. At least I hadn't picked a seat on the sunny side.

From Piazzale Roma I took the vaporetto to the Fondamenta Nuove. I labored with the bags as I went through the garden gate, said my usual "Ciao, cani," to Jack and Alice and began the long climb up. By the time I got to our landing I was damp with sweat and I was panting.

I put my canvas bag down on the floor and then, as I fished for my keys, a man opened the double metal doors and headed for the stairs. I looked up.

The man was Kris Kristofferson.

I felt like a woman in a housecoat and hair curlers who opens the door to find Cary Grant standing outside.

He's looking much older, I thought, as if that would make me feel less absurd. The same could be said of me, of course, but Kris wouldn't know that. He hadn't been looking down into the audience as I'd watched him romance Barbra Streisand in that sappy movie twenty or more years before. For that matter, he wasn't looking at me now. Kris was still a movie star, while I, a graying female holding a pink plastic handle from which hung a dozen rolls of toilet paper, wasn't even fan material anymore.

Nevertheless, there was that little something, that celebrity tingle. I smiled at Kris Kristofferson's back as he passed.

I reckoned he must be staying in Gaia and Giovanni's. If I had agreed to postpone our move into the stucchi, Kris now would be sleeping in my bed. I opened the door, hauled in my groceries and laughed.

Then I unpacked the groceries and took a bath. It was time to dress for the party on the roof of the PGC.

IT WAS A LITTLE AFTER SIX when Henry and I took the vaporetto from Rialto to Accademia. From there it was less than a five-minute walk to Palazzo Venier dei Leoni.

As we approached Campo San Vio, the small square which, with its leafy trees and wooden benches, is one of the few spots in Venice where a weary traveler can sit and look out onto the Grand Canal, I saw flashing lights exploding on the blue-black water. When we got to the PGC, I realized they were reflections of flashbulbs. Stage one of the party was taking place downstairs on the waterside terrace. Photographers were busily at work.

Practically the first person we saw was Bill Hollis in his navy blue blazer. Andrea, svelte in a beige suit, was at his side. They were talking to a brown-haired, brown-eyed woman wearing black slacks and a tailored jacket. She was fretting. She had made her husband wear a suit to the party.

"He hates suits," she was saying as we strolled up.

Bill gave each of us a big bear hug. Then he introduced us to the woman in black.

"This is Beverly Pepper," he said. We all shook hands.

Though the party was in her honor and her picture was being snapped every couple of minutes, Beverly Pepper was not only a youthful powerhouse in her seventies, she was down to earth. And, in spite of the fact that she and her husband had been living in Todi, near Florence, for decades, she still had a New York accent. I envied her that. Living with an Englishman had taken the edge off mine and I missed it.

Henry got into a conversation with Andrea. The guest of honor went off to speak to other people. Then, all of a sudden, Jane Rylands materialized. Immediately she insinuated herself between Henry and Andrea, turning her back to him. Jane had something urgent to discuss. She and Andrea were soon deep into discussion and when I got a drift of what it was, I smiled. It was about the difficulties (or was it the delights) of putting up marrows and tomatoes.

"She is cultivating Andrea with a vengeance," H. later observed.

I'll say. But why? Was Jane trying to make sure that Bill would be Philip's ally in any disputes with the foundation in New York? Or donate more money?

It was time for us all to go upstairs. We passed through the house and out into the garden. Metal stairs, very like those of a fire escape, at the far end of the palace led up to the roof. What a lovely sight it was when we got there.

Torches were lit along the terrace parapet. Long tables covered with cloths were laid out with rows of champagne flutes. Behind the tables were white-jacketed barmen. But best of all was the view.

To our left was the Accademia Bridge, while sweeping down to the right was the great, white-domed church of the Salute and beyond it the opening of the Grand Canal into the bacino. The sky was slashed with orange and yellow and then covered by geranium red squiggles. The sun set fast and by the time I was sipping a glass of Prosecco, stars gave us a wink from up in the inky sky.

The tidbits were delicate and varied. What were the delicious pale green, crispy leaves that crunched and were so aromatic?

"Deep-fried sage," someone said.

Deep-fried sage. . . . The food a little girl with culinary flair might prepare for her favorite dolly's dinner. Only here on the roof of Peggy's palace they were for real. And delicious.

ALL I HAD TO DO in order to complete my press registration for the Venice Film Festival was to go out to the Lido, collect my identification tag and hand over a fee, some $25, which the next morning is exactly what I did.

Along with my official I.D., I was given a list of films. There were going to be screenings every day from 8:00 A.M. until after midnight. It would be impossible to keep up with even half the previews, never mind the press conferences and other special events, unless a person was staying on the Lido. But what were these special events going to be? There was no advance information.

I walked across to the Excelsior to have a look around since I'd never been inside the hotel. I'd heard it was the poshest place on the Lido—the hotel of choice for Venetians and visitors who want to hire a beach cabana for the summer. But the season was over now. The hotel, in all its Cecil B. DeMille Egyptian Art Deco extravagance, had become a movie sellers' marketplace for the week.

The bar was crowded with men in collarless designer shirts and baseball hats—some with, some without, a ponytail sticking through the vent. Some wore the vents in front, of course.

I walked onto the terrace to have a look at the sea. A cool, brisk wind was blowing around the skirts of starlets in skimpy dresses. Bending over, with chests thrown forward, they were posing on a tacky, makeshift stage. There was a tent in the garden for private parties. It could just as easily have been an automobile dealers' convention.

I decided to go home. But I couldn't get out of the hotel. Crowds were blocking all the exits. Opposite the Excelsior was a private dock for its guests. An even bigger crowd was over there. All of them were teenage girls. There were hundreds of them.

I was not going to be a regular at this film festival. Besides everything else, it took an hour to get to or from it. Half my life would be spent on the vaporetto. But I certainly wasn't going to skip the next day's press preview. It was the new Merchant Ivory movie. I would just have time to fit in the press opening of the Maya exhibition at Palazzo Grassi before the film began.

A RESTLESS MOMENTUM WAS BUILDING UP as I rushed from one event to the next. I began to feel that I was turning into a brainless culture consumer. Or was all this culture consumption burning my brains out? I couldn't tell and didn't brood about it as I sped along.

The next morning I practically ran to Campo San Samuele where the press conference for the Maya exhibition was going to be held. I said hello to the contingent of British journalists brought over by Fiat. We would all meet up for drinks in the evening at the PGC and then go to dinner at Montin—where once Hemingway bent his elbow at the bar and Ezra Pound had dinner. Pilgrims have been turning up ever since.

The Mayan civilization is so alien to me that the objects I was looking at might as well have been moon rocks. I had no idea which ones were religious—if any of them were—and which items might have been strictly utilitarian. Usually in museums I want to look at, rather than read about, what's on view. But here a short, introductory lecture might have helped. The catalogue was informative but who was going to read five hundred pages on the hoof. It was so heavy that I'd left it in the press office to collect later.

Fiat is a generous provider. Prosecco, wine, tiny sandwiches filled with Parma ham, minuscule tarts, coffee and chocolate cake were set out on long tables in the museum café. After lunch, I toured the exhibition again and then rushed off to the Lido.

MERCHANT IVORY'S *A SOLDIER'S DAUGHTER NEVER CRIES* was being screened in a vast white tent in a field between the lagoon and the sea. Its entrance was done up like a movie lobby complete with candy counter. Today for the press the ice cream was free. All the journalists were licking fast-melting chocolate pops.

I sat down in the first row of the second tier of the plush movie theater seats and soon began gabbing with the people on my left. They were two Italian men more or less my age, dressed in crisply pressed sport clothes. They were television film critics, they told me.

What a good-natured, world-weary double act my companions were. It was as if they'd seen and done everything, possibly more than once, but were determined to have a grand old time as they saw it all over again. The film we soon were watching may have temporarily defeated even them.

It was quickly obvious that this story of a rich and famous American writer living an expatriate glamorous life in Paris with his brittle wife and their two children must be about James Jones, author of *From Here to Eternity*. Kris Kristofferson was playing Jim, the hard-drinking, poker-loving—and rich—novelist. But the movie didn't know if it was about him or his daughter.

The only engaging scene took place at the teenage Ms. Jones's private day school. One of her classmates, a real sweetie, was an imaginative and clever fellow but also gawky, both physically and socially. They are pals. He longs for more.

The high-strung, doting mother of this boy appears in the classroom. She sits herself down at the piano (don't ask how a piano happens to be in there), and gets ready to accompany the obviously reluctant son she has pushed into performing.

Looking helpless and miserable, yet managing to give young Ms. Jones a glance filled with yearning, he stands and composes himself. Mom hits the keyboard and from her boy out comes, "Non so più, cosa son, cosa faccio." Birdsong pure.

He was our soprano, the voice that came in through our bedroom window first thing every morning.

When the movie was over, everyone was glad to be set free. I may have been the only person who hadn't been entirely bored.

On the vaporetto back to Venice, I began to wonder. Had the singing been dubbed? Was the person we heard every morning this very fellow? If not, who was downstairs?

I climbed up to the stucchi, showered and changed. I told Henry about the film and the amazing boy. Then it was time to leave again.

We had drinks at the Guggenheim, where yet another large cocktail party was under way, and then we had dinner at Montin with the English journalists. It was relaxed, even fun. About midnight we said goodbye. H. and I walked home. We got to Ca' Donà at half past twelve. I was wrecked.

Pushed under our door was a note. I was to telephone Françoise Donà dalle Rose "before 10" to make an appointment for a meeting. Damn. Tomorrow I would have to talk about that contract again.

17

Battle Stations

I didn't want to see Françoise Donà, but of course I would. Ten A.M., however, was impossible. I wrote her a note proposing that we meet at two. Leaving our door ajar, I went out to slip it under Francesco's.

As I yanked at the heavy maroon barriers separating our landing from the hall, I heard a bang. The stucchi door had slammed shut. My keys were inside.

Well that was all right. So was Henry.

I went back to the stucchi and rang our bell. I didn't hear any footsteps. But I did hear a door open. I had a look through the porthole. Somebody was standing at the entrance to Francesco's apartment. It was Gaia. I walked over. She was looking very sleepy. I apologized for disturbing her. Then I went back to the stucchi and tried our bell again.

The only sound that followed was the opening of Francesco's door again. This time it was Giovanni standing there.

What a time to discover that the two apartments shared a single doorbell. Why hadn't they told me? Or even more to the point, why hadn't they installed separate bells?

Giovanni, in self-defense, quite sensibly suggested that I get into the stucchi through the internal door connecting the two apartments. Fortunately none of us had got around to locking it.

Henry was in bed. He'd never noticed I was gone. He'd just assumed I was in the kitchen or the bath. Well, yes, he had heard a bell, but what would I have been doing wandering around on the landing in the middle of the night? He'd reckoned that one of the film people had lost his way since quite a lot of that had been going on.

In the morning I phoned Françoise to confirm our appointment. That's when I discovered that with all the confusion about the doors—and all the Prosecco—I'd never actually left the note for her. We agreed to get together at half past two.

I went out for the papers. As I was going downstairs, the door to the piano nobile opened. A woman, middle-aged and trim, began speaking to me in American.

"Do you know where the buzzer is?" she asked. "I can't work out how to let people in when they ring the outside bell."

"Shall I have a look?" I offered.

I had no more idea than she did about where it was. But I wasn't going to pass up another chance to have a look at the portego of the piano nobile.

She opened the door wider.

I walked inside. A youth was coming out of the dining room. He was a dark-haired, slightly awkward-looking fellow—Ms. Jones's singing suitor.

"You were the star of the movie," I said. I meant it, too.

He smiled and thanked me.

"Was it you singing?" I asked, suddenly worried that it wasn't.

"Oh yes," he answered.

I beamed.

AFTER I GOT THE NEWSPAPERS and some vegetables at the fruttivendolo near the house, I went back to Ca' Donà. Just as I was about to shut the garden gate behind me, Françoise called out. She too was coming home with groceries and didn't want to have to put all her bags on the ground while she hunted for her keys. We smiled. Alas, I knew this was not an omen.

When I got back to the stucchi I went to my desk and booted up my

computer. I had been keeping a list of all the things that weren't functioning properly. Now I printed it out.

1. Bidet not working.

2. No hot water from bathroom sink.

3. One of the kitchen radiators doesn't give heat.

4. No replacement refrigerator, though new one promised.
   (Even at lowest temp, everything is coated with ice.)

5. No replacement iron. Iron so badly worn on bottom,
   catches on everything. Wire dangerously frayed. Need
   ironing board.

There was more.

Armed with this paper and whatever toughness I could muster, I
would enter the coming fight.

AT 2:30, FRANÇOISE RANG THE DOORBELL. Henry and I were sitting in
the salone. The three of us exchanged greetings, and then he left. I was
the one who wanted to live here; I would have to deal with the complications.

Françoise was stony-faced. I was nervous and angry. We pretended,
however, that we were two amiable adults having a normal conversation.

I began by observing that many things had been removed since our
last stay in the apartment, for example, the little velvet side chairs.

She agreed that more seating for guests would be desirable.

"There are a couple of small armchairs in the piano nobile near the
entrance to Titti's apartment," she told me. "Ask Gaia for them."

What would be gained if I told her that Gaia had a grudge against
me and would do no such thing. Françoise wouldn't have believed me.
Gaia would deny it. Either way I wouldn't get the small armchairs.
Scratch that one.

"It would be very nice to have the chaise longue back," I said.

"No, that is impossible," Françoise told me. "I have brought it next door because I must treat it for woodworm." End of the subject.

As for the works of art which had been removed . . .

"They are out being restored."

"You know, quite a few other things also are gone," I pointed out.

"We did not take photographs with a contract stating everything should be as it was. In this house furniture is always being moved around," Françoise retorted.

On the subject of the iron, things improved. It would be replaced. But an ironing board? "We never needed one," she said as if I were being frivolous.

Of course they didn't need one. Titti irons beautifully.

As for the new refrigerator, Françoise merely lifted an arm and lowered it again.

Discussion about my list was over. I could see from her face that the woman sitting across from me had now moved into implacable, rock-hard, let's-get-down-to-the-real-business, landladydom.

Françoise pulled a sheaf of forms from a large brown envelope. "These are for the inventory," she told me. "We must make one."

This was both annoying and so ridiculous that it was almost quaint. Henry and I had already lived in this same apartment without an inventory. And there had been many more precious items in it then. It was obvious to Françoise that I loved the place and longed to stay. She had to know by now that we were not going to make off with the family's possessions.

But no. We would have to march around the stucchi for hours counting all the dishes and sheets and so forth. Would we have to list every book, also? What a waste of time. The expression on her face and the tone of her voice made it clear that there was no point in making any comments.

"Let's do the inventory tomorrow," I proposed.

She agreed.

"The house must be put on another basis," Françoise declared. "In future it must be run as a business."

I understood that when Françoise had said "In future," she meant starting today, with me. I was their guinea pig.

To the so-called family committee, running Ca' Donà as a business seemed to mean one thing: Give less and get more out of the tenant.

First: The stucchi must be insured.

In response to my lack of enthusiasm, Françoise was, by her own description, magnanimous. "I will pay the general household insurance for the apartment this year," she told me. There was, however, the additional cost of insuring the stucchi's exceptional contents.

"We must cover the four paintings by Alessandro Longhi and the three most valuable items of furniture still remaining in the apartment," Françoise said.

These three items, I was told now, were the curvaceous secretary in the salone, the big, glass-fronted bookcase in the study and the decorated armadio in the bedroom.

"The paintings are the most valuable," she said, "but the insurers made me one price for everything. It will be cheaper that way."

Cheaper? This all-or-nothing insurance deal would cost me more than a thousand dollars—on top of what I'd already given them for rent and security. I did not speak.

"If you don't want to pay," said Françoise, who knew I did not, "we will remove the paintings and the furniture."

I stared at her. Then I asked, as casually as if I were asking a friend's opinion about a pair of shoes in a shop window, "And what will you put in place of what you take away?"

Only the smallest pause indicated that Françoise had not thought about this.

"We will find things from the magazzino or the other apartments," she said.

I sat and waited. It was evident that quite a lot more was on her mind. Besides I was in such a bad temper, if I'd opened my mouth the situation might have become far worse.

"This insurance only comes into effect if you are staying in the apartment as my guest," Françoise now informed me.

Ah, a guest. . . . I took that to be a euphemism for "off the books."

Françoise would pay the insurers directly and I would reimburse her for what she'd laid out. In cash. What was more, in future the rent was to be paid in cash, along with all other expenses.

"If you were to pay officially," she explained, "once you have stayed in the apartment more than a month, the family would have to register the contract."

Well, if they weren't planning to register the contract, what in the world was she carrying on about?

I didn't ask. I knew there would be no sensible, never mind businesslike, explanation. I also understood that this whole enterprise was a bizarre charade.

Once a month, I would have to go across Venice to my bank. I'd have to wait on a long, slow-moving line to draw out cash and walk back to the stucchi with loads of bills stuffed into my coat pocket. Well, paying cash for everything from wine to restaurant bills to plumbers is common in Venice. Venetians routinely walk around town with bundles of money on them, it seemed. At least the city is safe. It was a nuisance but I didn't object. I reckoned I'd better concentrate on the one issue here that was driving me wild: the insurance and her attitude about it.

How dare this woman threaten to remove the best of what still remained in the apartment if I didn't come up with more money. After we had agreed on the terms for the year. After I had moved in. It was extortion.

"This is not the time to tell me that I have to pay insurance or else," I said slowly. "In life there has to be give and take."

Françoise agreed. She then added, "There is no possibility of compromise."

That I had feelings, needs and a bank balance which might not be bottomless were matters not to be considered in our exchange. There was no exchange.

"I have the new contract which you must sign," she informed me.

"I will give you my answer tomorrow," I said.

The conversation had been so upsetting, I wanted time to calm down. And to think. I didn't know what to do. But I knew I didn't want to agree.

We made an appointment to meet at 1:30 the following afternoon. Françoise left.

I sat in the stucchi glum, furious and brokenhearted.

Less than a week before I had been living in an enchanted world. I'd spent my time in exile learning more about the history of the house and the family. I'd felt so lucky that this amazing chance had come to me and that I had been able to take it.

Now my life in Venice was being poisoned. How could these people behave this way?

I wasn't being excessively picky. I hadn't asked for the return of the linen sheets embroidered with coronets we'd had the first time, nor even the replacement of the worn-out items they gave us instead, one of which had holes in it already. Yes, I had kept a list of what was wrong with the place, but I hadn't been running to them with demands to repair and replace all these things. On the contrary, I understood they had their problems. I didn't want to add to the weight on Francesco's back. Yet they were turning me from an ally into an enemy. And for what? A phony piece of paper and a thousand dollars.

That night as I tried to sleep, I started crying.

"It's been a mistake," I said to Henry, snuffling. "I should never have rented this place. Let's leave."

My sense of alrightness in life had floated on the dream of coming to Venice. By now my love for the city seemed inseparable from my love for Ca' Donà and the stucchi. If I left the house, I wasn't sure there was any place in town I would want to live. I might have to abandon Venice, too.

I didn't want to go. But I felt so hounded by the family, the atmosphere had become so rancid, that leaving seemed my only choice.

Henry consoled me. He gave me encouragement. I was comforted and I was surprised. He had been against spending so much time in Venice; he didn't wish to live in count Donà's house. Yet he soothed me and he encouraged me to stick to what I wanted.

When I wasn't sobbing, I was resentful. And puzzled. If I went on battling with Françoise, would I win? I couldn't work her out.

The urge to go was genuine. It was in me to bolt.

I didn't.

I was stubborn and love-struck, even if the faded glamour of the stucchi now was giving me more misery than pleasure. London, where already the days were shrinking fast and the nights stretching out, did not beckon.

The next morning I asked Henry, "How do you say blackmail in French?"

"*Chantage,*" he said.

I wrote it down.

"Don't use it if you can possibly avoid it," he advised. "She won't like it. It will upset her."

I did not say "Good. That's the point." He knew how I felt.

I needed whatever weapons I could scrape together. And I wanted Françoise to understand how terrible her behavior was.

Enough. We decided to go out into Venice and inspect the preparations for the Regatta Storica being held later in the afternoon.

When we got to the androne, Françoise was just leaving the office. We all smiled, reflexively. No one spoke.

Henry and I decided to take the vaporetto from Ca' d'Oro down the Grand Canal and get off at San Marco. Then, after walking across the piazza, we'd pick up the boat that leaves from Zaccària, travels through the Arsenale into the north lagoon and along back to the Fondamenta Nuove. If anything was going on we were unlikely to miss it.

Nothing was. Or so we thought until the vaporetto passed my favorites lions in all of Venice: the four ancient white marble, larger-than-life-sized beasts guarding the entrance to the Arsenale.

We were now entering that part of the legendary boatyard which is off-limits to civilians on foot. It was here that Venice produced the ships—along with their anchors, oars and ropes—on which the wealth and power of the Most Serene Republic was built.

These days the Arsenale belongs to the Italian Navy. It doesn't need all its vast space anymore and there are many, as in endless, discussions in Venice about what is to be done with it. It would be the new home for the School of Architecture. It would be an expanded home for the art biennale. A conference center. A museum of boats, perhaps. . . .

"Look at that," I called out to Henry as our vaporetto approached the opening in the brick wall that separates the Arsenale from the lagoon beyond.

Seven or eight big rowing boats were parked outside one of the centuries-old, low storage sheds just to the left of the channel. Each one was decorated differently, although gold paint dominated in every case. There was a boat done up in aqua and red, another in a roll call of greens. All were bold and gaudy. And with no exceptions they were tacky, like props for some provincial summer theater's production of *H.M.S. Pinafore.*

The largest of these gigantic, if rowable, toys surely was meant to be the *Bucintoro,* the doge's ceremonial galley.

On the wall of the study in the stucchi there was a hand-colored etching of the grand and gilded Bucintoro in all its glory.

It was on the Bucintoro that the doge was taken into the bacino each year in May on Ascension Day for the ceremony that became known as the *Festa della Sensa.*

The doge, accompanied by those people judged to be most important at the time, whether Venetian or foreign, would be rowed into the lagoon followed by a flotilla of hundreds of boats and gondolas. When the Bucintoro reached the most northern mouth of the Adriatic, the Lido opening at San Nicolò, he would toss a gold ring into the water, reciting the words: *In segno di eterno dominio, Noi, Doge di Venezia ti sposiamo, o mare!* (As a sign of your eternal domination, we, Doge of Venice, marry you, o sea!)

The first of these weddings took place in 1177. And while, of course, the Adriatic, like all seas, had control over the destiny of men, Venice wasn't entirely powerless herself.

"Sea-girt City," wrote Shelley, "thou hast been ocean's child and then his Queen."

The last Bucintoro was built in 1729. It was thirty-four meters long and on two levels. The rowers sat below. There were 168 of them, four at each of its forty-two oars. The ship was encrusted with gold. Goethe, who saw it on his visit to Venice, observed, "This state-galley is a good index to show what the Venetians were, and what they considered themselves."

The Festa della Sensa ended with the fall of the Republic. The French, during their occupation of Venice, stripped the Bucintoro of its elaborately carved and gilded decorations and destroyed her. A fine model of the galley when it was still in its glory is displayed in the Naval Museum on the Riva degli Schiavoni near the Public Gardens, not very far from the Arsenale, where this kitschy creation was now bobbing up and down at its flimsy dock.

In 1986, it was decided to revive the ceremony and nowadays the mayor of Venice is rowed out to the Lido in this silly, plastic-embellished, oversized bucket. It, too, is a good index of what Venice has become. But I don't suppose the mayor wants to think so. He is, he says, trying to prevent the city from turning into Disneyland.

This Bucintoro was a disappointment. I'd expected something grander and certainly not grotesque. But then I began to think that these rowboats were gay in their fashion. Even the semiderelict sheds in the Arsenale seemed cheered up by their presence.

In the afternoon the boats would be rowed into the lagoon and around to the Grand Canal where they would lead a parade of historic vessels. They'd seem more like an entertainment than a joke when in the great procession. Or so I hoped. We would be there to see for ourselves.

Ah, but before that . . .

When she'd finished lunch, Françoise rang our bell.

I WAS FROSTY NOW AND SO WAS SHE. To me she was trouble. Nothing else. We sat at opposite ends of the sofa.

Françoise sounded almost vulnerable when she said, as much to herself as to me: "We have been acting like amateurs. Now we must be professional."

I'd heard it before and I knew what it meant. I got to the point.

"My fear is that if I agree to give you more money, you will just come up with another demand later on when the committee meets again and decides that, in order to run things professionally, they need even more money from me."

"You are dramatizing," said Françoise.

I raised an eyebrow.

Directness yielded nothing. I tried a small detour.

"To make a reasonable decision, I must know what the alternatives are," I told her. "I would like to see the furniture you will bring in to replace what you've said you will take away."

Out we went, Françoise leading the way, through the maroon metal doors and into Francesco's apartment.

Along the wall nearest the door was a row of floor-to-ceiling columns. In between some of them were built-in bookshelves. I wondered if this had been the stucchi's library, when, as I imagined, both apartments had been one. At the far end of the room, near the windows facing the garden, I saw the damask-covered chaise longue—recuperating from its woodworm treatment presumably. The place was so crowded with furniture, paintings and objects of art that it looked like Christie's collection department after an auction.

Overnight the list of items to be insured "or else" had been edited. The desk and chest of drawers in the study had been added and the armadio subtracted. Not that Françoise actually told me this. She merely led me to various items and then mentioned what they would be replacing.

How could she imagine I would accept her story about the insurer's "package deal," if the contents of the package were changed every day? It was as idiotic as it was infuriating.

The bookcase I was offered, though much smaller than the one we had, would be serviceable. But otherwise there wasn't a single piece of furniture I was shown that I liked or would consider living with.

I pointed out that if they removed the secretary now in the salone, the one in our bedroom would be a good replacement. She had no objection.

Françoise and I went back to the stucchi and sat down.

"You know," I began, "I would have thought the paintings by Longhi were much safer here in the frames made for them than they will be almost anywhere else in the house."

She saw the point.

"As for the furniture," I went on, "surely it's better not to move these old things around."

She agreed with me about that, too.

But her demand for insurance money "or else" seemed to have been locked in a lead safe where nothing I said could penetrate.

Well, let them damage their precious possessions if that's what they are determined to do. The stucchi, with its beautiful decorations and fine proportions, would continue to be grand without them. If they insisted on seeing me as a cash-dispensing machine, then to hell with them. Let them take the lot.

"I have no choice," I said to Françoise. "If I agree to your demands I will be subject to further requests."

She looked shocked. Then angry. I now gave her reason to be angrier.

"And I am not going to pay a second month's security," I added. "We agreed on one month. And that's it."

Our meeting was over.

Françoise told me that she must go back to Paris the next day. Giovanni and Francesco would be in touch about the removal of furniture and paintings. Gaia would see to the things that Françoise agreed must be provided: a better iron, for example. As for the refrigerator, now there wasn't even the fiction that it would be replaced.

But our business had not been concluded. Oh no. More torture was ahead. Françoise's demand that I sign a new contract had not been dropped. It was merely postponed.

We would attend to it in three weeks when she came back. And we'd do the inventory, too. She didn't see that it was absurd to write up an inventory after yet another month. She had a business plan and she was going to stick to it.

Françoise left.

Thank goodness.

ON OUR WAY OUT to find a place on the Grand Canal from which we could see the Regatta Storica, Henry and I noticed that the androne seemed emptier. Maybe some of the boats from the house were going to be part of the great procession. That would be very nice; provided our landlady wasn't riding in one of them.

I was not a cheerful person as we bounded along the sunny streets of Venice. But twenty minutes later I was smiling.

What a parade. It looked as if everyone in Venice who had a rowing boat had come out onto the Grand Canal. And not only were people in old boats, lots of them were in old-fashioned costumes—including Gaia and Giovanni. We saw them rowing along in one of the larger boats usually kept in the androne. They had piled it high with enormous, raffia-covered wine casks and draped it with fishing nets. The two of them had dressed as peasants. Gaia was wearing a ruffled blouse and long, full skirt with an apron over its front. Giovanni wore an open shirt and breeches. They looked expansive and happy. As all Venetians do, they were rowing standing up.

The whole of the city was in a party mood and I was too.

By evening I was back at Ca' Donà and soon feeling miserable again. That night I cried some more. But in the morning, I woke up feeling better. I'd started thinking of Françoise Donà as Lucrezia Borgia—and for some reason that cheered me up.

A WEEK PASSED. Francesco and Giovanni did not ring our bell. There was no sign of Gaia, either. No iron was left for us. No ironing board. No nothing.

So far, the only result of my skirmishes with Françoise was the arrival of a ratty, pale green plastic colander. She'd dropped it off just before she went to Paris. She also left me a copy of the contract to study and sign.

I had shoved the contract under a stack of papers on the soon-to-be-removed desk. But now I decided to read this document which she did not intend to file but which she continued insisting I must sign.

I was to agree to be responsible for the repair of any damage to the walls and floors of the stucchi; that work to be done in accordance with standards set by the Soprintendenza dei Bene arte. No mention was made of the existing water damage caused by holes in the roof, no mention was made of the landlord's responsibility to keep the fabric of the building in good repair. As for the floors, they had been patched up many times—and not expertly—in the centuries since they'd been made.

Maybe I should draw up a counter-contract. In it, the family Donà would be responsible for all damage to the floor or walls or furnishings—mine as well as theirs—caused by the elements and by their negligence—their failure to have the roof repaired or the plumbing and wiring done to current code.

A person would have to be very innocent or stupid to sign the document that had been left with me. I put it back under the other papers on the desk.

Weeks passed. I heard nothing from any of the Donà. I started to feel more relaxed. I began to feel my love for the stucchi again.

The exhibition in honor of Peggy Guggenheim was about to open. I was busy thinking about the show when bang, Françoise Donà telephoned. She was next door. She was coming over in an hour. We would tackle the inventory. Oh hell.

I warned H. that we were in for it. He then did an unexpected thing. He removed four wine glasses from the salone's china closet. There were dozens of these serviceable glasses lined up there.

"What are you doing?" I asked.

He explained that by putting these away, if any of the others were broken, we would have replacements.

I didn't object. We both had begun to have the mentality of tenants.

Françoise arrived. The three of us set to work making lists. Henry and I counted and Françoise re-counted, or vice versa.

"There are sixty-three," I said when we'd finished toting up the wine glasses.

Françoise looked surprised.

"I thought there were more," she said offhandedly. Then she shrugged.

So this, too, was a charade. She'd already done an inventory! She'd known precisely how many glasses were in that closet. Really, it was bizarre.

"You may find one or two of the glasses are broken," Françoise now volunteered. "Be careful."

When she'd done her private survey, she'd found broken glasses in the closet—and she'd left them there. I would never understand the way this woman's mind worked.

We counted every plate and cup and saucer in the closets. But there was no suggestion that we should count the sheets. Or the towels. Nor list the framed prints and books or note down the precious textiles and their condition. This inventory was as haphazard as it was amateurish. Then, as an afterthought, Lucrezia Borgia added to the list "one pair of blue and white Chinese vases with pink silk roses." The four eighteenth-century paintings by Alessandro Longhi—the reason the insurance was such a big deal—were not even on the list.

"Have you signed the contract?" Françoise asked when we had finished.

"Not yet," I told her. "I have to show it to my lawyer in New York." Very well. We would go over it the next time she came to Venice.

Françoise left. Two days later she went back to Paris.

Good riddance.

The wooden chap in painted breeches and white stockings was still standing outside Francesco's apartment. Nothing had been done to mend his base. Without saying a word, Henry walked over, picked him up and brought him back to the stucchi. He glued the crack, tied the base with rope to hold it while it set, and, two days later, the boys once again stood holding up their candles on either side of the arch as we ate dinner in the salone.

I did not mail the contract to Virgil, my lawyer in New York. I wasn't going to pay him $1000 to tell me that only a jerk would sign it.

18

Love or Money

Could the Donà get rid of me if I refused to sign their so-called contract? I asked everybody for advice. I wasn't just trying to find out about my rights, I kept hoping somebody might have an idea how I could get these people to leave me alone.

To my relief, it turned out that the fax Francesco sent me in London was legally binding. I was, of course, also pleased to hear that in Venice the person responsible for filing a rental contract is the landlord. I wouldn't be blamed, fined or charged if the authorities found out I was living in the stucchi without one. I learned something else, too. I was not the only one being messed around with by my landlord.

"We planned to do a lot of entertaining while we were in Venice," a rich American woman told me. "We were shown a large apartment with many rooms and baths, and we decided to rent it."

They went ahead and asked people to come and stay.

When they came back to town and moved in, they had a surprise.

"All the bathrooms were locked, except one," this woman said.

Their contessa had gone abroad, taking the keys to the locked bathrooms with her. Or maybe she'd just stashed them someplace. It amounted to the same thing; the bathrooms were unusable.

The woman and her husband were stuck with the apartment. Her invitations to houseguests had to be canceled.

Someone else told me about the apartment he'd rented in Dorsoduro. When he moved in, he discovered the owner had taken away the telephone. He challenged her about it but she refused to put it back. His landlady said a telephone had not been specified in their agreement.

Then there was the couple who rented an apartment in Castello for three months because it had a lovely long, wide view of a canal stretching into the distance; a view that all three living-room windows and both bedroom windows looked out on. Within days of their moving in, workmen began draining that picturesque canal. For the rest of their stay the view was of mud. From eight A.M. until four P.M., dredging equipment made a tremendous racket. There was dust everywhere and, depending on the wind, a terrible stench. The landlord, it turned out, knew this work was planned. A count, and a professor, he offered them no compensation. Or even an apology. And on top of it all, he refused to let the couple put their name on the downstairs door in case someone from the tax department came snooping. Too bad if people visiting couldn't work out which bell to ring.

I wasn't going to get sympathy from this lot. Or from anybody else in town.

"Venetians are spoiled," said Vivian. "They think they can get away with anything."

I ALREADY KNEW this was true of the people running Venice's restaurants. I received my first lesson in their high-handed ways during our summer stay.

I'd suggested to Filipo that we meet at a lively-looking place in the Calle Lunga Santa Maria Formosa for a reunion lunch. When we'd finished our meal and were given the bill, Filipo looked at the single figure written on it and frowned.

"I would like a detailed account," he told the waiter, in Venetian.

The man was reluctant. Filipo insisted.

This time the waiter noted each item we'd consumed, separately. His scowl developed new depths as he finished totting it up.

Filipo gave me the new figure. It was 30 percent less than the first one.

"That's what Venetians are like," he said as we went out into the busy, shop-lined calle. "We've been at it since the Fourth Crusade."

Crafty Venice had done very well out of the Fourth Crusade, I discovered when I read up on it after my lunch with Filipo. I could see what he meant.

In the thirteenth century, the French made a plan to set out for Jerusalem with thirty thousand men. They ordered two hundred ships and a year's provisions from the Serenissima. But Enrico Dandolo, the doge, had a hunch they'd never come up with the money. You could say he'd strung them along calculating that he would be able to put their default to the Republic's use. When ships and supplies were ready, the French did not have the money to settle their account and the doge was prepared.

The French would be allowed to sail for the Holy Land in the ships built at the Arsenale but only if they agreed to join Venice and her fifty armed galleys on a few military operations along the way.

In 1204, Dandolo was over eighty and blind. But he was brave as well as cunning. The doge himself led this enormous fleet to the capture of Constantinople. The conquerors created such mayhem that in 2001 the pope finally apologized to the Eastern Church, which was still outraged about the episode. The four Hellenistic gilded bronze horses which once had been taken to Constantinople as booty now became part of the Most Serene Republic's spoils of war. Placed above the central door of the basilica, they have been known as the horses of San Marco ever since. More important for Venice was her share of the captured dominions. The Republic now became a Mediterranean power, something she could not have achieved on her own.

Dandolo's will to profit, minus his heroism, characterizes Venetian restaurant owners today. "If you don't like the food or the prices, don't come back," appears to be their motto. Some other tourist will fill your seat tomorrow, no matter what awful stuff is on the plate and how much it costs. The high-handed tendency to gouge people applied not only to restaurants, I now understood. Or, as one friend of mine put it when I told her about my real estate troubles, "It's a very Venetian story."

The time had come for me to learn how to be a Venetian tenant.

This wasn't what I'd wanted but there was no point being soppy about it. Circumstances had changed, my attitude needed to as well.

From now on, I would not volunteer anything. In the future, when my landlady wanted to talk, we could meet next door at Francesco's or downstairs in the amministrazione. I had rented the stucchi for a year. I would have my privacy, at least, even if I couldn't have the peace of mind I longed for. And I settled on what I hoped would be an all-purpose negotiating strategy. I would act as if I agreed to whatever was asked of me—and then I would do absolutely nothing. This seemed to work for my landlady. Maybe it would work for me, too.

Uncertainty about the date of my showdown with Lucrezia Borgia, as well as the constant threat that Francesco and Giovanni would take away the furniture and paintings, made me anxious. But the longer Françoise stayed in Paris and the more time that passed without the furniture movers turning up, the more often my worries took a nap. I felt like branching out socially and sometimes a social life came to me.

"Hi, I'm Sally Spector," said a woman I didn't know when one morning I answered the phone. "Carole Rifkind gave me your number."

An American from outside Chicago, she sounded as if she had arrived in Venice the day before yesterday but, she explained, she'd been living in the city for twenty years. She proposed that we meet for coffee and we made a date to get together at Rosa Salva in Campo Ss. Giovanni e Paolo. The predictable heat of summer continues well into the fall in Venice but now the weather was changeable. We agreed that if it was warm enough, we'd sit outside.

A cold wind was blowing across the deserted campo when I got there. I went into Rosa Salva.

"Are you Sally?" I asked a woman sitting at a table in the backroom of the brightly lit caffè. She had a gray crew cut and blue eyes open so wide you could see the whites all around. She was wearing knitted gloves with the fingers cut off and a patchwork sweater.

"Yes, I am," she chirped.

VENETIANS SEEMED WARM, considerate and gossipy, but I was also finding them formal and reserved. (This isn't a contradiction: the stories

they repeat usually have to do with other people's lives—not their own.)
Foreigners, on the other hand, acted more like passengers on a long
ocean voyage. In no time, they were decanting their life stories. Sally
Spector, who by her own account lived a local's life, was in this respect
true to expatriate form. Within minutes of our meeting, I felt as if we
were in deck chairs waiting for the purser to bring us cups of bouillon.
The story she had to tell was amusing and revealing but in its way also
disconcerting.

In part, Sally's tale had to do with a subject I already was rather interested in—the small charities that exist in many countries to raise money
for the restoration of artworks in Venice. By the time I finished writing
about the National Trust, I began to think that a lot of charitable giving
is a form of social money laundering. People who donate cash to this
kind of worthy cause get a chance to rub shoulders with folk grander
than themselves and visit places they would never be invited to otherwise. I had a hunch that the Venetian restoration charities might provide me with material of a related kind.

Sally told me she'd studied art history in college and then married a
sociologist. He got a job teaching at McGill University in Montreal and
that's where they settled down. But Sally had always loved Venice and
in the early 1980s the two of them decided to spend a summer in the
city.

Not long after they arrived, she met Colonel James Gray. Sally didn't
say how they'd met but that wasn't important. More crucial was the
impact he made.

"He was charismatic," she told me.

The colonel had set up a charity called the International Fund for
Monuments. Among its first undertakings was aid for restoration work
on Easter Island. To help publicize his campaign, he'd even managed to
have one of the extraordinary colossal figures shipped to New York and
placed in front of the Seagram Building on Park Avenue.

"He just loved monuments," Sally said, admiringly. "He liked big
architectural jobs." And because he loved Italy, not long after the dramatic flood of 1966 had washed over the city, he organized the Venice
Project.

By the time Sally and her husband turned up for the summer some fifteen years later, the colonel had opened a small office for the Project upstairs in the Scuola Grande San Giovanni Evangelista. The restoration of this lyrical example of fifteenth-century architecture had been one of the Project's first undertakings in the city.

According to Sally, the colonel, who was no bureaucrat, decided to have an office in Venice for down-to-earth reasons.

"He thought American tourists should have a place they could go to use the toilet," she said, laughing.

Sally went to work for him, filling in for the woman who ran the office, who was on vacation. Clearly Sally had been, and was still, smitten. The colonel, she told me, had combined elegance with good manners, poise and clout, and he had a gift for raising money.

"He wasn't a rich man," she assured me. "He wasn't good-looking either." But, she added with some awe, "He was fantastic with rich women."

His flair with those of the female gender was not confined to the rich. Later I met a man who'd known the colonel well. "James would enter a party," he told me, "and you could be positive he would leave with the best-looking woman there."

The colonel, it turns out, had married five times before he retired from active duty as a groom.

What a pity not to have seen him in action, I thought as I listened to this account.

Naturally regard for Gray was less universal among men. John McAndrew, a well-to-do art historian, started out as a colleague of the colonel's on the Venice Project. But in 1971, he broke away and set up another American charity devoted to the restoration of the city. It was called Save Venice, Inc.

Some people say the split occurred because McAndrew wanted the Fund for Monuments to restrict its activities to Venice and the colonel didn't agree. The way Sally put it, the two men rubbed each other the wrong way. "They couldn't stand each other," was how someone later explained it to me.

(More than a quarter of a century later, another split and a messy one occurred. By then, Save Venice was contributing more to the restoration of Venice than all the other small charities combined. Yet again, differences of opinion, or temperament, led to the creation of a breakaway group, Venetian Heritage.)

It was apparent, as I listened to Sally's tale, that she had been one of the colonel's conquests. I don't mean they had an affair. I have no idea one way or the other about that. What I mean is that, having charmed her, the colonel saw his opening and took it.

As the summer came to an end the colonel had a chat with Sally.

"I don't want to break up your marriage," he said, "but I hope you will stay on and work here full-time."

I could almost see the old fox stroking his muzzle.

Sally Spector took the job as manager of the Venice Project's office. Her husband went back to McGill.

I knew what it felt like to be in love with Venice. But how could she give up her husband for a *city*?

"Half fairy tale; half snare," Thomas Mann called Venice. Other people, too, have written of Venice's power to entrap.

I hadn't felt frightened before. But listening to Sally, I began to wonder if Venice might be a dragon lying in wait to capture women. Would it capture me?

Well, there must have been some other reason why Sally stayed behind and her husband didn't. However, if there was, she certainly didn't seem to be aware of it.

"I am as simple as I seem," she told me.

I was not going to argue. Sally appeared to be swift and intelligent but also willfully naive. A friend of hers calls her "Peter Pan."

Sally went on working for the Venice Project, even after Colonel James Gray died. But then came a new boss, or bosses, people as complicated as they seemed. The charity changed its name to the World Monuments Fund. Its chairman was Marilyn Perry, whom the colonel, I'd heard, had helped get the job running the Samuel Kress Foundation in New York. The WMF's new executive head was Bonnie Birnham.

The colonel had been one-of-a-kind. The two women now in charge naturally had a more conventional, which is to say professional, approach. The World Monuments Fund was on its way to becoming a sophisticated operation. A fund-raiser was hired. The latter was paid something like $70,000, I was told. That sounded like a lot of money for a small charity in the early 1980s.

It wasn't long before Sally was fired.

"For insubordination," she says. The translation was that she no longer fitted in.

It was a blow from which she appears to have recovered fully.

Sally gives private English lessons and occasionally guides rich visiting North Americans around the treasures of Venice, but she considers her true calling to be art.

Unlike many painters and writers and musicians, Sally takes a robust pleasure in her artistic gifts and the expression she gives them. And though she doubtless felt it was deserved, she was nevertheless delighted by the success she was having with *Venice and Food,* a book with her illustrations and a facsimile handwritten text.

"I'm not much of a cook," Sally confessed, shrugging. That hadn't daunted her either. Neither did the spelling and grammar errors in the text. She wouldn't bother fixing them in later editions.

I was struck by the degree to which Sally accepted herself and her situation. For instance, because she had little money, she lived in a place too small to share with her boyfriend. They could only spend weekends together. While she might have preferred things otherwise, this didn't upset her. Indeed, there seemed to be no area in which Sally's expectations exceeded her circumstances. Sally was content.

"Venice is an asylum," she told me. "A refuge."

Sally was the first such refugee I met. But she wasn't the last.

WHAT IS IT ABOUT THESE SEASIDE SPOTS favored by nature or beautified by man, spots where the rich and successful dally and waifs hunker down hoping to find a safe harbor? Provincetown on Cape Cod is such a town. Key West, too. Much of the south coast of France is, or was, another.

In Venice the voluntary refugees I met were talented or intelligent, sometimes both. Some worked long hours at poorly paid jobs and all were willing to sacrifice many things—physical comfort, fashionable clothes, apartments suited to entertaining friends—in order to preserve what was more crucial: a view of themselves that could not have been maintained almost anywhere else.

Of course, you could say that seeking refuge is also a very Venetian story. After all, Venice was founded by refugees. If people on the mainland hadn't felt the need to flee from the Huns and the Goths and the Germanic Longobards, they would never have settled on these marshy mudflats. And if they had not endured the mosquitos and the floods—protected only by their determination and the extreme shallowness of the water out of which the tiny islands rose—there never would have been a Venice in the first place. A Most Serene Republic would never have emerged. But the first settlers, the people who built the Serenissima, were men and women with drive. Coming to these islands wasn't an end for them but a beginning.

And me? I wanted to live in Venice. I was fleeing London. But did this make me one of the people looking for a hideout? I didn't want to think so. And I didn't think so. But by the time Sally and I left the caffè, I was unnerved. Might Venice be as wanton as she is beautiful? Was she going to make mischief for me?

I was jittery as I gave Henry an abridged version of Sally's story; I wanted him to reassure me that my love for Venice wouldn't "somehow" force us to separate. I knew this sounded irrational but I didn't feel so sure.

From then on H. teased me about our imminent breakup. As a cool compress to a feverish forehead, it worked well enough. It was not, however, a cure.

Because of all the other uncertainties in my life—the contract, the furniture removal and so on—I was feeling vulnerable. The first time we'd lived in the stucchi, everything had seemed wonderfully cozy. But now, so much had changed.

Well, we might as well make the most of the apartment while it still had its furniture and paintings—and, I thought, while we still were a twosome. We began entertaining.

Vivian came for a drink. Next Bill and Andrea came to dinner. Then, at last, Beate was able to have a meal at our house.

Beate, in her early thirties, was born in Frankfurt. She speaks a lovely, lilting English. A tiny woman, her high forehead and big gray eyes dominate her face, which, while disproportionately large, is also delicate. There is something sprite-like about her but not cute. She was a peach of a guest. To start with, Beate was bowled over by the stucchi.

"They haven't overdone it," she exclaimed when we'd finished the house tour.

One evening soon after, Karole Vail, in Venice to set up her exhibition, came over for a drink. I'd invited her and her boyfriend but, after a couple of phone calls from her, this group had expanded to include half a dozen of her friends, Italian and American, who had gathered in Venice for the opening of "A Celebration."

We had plenty of Prosecco. Crostini with rosemary and olive ascolane, of course, were set out on the smoky glass top of the gilded coffee table.

"This is so much better than what the PGC has rented for me," Karole said, sounding both peevish and impressed. Her friends seemed to appreciate the stucchi too.

It gave me pleasure to share our place with other people. I liked Karole's crew and, in fact, came to be friendly with one of them, Adriana from Florence. However, this did not prevent me from noticing that I had been maneuvered into hosting a "Welcome to Venice" cocktail party on Karole's behalf, saving her the trouble, shall we say. Nor did I fail to notice that she had not even bothered contributing a solitary paper rose, of which there were dozens at the kiosk downstairs.

Sindbad, I had been told, had been notoriously stingy. But in this he was not worse than his mother. Everybody seemed to have stories about what a miser Peggy was. Jane Rylands had told us that Peggy Guggenheim, who had the last privately owned gondola in Venice, used to have her gondoliers, dressed in their white and turquoise uniforms, row her to Standa. The men would wait in the canal outside while the art-collecting heiress would go in and stock up on toilet paper. Standa was the cheapest place in Venice to buy it.

After we finished our Prosecco, all of us went out to dinner at a little restaurant near Ca' Donà.

Alla Frasca is in one of those miniature squares that are more abundant in Venice than a visitor might guess. It is so deeply embedded in the labyrinth of streets if you weren't going there on purpose, or weren't lost, you'd never see it.

Alla Frasca is tiny, too, with only four tables inside, but it has a terrace marked out by potted plants and that's where we sat. A green-and-white awning was unrolled and there were a couple of tall, chrome-colored, free-standing gas chimneys pouring out heat. It all came in handy because it was a drizzly night and chilly.

Marcello, a retired gondolier, was proprietor, cook, waiter and also drinking companion when every so often one of the neighborhood men dropped in and stood at the bar, which took up half the minuscule restaurant. He was in his fifties, I guessed, with graying, reddish hair and a happy-go-lucky grin.

Alla Frasca was every tourist's dream—and mine. It was an undiscovered local joint with reasonably good, plain food, decent wine and low prices, although the latter fluctuated according to Marcello's whim.

There was plenty of wine on the table. We had a mixed antipasto, followed by pasta and salad along with a gigantic platter of grilled meats. (This was Monday; the fish market was closed.) We finished with fragolino rosso, a slightly fizzy wine made from grapes that smell of strawberries. There were biscotti, too, with the coffee. The party broke up with everybody in a good mood.

KAROLE'S YOUNGER SISTER JULIA, her husband and little girl arrived in Venice in time for the press preview of "A Celebration." Although younger than Karole, she looked wan, and seemed very angry. The tense competitiveness between these sisters was not deeply buried. When Karole picked up Julia's daughter and smiled for the cameras, I thought Julia might smack her—or faint. Karole handed back the child fast.

Julia, to whom I'd introduced myself, turned to me at one point and said, "My father would have hated this." She looked as if she did, too.

That evening there was a gigantic cocktail party in the garden of Peggy Guggenheim's palace. Karole looked magnificent. She was dressed in the manner of Fortuny, with a long silk gown of tiny pleats over which she wore a swooping long velvet tunic. Julia was wearing khaki cotton, the safari version of sackcloth and ashes.

After cocktails, Peggy's grandchildren were off to the Gritti for a dinner, the re-creation of a birthday party held there for their grandmother. I went home shivering and blowing my nose.

VENICE
BELONGS TO
THE WORLD

19

Meeting Pinocchio

"What? What is this . . . ?" Michela would ask incredulously, as if she'd just picked up a particularly stinky piece of seaweed. She would then repeat some word I'd just spoken which she couldn't understand. She was teasing me; not being nasty. Michela wanted to help me make progress in Italian.

All too often when I tried to find a word, I would grab what seemed to me to be its nearest relative. This might turn out to be a cousin three times removed with no recognizable family resemblance to anybody except me.

I was giftless but I plugged away. I listened hard to what people were saying. I watched television, listened to the radio and I read. My conviction, or hope, was that if I accumulated a big enough vocabulary and was able to understand what was being written or said, complete sentences would one day just slide out of me. I would be speaking Italian.

I bought the *Gazzetino* every day now and, after skimming the national news, I tried to read every word of *Venezia*. In that section I never skipped the *Tacuino*. Although "Tacuino" means notebook I thought of it more as the bulletin board. It listed lectures, concerts, plays, exhibitions (including those which, it noted, were "by invitation only"). I went to many of these offerings; we both did.

Most events in the *Tacuino* took place on the day they were mentioned. But every so often something would be announced a few days in advance. Such notices were not repeated, so if you wanted to keep up with what was going on in Venice, which I surely did, you couldn't afford to skip a single issue of the paper.

Every day I also read at least a few pages of an Italian novel. I'd already finished Italo Calvino's surrealist/socialist *Marcovaldo*—episodes in the life of a working-class, holy fool. I heard the book was very popular with Italy's high school students, and it was with me, also. I enjoyed Calvino's style and wit. That I'd even grasped he had a sense of humor seemed a near miracle because I had to look up so many words on every page.

The next book I tackled might sound like a retrograde move since I found it in the children's section of the London Library. It wasn't.

On the library shelves there were half a dozen different editions of *Pinocchio*. Not one of them looked cartoonish. I riffled through each one as gently as I could, because they were old and printed on poor paper which was becoming brittle. One set of illustrations especially appealed to me. I took it down to the desk and signed it out.

Carlo Chiostri illustrated *Pinocchio* in 1901. I'd never heard of him. But then I hadn't known that the author of the book was named Collodi. Like millions of others, it was in a movie theater that I'd had my first and only meeting with Pinocchio, Geppetto and Jiminy Cricket in Walt Disney's Technicolor version of the tale.

Since I already knew the plot and the vocabulary was geared to children, I thought the book would be easy. Collodi, however, did not use a baby vocabulary. Indeed there is nothing infantile about his book— apart from what was done to it by Disney. *Le Avventure di Pinocchio: Storia di un burattino* is a powerful book. Even at its most entertaining it is not darling.

At five or six, *Pinocchio,* along with *Bambi* and *Dumbo,* had been as precious to me as my treasured stuffed panda. But unlike *Dumbo,* one of the twentieth century's great movies, the Disneyfied *Pinocchio* would make my teeth curl now. Gifted as Walt's animators were, the story of the puppet they'd been handed to work with was drowned in treacle.

There is a certain amount of bullying moralism in the book and that is its main drawback. But the loving *Fata turchina,* the fairy with vivid blue hair, is a far more important personage in the Collodi story than Mr. Superego, Jiminy Cricket. And his metaphors for dehumanized and dehumanizing states have stuck with me no less tenaciously than some of Kafka's.

Pinocchio is a rare and moving book. And Chiostri's drawings, like John Tenniel's for *Alice in Wonderland*, are so fine and so apt, they seem the product of a blessed collaboration.

When it was time to leave London for Venice, I wasn't very far into the story. But I didn't dare carry the precious London Library copy with me. As soon we had settled in to Ca' Donà, I began searching the bookshops of Venice for one of my own.

I couldn't find *Pinocchio* anywhere. Then, speeding along the Calle del Fumo, I saw in the window of Gianni Basso's shop two reproductions of Chiostri's drawings printed as cards. I went right in.

Gianni Basso smiled when I asked him about the images. He disappeared into the back of his shop. When he returned he held a beat-up copy of *Pinocchio*. Its spine was broken, the stitching undone. This is what he was printing from.

I bought the cards and then asked, "Where can I get a copy of the book?"

"Impossible," Gianni informed me. "It's out of print."

I was desolate. The one secondhand bookshop I'd seen in Venice sold only art books.

Though I believed Gianni Basso, I went on hunting, just in case. And in a bookstore behind the Rialto Bridge, a man told me about yet another one run by a *Pinocchio* enthusiast.

"She has everything," he said.

I was to look for a window filled with books about the *burattino* in a calle running from Campo San Luca toward San Marco.

There must have been a dozen or even twenty *Pinocchio*s set out in that window display. But not one was Chiostri's. The charming red-haired woman who runs the shop had never even heard of the illustrator. I was surprised that the edition was obscure. Being so taken with it, I assumed it must be a classic.

"I'll have a look on my computer," she said obligingly.

Eccolo! A publisher in Florence had recently reprinted it. The proprietress immediately ordered it. Two weeks later, *Pinocchio* became my daily companion.

I was so struck by the book that I couldn't stop telling people about it. A few of them looked as if they found my development far more arrested than they'd previously thought. But not Rosella. "*Pinocchio* is so wonderful," I said to Rosella.

"Yes," she agreed. Then she sighed. "But it's so sad."

Oh it is.

Pinocchio was written to be published in installments, which gave it a momentum that was perfect for me since I took so long to get from the top to the bottom of each page. Yet there were days when I was reluctant to pick it up where I'd left off. Dreadful things happen in the story as a result of the puppet boy's careless or willful betrayals of those who loved him. The extension of the wooden fellow's nose is the least of it.

Months later, while doing some armchair traveling in the pages of *The Rough Guide to Tuscany* I learned that near Lucca there is a town called Collodi. Evidently Carlo Lorenzini adopted his birthplace as his pen name. It seems that today the town is bursting with tributes to its native son and his creation. And it isn't only in Collodi that *Pinocchio* is celebrated.

"The tale's moral simplicity and exemplary Tuscan prose ensure it a massive following," the author of the guide writes. "The saintly Pope John Paul I used to address missives to the novel's hero," he goes on to say, "and a recent Italian newspaper poll to ascertain the Greatest Novel of All Time seriously included *Pinocchio* in its shortlist."

No wonder Roberto Benigni, after winning an Academy Award for *Life Is Beautiful,* chose to direct and star in one of the great books in his country's literature, *Pinocchio*. For such a very long time there had existed only two very different *Pinocchio*s—the Hollywood movie by Walt Disney and the extraordinary adventures written by Collodi.

It isn't stretching things too much, I believe, to say that in an oddly related way, there have existed also two very different Venices: The Venice of Venetians and the city visited by everybody else.

*   *   *

FOR OUTSIDERS, Venice is the grandest of playgrounds, not a real place. Reality, if you'll pardon the expression, whether it's mortgage payments or difficult relations, is what travelers to Venice leave home to forget about. It may be hard for tourists anywhere to avoid falsifying when they interpret what they're seeing. In beautiful Venice, it seems almost impossible and this, somehow, seems intended. It's as if Venice wants you to look at her cracking walls and think, How lovely. And so they often seem—if you're not the person who has to pay to repair them.

If you are Venetian, there is the thousand-year-long glory of the Serenissima superimposed on the life of the municipality with its problems of employment, flooding, housing and crowds. I have heard several people in Venice joke that there isn't a soul left in the city who can truthfully claim a Venetian great-grandfather. Venetians, however, don't behave or seem to feel like the offspring of recent immigrants.

When I was growing up, everyone I knew wanted to be an American yet none of us imagined our family history had anything to do with the men in breeches who dumped crates of tea into Boston Harbor and started a revolution. But I suspect that when a Venetian looks in a mirror, he or she sees a descendant of people who created the Most Serene Republic and made her powerful. I sometimes feel they take more pride in the achievements of the Venetian Republic than in those of their local government, the comune. And in fact they may have more interest in the Serenissima too.

For us, all the marble and white Istrian stone, the mosaics and watery reflections, the palaces and gondolas are splendid, gorgeous, soulful and heart-stirring. But to Venetians, all of this is the glorious past made manifest, both evidence of and a conduit to their family history. That, I think, is what makes crowded, slow, expensive Venice worth living in for Venetians today.

Dr. Laura Forlati, a Venetian lawyer and academic, taught me a phrase: *Andare alla deriva*. . . . "It means to be adrift," she said. "It's a nautical term used by Venetians to describe themselves. They are old in mind," she went on. "They have seen everything or, if they have not, their ancestors did. They are hypercritical and suspicious but they have a sense of humor—and of distinction. The distinction of being heirs to the great Republic. *Veneziano, il grande signore*."

*   *   *

OCCASIONALLY SPECIAL EVENTS announced in the *Gazzetino* were not
listed in the *Tacuino* but under a separate heading titled "Zoom." And
one day I was amazed to see a full-page ad for an upcoming concert. It
was a charity benefit. The musical performance would be held in San
Marco and then, for an extra sum, you could go to a grand dinner afterward in the Palazzo Ducale.

It sounded so enticing, I decided to splurge and go to both. After all,
the money would go to FAI, an Italian restoration charity. Since Henry
would be in London that night, I would have to go by myself. But the
thought of being at this gala—in such extravagantly romantic places—
all alone made it seem even more of an adventure.

When the evening came, I dressed up in my spiderweb sweater and
silky, gray skirt and dared the chill of those marble floors by going
stockingless in pink satin sandals. The concert was not superb, but sitting in San Marco with hours to look at its walls was reward enough. I
noticed Rose and Peter Lauritzen seated a couple of rows behind me.
With a covert intensity they scanned the crowd. If they were looking for
Venice's great and good who usually fill the front rows at major events
in the basilica they must have felt let down. Very few of those familiar
faces were on view. I had the uncharitable thought that this might be
because only a handful of free tickets are given out for benefits, no matter what position in the city a person holds.

After the concert most people drifted into the piazza. I followed
those who were making their way toward the Porta della Carta, the
principal entrance to the Doge's Palace next door. This was one evening
when I would not be able to avoid speaking Italian. Upstairs, in the Sala
dello Scrutinio, which had been outfitted with big round dinner tables,
there were a hundred or more people circulating and I didn't hear a single word of my native tongue.

Not knowing in advance where in the palace the dinner would be, I
hadn't been able to read about it beforehand. As I milled around, sipping Prosecco and nibbling canapés, I longed to know more about the
melodramatic paintings in thick gilded frames that covered the ceilings
and the walls of the enormous room where I would be having dinner.

I noticed a dark-haired woman in a black suit standing alone. She looked familiar. I was sure I'd seen her at an art history lecture I'd been to not long before. I didn't know her name. But when I approached her, she was kind, friendly and wanted to be helpful.

From her I learned something about this room, in which commissioners who oversaw the election of doges once sat. Many of the paintings heaving with ships turned out to be portrayals of Venice's triumphant naval battles in the East. As we talked, we strolled across the room and when we came to the wall which was cut with wide windows, we leaned on one of the generous sills. My companion turned and looked out at the majestic white stone façades enclosing the courtyard and the great expanse of its pale marble floor.

"It's best seen by moonlight," she said.

At once the noise behind us was wiped away by a lunar silence. I looked out the window and I too could see the ghostly, pearly glow of a white garden made of stone.

For an instant I saw the senators and councillors who centuries before had crossed this courtyard lit by the moon and then climbed the broad stairway to the room where I was now standing; a room where in a few minutes waiters would begin to serve asparagus risotto.

I was moved and felt grateful, also. Only a Venetian, I thought, would have such an intimate experience of the Ducal Palace. How very kind this woman was and how lucky I was that she'd cared to share it.

For centuries, the Serenissima knew how to arouse such cravings and how to profit from them. I don't mean in any way to belittle the feelings I had in the Palazzo Ducale when I say this. But the fact is, a Venetian Venice and a foreigner's Venice have existed for half a millennium or more. And as long as the Most Serene Republic endured, her aim was to bedazzle those who visited. She spent lavishly to achieve that goal. The Serenissima understood, long before historian Jacob Burckhardt made his observation that "her stupendous energy—and the world's prejudice in her favor" are what carried Venice to greatness. Whether she was at the height of her powers or in her decline, the Republic was determined to keep that prejudice alive.

"Such is the rareness of the situation, that it doth even amaze and drive into admiration all strangers," Thomas Coryat noted when he visited Venice in 1608.

And indeed many strangers came to the islands of the lagoon to do business of one kind and another. Some, like Richard Lassels, an English priest and traveling tutor, made the then arduous journey to Italy repeatedly. Lassels went to Venice five times before his death in 1668 and it was in his much praised guide that the term "Grand Tour" appears for the first time. In it he writes of the piazzetta: "There are dayly to be seen walking here a world of strangers of severall nations and attires, as, Polonians, Grecians, Albanians, Slavonians, Armenians and Turks, all merchants and talking of traffic and traiding. . . ."

These foreigners, dazzled by the jewels and marble palaces of Venice, were entertained by their hosts and made to feel welcome. But the Serenissima wished not only to attract them but to seduce them and thereby keep the balance of power in her favor. To that end, she used a venerable seductress's trick: She both made herself magnificent and held herself aloof. Visitors to Venice were not given uncontrolled access to the city or its residents. Contact between her own people and foreign visitors was carefully regulated by the Most Serene Republic.

German traders lived and kept their goods in the sixteenth-century Fondaco dei Tedeschi on the Grand Canal near the Rialto Bridge. (Today it is the main post office.) And on the fish market side of the canal, from 1621 until 1838, the Turks were confined to a fourteenth-century building which has been called the Fondaco dei Turchi ever since. (In the nineteenth century, the crumbling Fondaco was subjected to a deadly, trumped-up re-creation of its former self. Today it is the Museum of Natural History.) And to make sure its secrets stayed that way, the Serenissima barred Venetians from talking privately with foreign ambassadors.

The Republic had been vastly rich and powerful, but by the eighteenth century she was no longer either. Trade no longer produced great wealth. Her skill in marketing her image turned in a new direction, tourism. Rome, Florence and Naples were established as cities that Dutchmen, Poles, the French and Germans and, above all, many British felt they must stop at during their Italian tours; it would be most useful economically if Venice were added to this list.

Venice did not have classical antiquities to lure these well-off, curious visitors. But she knew how to throw a party. So out came the makeup, props and musicians. The festivities lasted for most of the eighteenth century.

Foreigners who went to Venice at that time took their pleasure in her small, exquisitely decorated and charmingly painted gaming houses; the company of her handsome and clever courtesans made giantesses by their skyscraper shoes was sought. The visitors went to performances of the many operas for which Venice became famous. (Venice was the first city where opera was performed for the public rather than being restricted to the court.) Her fêtes and festooned outings on the water, accompanied by musicians on floating stages, were intended to delight and did.

Nowadays millions return from their trip to Venice carrying masks in their suitcases. In those days, when the numbers of visitors were smaller and their average wealth greater, many of the souvenirs that were produced for them were paintings. Most famously, Canaletto fashioned his views of the city chiefly for export.

Canaletto's *vedutas,* crafted with considerable skill, did not necessarily faithfully reproduce the city. This did not put off buyers. On the contrary, it contributed to his success. When a Canaletto hung on the wall of an English country house (the destination for many of his paintings), the scene appeared to its owner a perfect representation of Venice. Indeed, Canaletto's Venice seemed more enchantingly, more satisfyingly, Venice-like than the city they'd seen with their own eyes.

There were other painters also, of course, including the charming Francesco Guardi, said to have been more favored by the French. And then there were the pictures made for home consumption—among them the series of almost one hundred paintings, called the "Functions of Venice," done by Gabriel Bella.

In the catalogue to a late twentieth-century exhibition called "The Grand Tour," Ilaria Begniamini, one of the curators, observes that "Canalettos were exported while naive Bellas were kept to preserve the memory of the age." What Venetian songs in dialect were in music, she suggests, Bella was in painting. These were native products for the native audience. It is in his eighteenth-century scenes, whether

they are of dinners and dances or boat races on the Grand Canal, that
Bella shows us the Venice of Venetians.

But who was this Bella?

It is hardly surprising that in a city that produced Titian, Bellini,
Carpaccio and Tintoretto, Bella's name is scarcely known outside
Venice. He wasn't a major artist, and some would say he wasn't even a
good one. I remember sitting one afternoon with Bill and Andrea
Hollis in their apartment overlooking the Grand Canal. We were hav-
ing a drink and Bill was in a state.

"We just spent the afternoon in the most awful museum. I've never
seen so many terrible paintings in one place before," he spluttered.

Where was that, Henry and I wondered.

"It was in a palace near Santa Maria Formosa," he said.

They had just come from the Querini-Stampalia. It is upstairs in that
museum that the Bellas hang.

I didn't argue. What would have been the point? But when I look at
a Canaletto, I feel the faintly cold pleasure of peering across a great distance to an elegant, fantastical town. I never have the sensation I am seeing Venice. Coming upon a Bella, for me, is like finding a small square
opening in the wall of time. Stepping closer, I feel I can make out what
Venice was like for Venetians, and even for her foreign guests. For in
some pictures they are present, too.

20

A Case of Mistaken Identity

"Venice is sinking, she is going to die." I heard this from people in London and New York and from other foreigners in Venice. Only once did I hear it from a Venetian.

It was on a vaporetto, going to Murano. I couldn't help eavesdropping as a man in his twenties gave a dramatic speech to friends he was showing around town.

"In ten years," he said stretching out his hands dramatically, "I will tell my sons about Venice; the city that used to be here. It will be gone." He seemed to be taking a strange pleasure in imagining this terrible loss: Venice turned into the most glorious aquarium in the world.

Venice submerged. The anxiety that this will be the fate of the city, particularly intense among foreigners, is one of the aftereffects of the floods of 1966. It is a fear fueled by misconceptions, which, in turn, have fired the conviction that, whatever the costs, measures must be taken to prevent another such destructive flood.

On November 4, 1966, both Florence and Venice, for quite different reasons, were flooded. In Venice, however, no one was seriously injured, not a single work of art was destroyed or even severely damaged as a result. Nevertheless thousands of people, more likely millions, including many who have given money to help the city, believe that it caused terrible damage to Venice. Even Save Venice, the American charity that split off from the colonel's Venice Project, seemed to be muddled on this point. The fancy color brochure they published to celebrate twenty-five years of contributing to the restoration of artworks and monuments in Venice opened with the words: "Save Venice, Inc. was organized . . . in response to the terrible damage caused by the floods of November, 1966. . . . The flood damage was so devastating that, beginning in 1967, more than thirty national committees around the world were formed to restore and protect Venice's masterpieces."

Donors to Save Venice, which no longer presents history in this inaccurate way, have given tens of millions of dollars to help the city. Henry and I were lucky to be living near the church of Santa Maria dei Miracoli, one of the loveliest examples of what its gifts helped achieve. Inside and out the marble glows now; its gilded ceiling shines even in dim light. But neither the Miracoli nor any of the other projects to which Save Venice—and the many other private charities created to help Venice—has given money were ravaged by the flood.

What happened in Venice on November 4 was that water rose to 194 centimeters above mean sea level. Now flooding becomes visible in the piazza, the city's lowest point, only after water reaches eighty centimeters above mean sea level. That November day, Piazza San Marco was under 114 centimeters of water (four feet) for a total of ten minutes. It was covered by up to seventy centimeters of water for the following ten hours. Yes, the whole of Venice was flooded for a time, but even at its most severe, one-third of the city was covered by less than forty centimeters, which is 16 inches, of water. Of course that was troublesome. There was damage caused by thick, black gook from heating oil when the contents of ground-level fuel tanks tipped into the rising floodwater. But to call this life-threatening? A menace to works of art? Tantamount to nearly having perished?

Emotionally and imaginatively people mixed up what happened in Florence with what went on in Venice the same day. It was in Florence—*not Venice*— that flooding had devastating and indeed tragic results. It was in Florence that floodwaters were so deep and fast moving that people drowned; more than thirty lost their lives. Water not only spilled over the banks of the River Arno but it moved with such velocity that it broke through embankments and carried uprooted trees and overturned cars, as well as mud and oil, into the streets and buildings at the center of Florence. There was even rubble washed up on the road across the shop-lined Ponte Vecchio.

It was in Florence that art, artifacts and thousands, perhaps hundreds of thousands, of books were damaged and some cherished works, most notably "The Crucifixion" by Cimabue, were ruined. Nothing comparable happened to Venice. Yet people go on believing that it did—and that any minute it could—indeed *is* bound to—happen again.

Why?

Because tragic accidents happen to tragic heroines. Robust creatures like Florence aren't perceived to be in mortal danger, even when natural disasters have calamitous results. But Venice by 1966, while still beautiful, was poor and weak, an expiring Puccini heroine of a city. 'Venice in Peril' is what the English called the charity they established to try to save her.

Venice has been flooded ever since people went to live on these islands in the lagoon. For Venetians, November 4 was another day; the same as usual only rather more so. According to one observer who was there soon after the flood, people didn't panic. In fact, they didn't think anything so very exceptional had happened. It was only months later, when they saw rising damp creeping up the walls of the palaces that many Venetians realized the November flood had caused exceptional problems. It was people elsewhere looking at television, newspaper and magazine images of Venice flooded who panicked and were in despair.

Water washing onto the islands of the lagoon is as typically Venetian as fog in December and sticky heat in July. People in Venice have always had to coexist with *acqua alta,* the type of flooding peculiar to the region.

In Montana or Moscow, residents make a distinction between snow flurries and a blizzard, so in Venice where flooding is common, people have different expressions to describe different degrees of it. When water rises to between 80 and 110 centimeters above mean sea level, it is called *alta marea.* When it rises above 110 centimeters, it is *alta marea eccezionale* or more commonly, *acqua alta,* high water.

But why do these particular terms exist? Italian already has *diluvio* and *alluvione* to describe a flood, while "to flood" is *inondare*. The answer is that when there is water in the squares of Venice the cause is not entirely the same as when the Po River breaks its banks. Although heavy rain may contribute to acqua alta, it is not the only factor.

Venice sits in a thirty-five-mile-long lagoon (540 square kilometers), which is the largest lagoon in Italy and some say in all of Europe.

This body of water—and the treasured city from which it rises—is protected from the northern Adriatic, which has the highest tides in the Mediterranean, by two long narrow sand bars: islands called the Lido and Pellestrina. The sea enters the lagoon and rolls out again through three openings in this sandy strip: at San Nicolò (sometimes rather confusingly called the Lido, through which it cuts), Malamocco and Chioggia.

Two times a day, Adriatic tides enter and leave the brackish lagoon. This, as it always has been, is the drainage system for Venice. (That's right, just as many tourists and their noses suspect, there are no sewers in the city, although there are septic tanks.) Acqua alta, which typically occurs in winter, is the result of a very high tide often pushed up the Adriatic by the *scirocco,* the south wind. A rare flood like the one in 1966, however, is caused by further abnormalities in the twice daily tidal exchanges.

The scirocco, if it blows hard enough and long enough, can prevent water that ought to flow out of the lagoon on the ebb tide from doing so. As a result, the next sea tide, when it comes in, has to ride on top of the unusual volume of water trapped in the lagoon. High water pouring in on top of high water has to go somewhere. It spills over from the lagoon into the canals and from the canals onto the streets and squares of Venice. (Other conditions also contribute to acqua alta, among them a sort of false tidal wave peculiar to the northern Adriatic.)

ON NOVEMBER 4, 1966, Venice suffered from an exceptional acqua alta. But the disruption following the flood, for all but those who lived in ground-floor apartments, was short-lived. Some Venetians even clucked that no one ought to have been living on the street level in the first place:

Those spaces had been intended for storage not for human dwelling.

Obviously new arrangements had to be made for housing the people who'd been flooded out. Venice also switched from heating with oil to using gas and moved its heating systems upstairs. But Venetians, used to acqua alta, were back to their normal routines within days.

Some Florentines were without electricity, heat or water for weeks. They had difficulty getting food. Many lost property, including their cars.

In December 1966, Rene Maheu, Director General of UNESCO, responding to an appeal by the president of Italy, sent out a call to the writers, artists, musicians, critics and historians, museums, foundations and collectors "whose works have been inspired by the treasures of Florence or Venice," asking them to give "whatever they can."

"Venice sinking into the waves," he cried out. "It is as if one of the most radiant stars of beauty were suddenly engulfed. . . ."

The response was immediate and generous. It came in the form of money but also goods and volunteers, both amateur and professional.

Within weeks of the floods, the American Committee to Rescue Italian Art (C.R.I.A.) and Britain's Italian Art and Archives Rescue Fund (I.A.A.R.F.) came into existence and were sending aid to Florence and within months to Venice. Very soon, people were at work lifting what might be salvageable out of the mud of Florence. Inventories of the damage were compiled. New restoration techniques were developed to cope with the many new problems. Some projects, like the restoration of the Uccello frescoes in the cloisters of Santa Maria Novella, took many years to complete.

Florence had been overwhelmed by a freakish disaster. It was a long time before life in the city could get back to normal. But Florence was a robust, flourishing town. In just over a year, Florentines felt they had recovered sufficiently to carry on restoring their treasures without the ongoing care and attention of international charities. The I.A.A.R.F., for instance, after fourteen months of contributing to the recovery of Florence "withdrew from the city," according to the account of its chairman, formerly Britain's ambassador to Italy, Sir Ashley Clarke. This is not what happened in Venice.

No one would use the word robust to describe the condition or the mood of Venice in 1966. At the end of the Second World War some 180,000 people lived in the city. At the time of the flood the population was 125,000 and falling. Those who had remained lived in conditions that could be called basic. Even twenty years after the flood, nearly half the houses in the city lacked a bathroom, according to Peter Lauritzen's *Venice Preserved*, while "the toilet, behind a screen or curtain in the kitchen, drains through a pipe directly into the canal outside."

After the flood, fifty charities came into being to help Venice. More than half that number continue their money-raising activities today. And new ones still start up.

But if Venice was not badly damaged by the flood, what in the world was all this money being raised for and what has it been spent on? The answer in both cases is: restoration.

The year after the flood, UNESCO, together with the office of the Superintendent of Galleries, made a survey of the current condition of all the works of art and the monuments in the city. Lauritzen writes that a catalogue of sixteen thousand index cards was produced. What those cards revealed was that a third or more of the works examined were seriously damaged and urgently in need of work.

A second phase of research was then undertaken by UNESCO, this time along with the Superintendent of Monuments. It examined the state of four hundred palaces, some hundred churches, thirty convents, and twenty scuolas. More cards were produced.

It isn't necessary to go into a detailed account of what was found. It is enough in this case to get right to the punch line: Inside and out, Venice was falling apart.

It wasn't floodwater that was killing Venice. Venice was dying of poverty and neglect.

The entire marble-and-gold structure of the city, along with a great deal of what was inside its palaces, churches and public squares, was threatened—not because of acqua alta but because, one way and another, almost all of it had been left to rot.

NAPOLEON BROUGHT ABOUT *LA CADUTA,* the fall of the Most Serene Republic. In 1797, Venice for the first time belonged to strangers.

Venetians lost the liberty to which the Republic was devoted for a thousand years. Venetians mourned their lost freedom. It was mourning seemingly without end. You could say it lasted a century and a half. The pride of her nobility was mortally wounded. Literally. Many of these families, the people who since the twelfth century had been listed in the *libro d'Oro,* and the very few others who managed to get their names added to the Golden Book afterward, could not live with the shame of it.

"More than one third of all the families inscribed in the Golden Book in 1797, were extinct within the space of a generation," Lauritzen notes.

After the fall, Venetian nobles simply stopped reproducing. Within twenty years, one noble family in every three—among them the Barbarigos and the Corners—died out.

In those noble houses that did not commit this extraordinary form of class suicide many people fled to their mainland properties. Those who stayed in Venice seemed exhausted by the effort of hanging on.

In 1818, in his "Ode on Venice," Byron described what had happened to these offspring of such heroic, vigorous and fearless fathers. ". . . They only murmur in their sleep," he wrote. "They creep, crouching and crab-like, through their sapping streets. . . ."

The poor, of course, had little choice but to stay and they were far more vulnerable than the nobility.

Some foreigners with a taste for melancholy beauty traveled to Venice during its occupation, but most Grand Tourists stayed away from what now was a gloomy town.

Poor people had lost a source of income: there were no jobs carrying the luggage of visitors, no tips for running their errands, no payments for rowing them about in gondolas. And with fewer nobles in Venice, the poor also lost the housing the nobility had provided for them. Within a generation of the defeat of the Republic, 25 percent of the people in Venice had become beggars. Quite a few of them slept in the streets.

Napoleon not only had the city's treasures sent to Paris (including the bronze horses of San Marco, which had been looted from Constantinople), he shut down more than half of the city's parish churches and closed many monasteries and scuolas. The Scuola Grande di San Marco, next to the church of Ss. Giovanni e Paolo, was turned into a hospital, but other religious buildings were abandoned or destroyed.

The French undertook slum clearance projects resulting in the creation of the Public Gardens in Castello after houses in the area were pulled down. The Giardinetto Reale on the waterfront around the corner from San Marco followed the leveling of granaries on that site. Elsewhere buildings were flattened and canals filled in to build those long, wide and straight streets so uncharacteristic of Venice—the Via Garibaldi and the Strada Nova. (The street names themselves are atypical. While *via* and *strada* are commonplace elsewhere in Italy, Venetians chose to call a street *calle* instead.)

Then in 1814, the Austrians, who had briefly occupied the city earlier, were back in the coffee shops of Venice following their defeat of Napoleon. And the Austrians kept control of the city pretty much until it became part of a unified Italy in 1866. Some cultural treasures were returned to Venice from Paris, including the horses. But if the French saw Venice as a cornucopia of riches to scoop out and ship north, the Austrians used Venice as a military camp. The city was fortified, filled with troops, and its outer islands were used to store explosives.

Nothing was done that might create economic vitality. Instead Venice suffered terrible impoverishment. A trickle of tourists continued to come. As before (and after), there was the Venice perceived by others and the Venice of Venetians.

". . . This populace of fishermen, sleeping on the pavement, winter as well as summer, with no other pillow than one of granite, no other mattress than a tattered cloak," Georges Sand wrote in 1834, "is not such a populace a great example of philosophy? When it has no longer wherewithal to purchase a pound of rice, it sings a chorus to drive away the pangs of hunger. . . . Existence is still so easy at Venice!" Another writer named the "merry" homeless souls who did odd jobs for him his "Open-Air Club."

When Venice became part of a unified Italy in 1866, the numbers of tourists increased. Byron was speaking for many when he wrote that the dilapidated, impoverished town they found was, "Perchance even dearer in her day of woe, Than when she was a boast, a marvel, and a show."

Venice began her new career as one of the most sought after and one of the most long-lived of the world's about-to-expire romantic heroines. The myth flourished while the stones of Venice and the shallow, delicate lagoon were all but abandoned. The more the city deteriorated, the closer she seemed to her last breath, the more alluring strangers seemed to find her.

But following the flood in 1966, and the surveys done not long afterward, both Venetians and foreigners began to see that the peeling walls and run-down atmosphere that made Venice look so appealing to visitors was evidence that she'd reached an extremely dangerous state.

It is a measure of the grip Venice has had on the imagination of so many people and the passion they feel for her, that help came quickly and was given lavishly. Not least of all, but maybe most surprisingly to outsiders, from Italy itself.

The reason that Henry and I and so many other travelers to Italy adopted the "Don't pass a church without going in" rule is that there is no country in the world endowed with so many treasured paintings, buildings, monuments and sculptures as Italy. Almost anywhere you go, tiny villages or provincial towns, there are marvelous things to see. There are shrines worth stopping at in the middle of the countryside. There seems to be far too much for any government to maintain. Yet Italy did not react to the news that Venice was falling apart with a governmental shrug. In 1973, it passed the first of its Special Laws for the Safeguarding of Venice. Because of her unique beauty, her singular position, her desperate situation and her special needs (all that water and salty air not only causes erosion but it starts eroding again as soon as the damage has been repaired), Venice would be given large amounts of money to help with the restoration of the city and her lagoon.

So, as you might expect in a fairy tale, the scirocco that blew and blew and carried into the streets of Venice the exceptional acqua alta of November 1966 seems to have had magical properties. That fierce, warm wind shook money trees all over the world. Gold for Venice rained down from Rome, Canberra, Paris, Boston, Bonn, Tokyo, New York, London and Stockholm. And it hasn't stopped yet.

*   *   *

LARGE NUMBERS OF PALACES AND CHURCHES, paintings and sculpture have been restored in the years since the flood. "Venice has become the most restored city in Italy," Philip Rylands once wryly commented in the days when he was still speaking to me.

But while its buildings were being restored, its population was declining and the number of tourists growing. Now local people are beginning to wonder: Is the interest in Venice since the flood of 1966 too much of a good thing?

Every action Venetians take to improve their city, including the restoration of its buildings, churches, bridges and monuments, makes it a better town for its residents—and an even more attractive destination for ever larger numbers of foreigners.

More tourists, in turn, make life in Venice more difficult for its residents.

So we come to the obvious, if cruel, question. What if Venice was no longer a city for Venetians? What if the city were to become a series of superbly restored façades? What if, behind each marble palace, everything old was stripped out and brand new, air-conditioned suites of rooms with wall-to-wall carpet were installed?

Ah, at last Venice will have enough hotel rooms. Maybe prices will come down as supply approaches demand. As for the day-trippers, or even the couple spending a romantic weekend in Venice, will they notice? And if they do, will they care?

Plastic garbage bags could be thrown into the canals to lend verisimilitude. Stinky, anti-perfume could be sprayed at the bases of certain bridges in the hottest season to augment the Venetian experience.

The gondoliers could carry on their trade as usual. After all, they have been warbling *"O sole mio"* as if it were a Venetian, not a Neapolitan, song since at least the time Proust visited.

Does it matter if the city has people in it who go to work? Does it matter if there are schools, offices, law courts, a university? Butchers? Shoe repair shops?

Obviously it matters to Venetians. It's their home. But I think even transient tourists would feel the difference if all the Venetians left and the city was transformed, 100 percent, into Disneyland.

If that were to happen, Venice really would be a corpse. And I think visitors strolling along her alleys or riding in her gondolas would not be able to escape being touched by the clammy, mortuary feeling of the place. Dead rather than dying, the romance of Venice would evaporate.

But maybe I am being naive. Maybe plenty of visitors would like the city better if there weren't all those Venetians walking so quickly up and down the calles with their shopping baskets and briefcases and baby carriages. Getting in the way.

21

Sliding Doors

"I sent the contract to my lawyer in New York. I haven't heard from him yet." This was my new weapon and shield against the next Donà assault.

Delay was all I had managed to come up with to protect myself. Whenever Henry flew back to London, I felt even more vulnerable. And I missed him. We'd had little practice in being apart.

The first time he flew off was hard. All of a sudden the hours turned elastic and I was overwhelmed by how many more of them there were each day. For years we had been so much together, I hadn't realized being a couple is so time-consuming. But pretty soon there were moments when being alone in Venice seemed like a lark.

I could drift around the house and drift around town without a dinner hour to stop me. There was a freedom in making plans without checking in with anyone else. I thought living alone in such enormous rooms would be daunting. I was surprised to find how much I liked being in the stucchi by myself. I mentioned this to Marino Zorzi.

"Ah the Venetians understood how to build," he replied.

I had to agree. There was something about the proportions of the rooms and their decoration that was cosseting.

Although I fancied I would indulge in solitary pursuits—reading at five in the morning with a glass of Prosecco and olive ascolane to keep me company—as soon as I was alone, I found myself on the telephone. I made dates for lunch, for a drink, to visit an artist's studio. And I got in touch with people I'd meant to call but hadn't contacted before. That's how I happened to phone John Millerchip, whose name I'd been given by Frances Clarke.

Lady Clarke's late husband, Sir Ashley, had founded Venice in Peril and she now was one of its presidents. I'd spoken to her early on, when I first was trying to find a place to live in Venice, but I can't remember when we actually met. However, once we were introduced, I seemed to see her everywhere—lectures, performances, openings of art exhibitions, cocktail parties. She was indefatigable.

A slight woman in her sixties, I would guess, Frances Clarke looked like a painting in grisaille. Although I could plainly see she was partial to wearing navy, I only saw her in shades of gray. She didn't appear to be either an intellectual or a sybarite. Rather, she seemed driven toward a goal, or by demons I could not identify. Why did she go out on an evening when she was so exhausted she sometimes fell asleep on the job? And why did she go to virtually everything?

Henry and I were trying to learn Italian, to find out all we could about Venice and to see the inside of every palace—insofar as we were able to manage it. We trekked to the opening of every envelope. We went to lectures on poets we'd never heard of or on historic Venetian fortifications in Dalmatia. If we'd been in London or New York, we never would have left the house for some of these events.

Lady Clarke, fluent in Italian, has had a home in Venice for decades. She knew everybody or certainly most everyone she was going to know. So why did she keep going out so much? Was she paying homage to her late husband? Was it the loneliness of a widow? Perhaps. But her taste seemed so catholic it bordered on having none at all.

"She has a sense of duty," Sally Spector explained, when I joined her for coffee and gossip at what had become our regular meeting place, Rosa Salva. "She believes it's her duty to support culture."

I could see this explanation was plausible. For such a small town, there are a great many cultural events in Venice and most of them are well attended. One cool, wet night, for example, I went to a palace off

Campo San Stefano to hear a talk about Titian. More than a hundred people were packed into the room when I got there. These were not down-and-outs sheltering until the storm had passed. They were well dressed and they were attentive: In Venice, the audience stays to the end.

I saw Lady Clarke and mentioned I was writing about Venice and its future. I said this because I assumed she would have opinions and ideas she might like to pass along.

"Oh, if you want to know about Venice," she ducked, "you ought to speak to John Millerchip. He will tell you what is going on."

Being fobbed off on Mr. Millerchip was my great good fortune. He is a trustee of Venice in Peril. And he is also secretary to all the private charities raising money for the restoration of the city, the liaison between the charities who raise the money and the people who put it to use. I came to like and respect him. I was to learn a lot from him as well as from the people he generously put me in touch with. Many of them were Venetians I might otherwise never have met.

I TELEPHONED, introduced myself and said I was going to write about Venice. John Millerchip and I made an appointment to meet. I would find him in the UNESCO office in the Procuratie Nuove on Piazza San Marco.

"It's a big black door," Millerchip told me. "If you pass Florian's, you've gone too far."

The big black wooden door was impossible to miss. It seemed high enough for a man on a horse to ride through without getting a knock on the head. But this was a sixteenth-century building and horses were banned from Venice by that time, so if the scale was right my idea about the reason for it wasn't.

I rang UNESCO's bell.

"Chi'è," asked a voice which seemed to be emerging from the mouth of the brass lion that held the hefty door knocker.

I gave my name and then, as soon as I heard a click, I gave the door a good hard shove.

I entered a gloomy passage and followed alongside what looked like a concierge's office. No one was there. Very soon I came into a large, stone-floored, roofless courtyard. Here dusty potted palm trees brushed against substantial marble statues. Straight ahead was a large stone relief of the Lion of Venice so badly eroded—by wind? pollution?—that almost half of him was gone. Against the wall to my left was a statue of a charming woman accompanied by a life-sized baby elephant. (The sculptor may never have laid eyes on a representative of the species but the results were delightful if not exactly elephant-like, just the same.) The statue looked abandoned, as if, on its way to its destination, the delivery men got tired, plunked it down and walked off. This too contributed to the melancholy feel of the place.

The courtyard, both to the right and left, opened onto others, forming a string of interconnecting open spaces running through the middle of the entire length of the Procuratie Nuove.

It was exciting to be standing in this strangely sad space that felt derelict but wasn't, with its marvelous stone carvings and, high above, the open sky. I felt as if I were behind the scenes in a mad king's opera house. And I felt privileged. Here I was inside the life of Piazza San Marco; I was no longer just one of the millions of foreigners shuffling across the square on the other side of the heavy, black door. Alas, I was still confused. I didn't know which way to turn. How was I supposed to find UNESCO?

A man appeared in the courtyard. Immediately I asked for directions. He pointed toward a narrow staircase diagonally to my right. I thanked him and started climbing. There was no bell outside the honey-colored wood door at the top. I walked in.

I came into a long corridor lined with tall, ornate, gilded mirrors. The ceiling must have been twenty feet high, maybe more. This passage opened out into a hall that was equally ornate, though its furnishings included a pair of prosaic, heavy wood library tables. Both of them were covered with fanned-out pamphlets and piles of old posters—promotional material for UNESCO and the various charities working "under the umbrella" of UNESCO.

If the stucchi had funky grandeur, this place was grandeur in near collapse. The once exquisite fleur-de-lis–patterned wall coverings, woven with gold, seaweed green and cerulean blue silk thread, were now hanging down in rippling shreds. In some places you could see the strips of lathing underneath. This wasn't in one patch only. It was the condition of the walls everywhere I looked.

At the far end of the room were floor-to-ceiling windows. This place had a stupendous view overlooking the bacino.

A woman emerged from an office on the left. Mr. Millerchip had waited for me but since I was late—having taken one of my many unplanned detours—he'd gone out.

"Would you like to take a seat until he returns?" she asked.

"Yes," I said.

"You can read the pamphlets and books on these tables, if you choose," she said returning to her office.

Instead of sitting down and riffling through the reading matter right away, I went straight to the windows.

To the left was the tiny island of San Giorgio Maggiore with its church and cloisters. The burial place of Doge Leonardo Donà. Over to the right, on the long skinny chain of islands of the Guidecca, there was another church designed by Palladio, the Redentore.

Looking straight down from the windows, I saw that a canal runs behind the Procuratie Nuove. I couldn't see the watergates but I was sure they must be there. Across the canal was the Giardinetto Reale, thickly planted with now venerable trees. These days it is one of the only places near San Marco where a tourist can sit down and rest—free of charge.

On the far side of the garden was the *molo*—the broad pavement that follows the water's edge all the way to the Bridge of Sighs beyond the Palazzo Ducale. I could see that, as usual, it was covered by a swarm of tourists on their way from the piazzetta to the San Marco vaporetto stop. I knew, even if mercifully I couldn't see them, that beyond the garden gates, there was an unbroken string of tacky souvenir kiosks.

Dense and full of movement in the foreground, the view opened out serenely onto the lagoon, the sky, the islands and the sea beyond. I could happily have pulled up a chair and sat staring out the window while I did my waiting. But I was too self-conscious. I sat down at one of the library tables and started browsing. I had a good long read since it was almost an hour before John Millerchip bounded in. (I couldn't know it yet, but John Millerchip is a man who doesn't walk. A sort of gliding run is his slowest speed.)

He apologized for being late. Since I had been late myself, I could hardly complain. Besides even if an hour is a long time to wait, it isn't as long in Venice as it would be almost anywhere else. I don't mean only because the views are so good. Punctuality is not a local preoccupation.

I followed John Millerchip into his office. This room turned out to be as immense as our salone at Ca' Donà but it seemed even larger because its ceilings were much higher.

No sooner did we approach his desk, piled with papers, books, letters and heaven knows what else, than his telephone rang. What an amazing-looking instrument it was: Huge, ancient and heavy it could have weighed ten pounds—it was enameled in a shiny, Hollywood boudoir, turquoise.

John Millerchip waved me toward a chair. I sat down and had a look around while he chatted away in fluent, melodious Italian.

There were a couple of tables made of sawhorses and boards. These were the "offices" of the World Monuments Fund and of an English photographer specializing in Venice scenes, Sarah Quill. Elsewhere, the room was studded with gilded tables that had golden vines growing up their legs and mirrors framed by golden Medusa-like curls. The walls were blue-green silk woven with a pattern of fleur de lis that was finding it impossible to stay attached to the walls or even to itself. I don't think I've ever been in the company of so much fraying, shredded fabric.

No set designer could have produced an atmosphere better calculated to convey the decay of Venice's glorious treasures and, by implication, the need to give money to restore them.

John Millerchip, his straight white hair brushed back from his face, has a bushy white beard, too, but the evidence of the black hair he must have had before is still there in his furry eyebrows. I suppose he was about sixty when we met but, lithe and quick in his movements, he looked like a younger man gone prematurely gray. He and Chris, his wife, had lived in Venice for twenty-five years, where they raised four daughters before the high cost of renting led them into the hills beyond Conegliano. There they built a house.

A Welshman, John Millerchip is decidedly not taciturn in the English way. He talked away on the telephone and when he'd hung up we were off on a conversation that went on well over an hour. Later our exchanges lasted even longer. There was so much ground to cover—on land and in the water.

I, the student of Venice, would ask a question and he, my teacher, would set off across terrain that was not only new to me, but full of sudden twists and unanticipated views. There was so much about Venice I didn't know; so many explanations I'd made up without even being aware of it as I'd tried to provide logical explanations for things I'd noticed but hadn't understood.

John and I began by talking about the Fenice. The story of attempts to re-create it after arsonists had set it on fire and the whole of the interior had burned out was itself a black comedy that went on and on. Though to lovers of Venice it was simply tragic.

From all over the world people had rushed to send money for the Fenice's restoration; ritzy galas had been staged, benefit concerts performed. In fact more money poured in than was needed, since the government would pay for most of the work. But how wonderful that the opera house was going to be rebuilt exactly as it had been. Wasn't it?

"Is it necessary to spend so much replicating the theater?" John Millerchip was now asking. "Does Venice need a theater with room for an orchestra of 120? What if the quality of performances is poor. Is such an outlay justified?"

It was lucky these probing questions were rhetorical. I had no idea what the answers should be. Maybe the singers, the staging, the orchestra of the Fenice didn't warrant such a glittering theater. Maybe, as someone later suggested, an international architectural competition should have been held for an entirely new opera house—something sensational and stunning, rivaling what had been built in Sydney, say. All I knew is that Henry and I had been looking forward to going to operas at this world-famous theater but instead had to take the vaporetto to the parking lot island of Tronchetto and listen to the Fenice-in-exile under a gigantic white tent. Sometimes it was terrific and always it was enjoyable because the people sitting near us would comment on Mario or Lisabetta's performance with the combination of knowledge and personal entitlement that I recognized from my childhood outings to Yankee Stadium. But the Fenice in a tent never could be called glamorous.

"Just yesterday," John Millerchip continued, "there was a meeting of the artisans in Venice who are going to work on the restoration of the Fenice. They have decided, at last, to band together to form some sort of registry."

"Oh that's great," said I, the granddaughter of a union organizer.

"Why?" Millerchip shot back. "For what will this registry be useful? For the next disaster? Otherwise, there is not enough work in Venice to make such an enterprise useful."

There was so much I didn't know.

In spite of the beautiful surroundings, and the advantages they may have been given, the high cost of doing business in Venice had driven many companies away. *Il Gazzetino* had left and set up its offices in Mestre. The Assicurazione Generale, the giant insurance company with offices in the Procuratie Vecchio in Piazza San Marco, had moved out, too. Alitalia and Telecom Italia and IBM also. As for the small shops, many of them didn't relocate. They just closed. In their place knick-knack shops open. You can't eat knickknacks. Already three-quarters of the stores in Venice were occupied by "nonfood" enterprises.

Well, wasn't the comune trying to keep businesses in the city? Everyone I talked to seemed optimistic about the current government, if at the same time cynical.

"The town council is vigorous and full of ideas," Millerchip assured me. "They want to capitalize on Venice's 'liabilities.' " One of these was its isolation.

Isolated? Venice?

The city has been connected to the mainland by rail since 1846, and people have been able to drive to Piazzale Roma since 1932. More than ten million tourists pile into Venice during the year. How can the people running the city, and those managing its businesses, say Venice is cut off?

The answer is that almost everything has to be brought into the city by boat and everything is shipped out the same way. This has become too costly in terms of time as well as money. I already had experienced something of this when documents sent from New York by air courier took a week to arrive at Ca' Donà, as if I'd been living at the end of a dirt track on a mountaintop.

If I understood Millerchip correctly, the comune was trying to attract those who would be drawn to the slower pace of life in the city because the speed at which they did their business—and the costs—wouldn't be affected by such things as water transport. Their principal target was people who were more dependent on technology than hard goods. Venice, the municipality believed, would be just the place for institutes or individuals who do their importing and exploring via the Internet.

I was tempted to laugh. I'd already had the opportunity to discover Venice's pitiful failure to deliver in this department. Even when I was up and running, I was, in fact, only up and hobbling. From Venice, connection is slow. People elsewhere must have suspected as much, because this idea, promoted for decades, hasn't caught on yet. Instead tourism remains the number one source of income and it is choking the life out of the town.

"The mausoleum has a turnstile at the door," Henry James wrote of Venice in 1892. But nowadays people are passing through it all year long and many are fare dodgers. The majority of visitors to Venice are day-trippers and quite a few spend almost nothing; they arrive with packed lunches and leave before dinner. Above all, there are too many.

Always there have been people who go abroad because they think they should, and others who are eager to learn about new places and ways. Some travelers are oafs, others are charmers. But crowds lack all variety and therefore interest. It doesn't matter if the language they are speaking is Japanese or Polish, American, French or German, a crowd of tourists is a big, slow-moving mass and, like mud, they clog things up.

Venetians are remarkably forbearing people. I think they are prepared to put up with more even than the English before they start complaining. I sometimes wondered, as I watched young mothers leveraging their baby strollers up the steps of the city's many bridges and then bouncing them down to the calle beyond, if this teaches Venetian infants to have equanimity long, long before they learn to recognize words or can walk. But even equanimity has its limits. And as I began to know more Venetian grown-ups, I began to hear remarks.

"Don't you think Venice is getting too crowded?" some people muttered with an uneasy look on their faces. Not Filipo. He didn't mess around. One day he was feeling so fed up he turned to me and said, "I'd like to throw all the Japanese into a canal."

Just you wait, Filipo. The Chinese have yet to hit Venice in a big way.

*   *   *

YOU CAN'T EXPECT tourists to give up Venice because the city is over-whelmed by them. Of course, people taking a cruise will want to sail right into the lagoon to enjoy the magnificent view. But something has to be done.

"Why isn't the government doing more to control tourism?" I asked John Millerchip.

"They think it's more important to revitalize the economy of Venice for the Venetians," he explained. "If they can achieve that, it will be much easier to talk about changes in the management of tourism. Until they do, the people in Venice making their living from tourism will resent any move that reduces the numbers—and that would mean the government in power will lose votes."

That seemed intelligent. Even wise. People won't give up the chance of making money from transients unless they have a reasonable alterna-tive. First you need to create other possibilities and then you can push for change. Okay. But if people who are making a living selling plastic gon-dolas, overpriced snacks and sequined masks are to switch to other enter-prises, the comune has to offer opportunities that are more than hot air.

Well maybe that was too glib. I needed to find out more. I wanted to understand what was happening in Venice and why. John Millerchip was not only a good teacher, he was extravagantly helpful. I left the office with a list of local people he thought might talk to me about the city. I was to mention his name. I understood without him saying so that if I didn't, they might not wish to take the time to educate an ill-informed stranger. I also understood that being secretary to the Private Committees wasn't only a job for John Millerchip, it was a vocation.

"Would you like me to keep you up-to-date on what is going on?" John asked as I headed toward the hall.

Indeed, I would.

I went downstairs, gave a nod to the funny-faced baby elephant and pulled open the high, heavy door. I was back in Piazza San Marco, once again part of the anonymous crowd.

22

Dead in Venice

I still had not ridden in a gondola. It seemed such a corny idea, so expensive and so phony. It's been decades since Venetians used gondolas to get around their city. But when friends gave me the name of a gondolier with whom we could make up our own itinerary, I gave in. I telephoned Tito. We arranged a nighttime outing. He would pick us up near Ca' Donà at half past eight.

Tito in his white cotton sailor suit quickly explained that his gondola was, in fact, a *sandalo,* a smaller skiff-like craft. However, it was fitted out with suitably romantic-looking velvet cushions and neither Henry nor I could tell the difference really.

Sitting low in the water, and rocking gently, we set off into the watery backstreets of Castello. The more out of the way, the better, I had told Tito, who was good-natured and obliging.

This was marvelous. There were so many illuminated windows to peer into, so many shadows playing on the crumbling walls. Much of this we otherwise would never have seen. Many of the rios we rode along had no fondamentas, these façades could be seen only from a boat.

It was such a peaceful journey. The only sound we heard as we rode through the narrow byways of Venice was made by Tito's oar as it cut through the black water. That and, occasionally, his shouts of *"Oyyeh, oyyeh"* when he approached a blind corner.

We were lucky with the timing of this first outing as well as with the route. We never met one of those caravans of gondolas, each boat packed with men and women clapping in time with a singer and his accordion accompanist.

I became a convert. I even felt grateful to tourism for a moment. Because surely it is tourists who have saved the gondola and kept gondoliers in business. As an observer of boat life in Venice, however, gondolas played no part in my experience.

In all the many hours I spent staring at the lagoon from our windows, I saw only one gondola. It had been hired for a movie. Tourists don't hire them for trips into the northern lagoon anymore. When people want to go to Murano, Torcello or the airport, they take boats with motors; taxis, water buses or speedboats of their own. I did see some boats rowed for sport from our windows, but most of the craft had motors. The most eye-catching of them were the hearses.

The funeral boats carrying the dead to their burial on the cemetery island of San Michele are painted acid blue and have a singular design. The boatman has a small enclosure at the front, while in the rear there's a large, squat rectangular cabin for the nearest and dearest. In between, on the open deck, rests a metal frame that can be raised or lowered for the coffin. These coffins were often piled high with lavish floral creations, draped with satin sashes on which were written messages in a gold or silver glitter italic script.

San Michele, the island closest to Venice in the northern lagoon, has housed a monastery since the thirteenth century. Once its brothers were esteemed for their scholarship. A handful of frati still tend the garden there today. It was only after the fall of the Republic and the closing of half the parish churches that San Michele became the conquered city's cemetery.

The island is surrounded by pale, redbrick walls. Those on the side facing us are the most elaborate. Pointy arches and turrets made of white stone interrupt what otherwise would be a long straight expanse of brick. Near the tip of the island farthest from the Fondamenta Nuove stands a handsome, white stone Renaissance church and, jutting out adjacent to it, looking as if it is straining to break away and drift off into the sea, is a delicate chapel, a marble-lined, white stone hexagon topped by a plump beehive-shaped dome. Inside the cemetery, towering above the pink-and-white walls, stand many yews and cypresses, some of which are bluish and others nearly black.

"Don't you mind facing the cemetery," Jane Rylands asked in her high-pitched midwestern voice, when she and Philip came to dinner.

"We are all going to die," said Henry who did not treat the question as rhetorical. "I don't mind being reminded."

For myself, although I didn't say so, I did not see a memento mori when I looked at San Michele. The colors and shapes seemed to have subsided into a harmony with one another over the centuries: green merging into navy, white stone against the gray sky, a delicate Renaissance chapel crowned by clouds. It was a lovely view. Dramatic in a tempest, mysteriously melancholic in the fog.

I wasn't pretending that death doesn't exist; I merely failed to connect it with San Michele. You see, to be buried on the island you must be a resident of Venice—and you cannot be Jewish. For all that it's called the island of the dead, San Michele had nothing to do with the death of me or mine. So while I knew it was a cemetery, I didn't feel it was.

Of course, this being Italy, there turned out to be exceptions to the restrictions on who can be buried on the island. I discovered that one section of the cemetery is given over to the Evangelicals. I believe that means Protestants, although I took to thinking of it as "The Miscellaneous." Another is reserved for the Greek Orthodox. It is to those zones that culture pilgrims make their emotional or simply curious journeys to see the graves of Stravinsky, Diaghilev, Ezra Pound, Josef Brodsky.

I first went to San Michele on the feast of *Ognisanti,* November first, the day of the dead. Ognisanti is when people visit their dead. It is not merely when they ought to, but when by the thousands they do. The All Saints commemoration, in fact, lasts for nearly a week.

In the window of a shop selling gravestones near our house there is a nineteenth-century photograph of the bridge of boats that connected San Michele and the Fondamenta Nuove during Ognisanti. Now there is a continuous free shuttle service. For a period of four or five days, the vaporettos are packed with people carrying flowers.

When I got to the cemetery, the ground was already covered with bouquets. People were climbing ladders to attach their flowers to the appropriate container of ashes in the stacked white cement chambers. These grim skyscrapers are not a pleasing sight.

The Evangelical section, however, looks like a leafy New England graveyard. There I came upon a plain white stone, rounded at the top, with what looked like a shrine at its base. "Josef Brodsky" was carved in the rock followed by something short in Russian and his dates: 1940–1996. A black-and-white photo of the poet was under this. A woman was fussing around. I have no idea if she was hired to look after the grave or if it was a labor of love. I stood at a distance and heard her explain to a tall man hovering nearby that Brodsky was Russian and had won the Nobel Prize. She did not mention that he was also a Jew. Her Italian was shaky; I thought the man probably didn't know any. He very politely listened to every word.

In front of the poet's gravestone were densely planted flowers; they were nail polish red and margarine yellow. Marking the end of this garish carpet was a row of little votive lights. On top of the stone, a handful of seashells had been left. I watched as the woman dusted each and every one. I am not a Brodsky groupie and I didn't like to make a mess, but I felt impelled to pick up a pebble and put it among the shells to mark yet another visitor. I imagine as soon as I moved on, it was being flicked to remove any dirt.

I then saw an extraordinary grave—an enormous stone tabletop was being held up by four sturdy legs ending in lion's paws. A spray of white-tipped, purple mums rested on it. This was the grave of Sir Ashley Clarke. Not far from it I came on the graves of two Americans who had also loved Venice and given a good deal to help her: John McAndrew, who had started Save Venice, and his wife Betty.

I could understand why Brodsky wanted to be buried on San Michele. Life in Venice so often seems to have been sprinkled with glamour dust, why not death, too? I might have had the same wish, if I'd thought such a thing possible. But I was 100 percent sure that I would not be made an honorary citizen of Venice, as Sir Ashley had been, nor win the Nobel Prize. My Jewishness along with my actual shortcomings would keep me out of this place.

Then one winter day, quite by chance, I found out that Venice has a cemetery for Jews. I learned about it as a result of my trek to the first, and optimistically named biannual, *festa Ebraica*. I'd seen the Hebrew Festival advertised on a poster near Ca' Donà and on the following Sunday I made my way north to the Campo Ghetto Nuovo.

IT WAS IN THE FOURTEENTH CENTURY that the pope gave the Jews permission to travel north of Rome. The Church had begun a vigorous campaign against usury but since this didn't stop people from wanting to borrow money, Jewish moneylenders were in demand.

The first Jews to settle in Venice were Ashkenazy. Afterward came the Sephardic Jews from Spain. For more than a hundred years there was no restriction on where Jews could live. Then in 1527 they were told they would be confined to a small district in the north of the city known as the ghetto, taking its name perhaps from the foundry there. This was the first ghetto and gave its name to others which followed beginning in 1555, when Paul IV created more in the Papal States.

As the Jewish population grew, people had no choice but to build up. And because the Serenissima restricted the height of all dwellings in Venice, when Jews ran out of living space, they had to cram more apartments into what buildings they had. Their apartments, as if squashed by a giant fist pushing down from the sky, have very low ceilings as a result. The Campo Ghetto Nuovo is the only open, airy space.

Napoleon put an end to the Republic—and to the ghetto. Today there is very little left there that is Jewish. A few shops sell religious objects, not necessarily made in Italy, never mind in Venice. And in one corner of the Campo Ghetto Nuovo a storefront has become the Lubavitcher headquarters in town. On a façade nearby is a series of bas reliefs, a Holocaust memorial by the sculptor Arbit Blatas. The Jewish old age home is still in operation, but only just. I believe four people lived there. The entire population of the Jewish community of Venice (Conservative or Orthodox Jews who elect to so register) is 433 people. That includes the Jews of Venice and Mestre and also of Treviso and as far away as Conegliano, up in the hills.

Fortunately five synagogues survive. Two of them, in the Campo

Ghetto Vecchio, are still used. The congregation of about sixty worships in the handsome sixteenth-century Levantine synagogue in summer. When winter comes, they cross the small square to the more opulent Spanish synagogue the Sephardic Jews built a hundred years later. (Presumably, it alone is heated.)

I HAD ALREADY BEEN TO SERVICES at the Spanish synagogue. I'd turned up without a letter of introduction—who knew you needed one? I didn't have my passport either. This was seen as suspicious. Only after a lot of wrangling was I allowed inside. I joined the other females upstairs.

In my childhood I had gone to Orthodox services in a small plain synagogue with my mother's parents. My grandmother and I had sat upstairs among the women in the balcony who had followed the service carefully with their prayer books.

Now, as I sat in the Spanish synagogue, I remembered food writer Claudia Rodin's reminiscences of going to High Holy Day services during her childhood in Cairo: "The room glittered with chandeliers and velvet ropes embroidered with gold and silver thread," she wrote. "The women sat . . . on golden chairs under a pergola. Dressed in colored silks, perfumed and bejewelled, they exchanged the latest gossip about matches, dowries, and infidelities and visits to saintly tombs. Every so often, a face would appear at the window and shout 'Taisez-vous les dames!' ('Shut up, ladies!') and they would stop for a while and intone 'Amen!!' "

In Venice the women were not in a garden and in Venice no one told the ladies to shut up. Whether brides or grandmas, they talked nonstop while the service went on below.

THE GERMAN SYNAGOGUE in the ghetto, now being restored, is said to be one of the earliest in Europe. It was built in 1528. It is located at the top of one of the apartment buildings on the Campo Ghetto Nuove. At street level, the building houses the Jewish Museum. That is where the mayor of Venice officially declared open this first Festa Ebraica, a week of plays, concerts, performances and art exhibitions. It was announced that every morning there were guided tours of the Ancient Jewish Cemetery on the Lido. I had read about the cemetery and walked past it, but it was derelict and always shut. I didn't want to miss my chance to get inside, so I signed up for the Tuesday tour.

My alarm rang at 7:30 on Tuesday morning. The next thing I heard was thunder and the metallic sound of rain as it smashed against our windows. I could see bursts of lightning. For a person who would rather be asleep, jumping out of bed did not seem appetizing.

I wondered if the visit to the cemetery would be canceled. But since there was no way to check and since I was, after all, awake, I got dressed, had a glass of grapefruit juice and went to the vaporetto.

Outside, on the fondamenta, the sky was dark gray. But to the north it was brightening up. Rays of sun were shining down near the airport.

As the boat approached the Lido, I could see blue sky above San Marco and fluffy clouds, pink and yellow, exactly like in a Tiepolo. It was so beautiful, I felt that getting up and out so early in such nasty weather hadn't been a total loss no matter what followed.

The vaporetto docked at Santa Elisabetta. I went out to the street where many buses stop. But which one would take me to the Cimitero Ebraico?

I approached a man wearing the blue uniform of the ACTV. When he heard my question he pointed to a fellow walking away.

"Ask him. I've just given him directions."

I raced ahead.

"It's only a ten-minute walk," the dark-haired man told me when I caught up with him. So we carried on together, following the path along the edge of the lagoon.

Jakob, in his twenties, was from Warsaw. He told me that his parents had survived the war by escaping to Russia. Afterward they went back.

I don't suppose his parents had known how many returning Jews were being killed by the Poles. But I didn't pursue any anti-Polish talk with Jakob, who had better reason to know what had happened and clearly wasn't bearing grudges.

Jakob was an actor. He said he'd performed the night before at the Teatro Fondamenta Nuove. The play was based on Isaac Babel short stories. The theater was a two-minute walk from Ca' Donà. While I had seen a notice for the performance, I thought that Isaac Babel in Italian was too much for me.

"And I speak Italian with a Polish accent," Jakob said laughing.

We walked along. The sound of cars whizzing by on the road to our right and the smell of their gasoline were now as strange to me as the sight of so much grass and so many trees.

The storm was over. Looking north over the lagoon, we saw the silhouette of the Dolomites, craggy and snow-topped on the horizon. Ahead of us was the church of San Nicolò. Across the street, on the corner, several people were gathered in front of the brick walls and iron gate of the Ancient Jewish Cemetery.

Jakob and I joined them. We were about ten altogether. Everyone, including several others who were American, understood and spoke Italian well. All but me. Therefore the tour was going to be in the language of our guide, Capitano Aldo Izzo.

The captain, a Jewish Venetian, knew a great deal and wanted to share all of it. Or so it seemed as he talked and talked about the history of the cemetery. He was proud of his people, both Jewish and Venetian. As he conceived it, the history of the cemetery was at the same time the history of Venice. None of us was going to disagree.

It seems that even at the beginning when Jews could live anywhere in Venice, they were not allowed to, nor would they have wanted to, bury their dead in churchyards. Therefore, in 1386, the Jews were given some orchards and vegetable gardens, the land on which we were standing.

In the sixteenth century the Jewish population expanded. (Not coincidentally, that is when they were forced into the ghetto.) The cemetery necessarily had been extended.

The captain had more to tell us. Quite a lot more. The ten of us stood, feet planted in the mossy earth just inside the entrance of the Ancient Jewish Cemetery, and we listened. We shifted our feet as we waited under the tall trees and hanging vines. The tour I had hoped for hadn't yet begun, but at least it wasn't raining. And really Captain Izzo knew so much and cared so much and there was so much to learn that I did my best to listen without fidgeting. Nevertheless, I couldn't always keep my mind on what he was saying.

From books about Venice, I'd learned that by the middle of the eighteenth century, this cemetery was so crowded it was closed to further burials. After that it was neglected. Sand blew over it, tombstones fell down. In his letters, Lord Byron writes that he rode his horse over the toppled graves.

The Ancient Jewish Cemetery became a place visited by tourists who enjoyed its exotic, romantic gloom. Though not all were insensitive to its fate. "Pathetic as it was beautiful," one writer said. Another, Louisa Stuart Costello, wrote that "two shabby little tenements are erected here for the convenience of the Duke of Brunswick, who comes to this spot to bathe, smoke, and breakfast. . . . It is in the midst of the Jews' burial ground, and a place for a party where conversation should be, 'Of graves, and epitaphs, and worms.' "

The cemetery had further deteriorated since then and had become smaller. Gravestones were lost; some used for fortifications, others removed to make room for the road that was built along the edge of the lagoon in the 1920s. By now, the back third of what was left had sunk down and turned to marsh.

Ah, Capitano Izzo was moving forward. We trailed behind him and began to look at the graves.

All the Jewish cemeteries I know are windswept prairies of unembellished stones modestly incised with Hebrew letters. But here the stones were of all dimensions and some were beautifully shapely. Several were round columns that rose about four feet from the ground. These belonged to a single family of Venetians about whom all that was known was that they shared their name with Cividale, a small town in Friuli to the north.

Many of the stones had carved emblems or small pictures. On some we could see the image of two hands with their digits separated into two pairs. This, Izzo said, was the sign of the Cohens. On other stones, there were carvings of water being poured into a vessel or into cupped hands. This was the sign of the Levis, the priestly caste. I was particularly captivated by the carving of a deer standing upright in a boat. I asked Captain Izzo about it. He said no one knew what or who this signified. On another stone, "for poor persons," he said, there was a handful of carved stars. The most humorous sight was a stone close to the entrance of the cemetery. It portrayed two little men in pointy caps who looked like refugees from the Seven Dwarfs. Between them they held a pole from which hung down the heavy weight of a bunch of grapes almost as large as they were. This was inspired, supposedly, by a biblical reference to Moses' sighting of the promised land.

The ground was covered in weeds; the trees had self-seeded and some seemed to emerge from the stones. Mr. Izzo told us that the oldest gravestones had been removed for restoration, paid for by Save Venice. In fact, restoration of the entire lovely, but sad looking, Ancient Jewish Cemetery was under way.

The tour was over. The captain, however, was full of energy and prepared to continue.

"Would you like to visit the new cemetery?" he asked our little band. "It's only a short walk."

A new cemetery? We were all keen to go. Aldo Izzo locked the gate, turned the corner, and led us down the street to a solid, redbrick gatehouse. We arrived at a place I hadn't heard about before, the cemetery where the Jews of Venice have been buried since the older one closed and where they are still being buried today.

We strolled around. It was larger than the ancient cemetery and in some areas it, too, was badly overgrown. I was startled by how many headstones held photographs of the dead. What was going on with all these graven images?

Aldo Izzo explained that in Italy, toward the end of the nineteenth century and into the twentieth, the Jews of Italy were relaxed about their religion. They had just ignored the prohibition. "But now," he said shaking his head, "now unless you are Orthodox you cannot be a member of the Jewish community of Rome."

You did not, however, have to be Orthodox here. Could I be buried in Venice between the lagoon and the sea? I didn't expect my grave to be visited whether it was on the Lido or in the bleak New Jersey acreage where my family had reserved a place for me. Would it be possible?

The next time I saw John Millerchip I asked him how I could find out about being buried on the Lido. He suggested I see Paolo Gnignati, the head of the Jewish community. Then John and I talked about the restoration of the old cemetery. He told me a site meeting was coming up and a number of people involved in the project would be there. Did I want to join them?

Suddenly I felt like a commuter to the place. Again the meeting was early in the morning—and in rotten weather. This time when the alarm went off the wind was making a tremendous noise, a kind of wolfish howling, and it was snowing.

An igloo would have been warmer, I thought as I wrapped myself in a shawl and padded across the apartment to where the caldaia was hidden. I turned up the heat. Francesco, heaven knows why, decided not to install a thermostat when he'd bought the new hot water heater. So we had to turn the heating down every night and get it going again in the morning. This meant the house was frigid for hours until a little warmth wafted out of the few, prodigiously inefficient radiators. (They might be small but the heating bill was huge.) When left on all day, the radiators never made the salone warm and the studio was always so cold and drafty I couldn't sit at my desk for more than half an hour.

I went into the kitchen. The snow was blowing in off the lagoon.

This is ridiculous, I thought, shivering. The cemetery is at the water's edge. The wind would be savage; the ground under the snow all slushy mud. No one would turn up. Back under the quilt I went.

But I didn't sleep, I brooded. . . . Maybe Venetians are like the English. In England nothing is ever canceled because of bad weather. If I stayed home it would be too cold in the house to get much done. Did I want to sleep my life away?

In this way I goaded myself until I was out of bed, washed and dressed. I plunked my ancient Tibetan fox–trimmed hat on the top of my head and went downstairs. When I got to the Fondamenta Nuove, icy wind cruelly cut into my face. I raced to the vaporetto.

When I arrived at the cemetery, its gate was open. A woman was just walking in. She was blond, fine looking, neither old nor young. I couldn't guess her age. I followed some distance behind her, slithering in the mud. I had no idea where the meeting could be.

In the far left of the burial ground, a large sheet of corrugated iron was propped up. Behind it was the storage area for the building works that would soon begin. At the rear was a hut and I walked inside. The little room was crowded but there was no John Millerchip.

The woman I'd followed was Donatella Asta. She runs the World Monument Fund office in Venice. Near her stood Melissa Conn, in her early twenties, who oversees the local office of Save Venice. We said hello. She introduced me to Dottore Cesare Vivanti. For twenty-five years, he'd been pressing people to restore the Ancient Jewish Cemetery. He was more than eighty now and, finally, it was happening.

John materialized. He was carrying a big umbrella. But where was his coat?

"Never wear one. Don't have one," he said softly, not wanting to disturb the discussion going on. He told me he was late because he'd had to walk to the station. He couldn't use his car because it had snowed so much up in the hills that the road down from his house was impassable. Nobody along the way had offered him a lift and he wasn't wearing boots. It took him an hour to walk to the train. From there it is an hour to Venice in good weather. And then, of course, there'd been the journey from the ferrovia to the Lido.

Landscaping was the main topic. Everyone agreed that while it was essential to drain the swamp and restore the headstones, the romantic atmosphere of the cemetery mustn't be destroyed. There was a good feeling in the hut. After years of talk, the project was under way. And when the meeting finished, we all decamped to a caffè for a round of hot chocolate. Our host, the man in charge of the building work, was a former student and long-time admirer of Vivanti's.

Dottore Vivanti and I chatted briefly. I asked if I could phone him to talk more. He gave me his number.

CESARE VIVANTI INVITED ME to his house. He has a round, gentle face and he spoke so quietly I had to lean forward to catch what he was saying as he began his story. He had been born and raised in Venice, he told me. Evidently at the start of the war things were all right for Jews in Venice but when he was in his late teens, the campaign against Jews began in earnest. He had to flee. He and his younger sister walked north to Italy's border with Switzerland.

When they got to the border they were stopped and turned back.

"One of the soldiers was about the same age as me," Vivanti said. "I told him that if we returned to Italy, we would be killed. He took me to one side and in a soft voice told us to go away and hide and return again to this same place at midnight." This the young Vivantis did and, with the young soldier alone on guard duty, they were able to walk into Switzerland. He spent the remainder of the war in Lausanne.

After the war, Vivanti returned to Venice and became a teacher. It was only in the 1970s that he got involved with the Ancient Jewish Cemetery.

"My sister had died," he explained. He felt that with her he had lost his link to his family and to their past. He felt compelled to investigate his family history. This took him to the ghetto where the archives of Venice's Jewish community are kept. For the first time Dottore Vivanti became aware of the decayed state of the ghetto. But he saw that at least some money was beginning to come in for its restoration. There was none for the derelict old cemetery. Very soon he'd found himself detoured. He stopped doing research about his family and began working to save what was left of the old cemetery.

"Were any of your family buried there?" I asked him as we talked in his comfortable house not far from Palazzo Grassi.

"No. They got here late," he said. "They only came to Venice from Corfu in the eighteenth century."

He, a representative of the Old World, and I of the New, where "late" might mean, say, 1920, now exchanged a smile.

Vivanti told me that the first person to show both an interest in his restoration project, and a willingness to give money toward it, was a member of the regional government. Curiously, this man belonged to the Alleanza Nazionale, the former Fascist party.

The Veneto region gave money for the cataloguing of all the gravestones, making a record of the names of the dead, the iconography of the stones, whatever could be found out about the families.

Once the region began contributing, the Comune of Venice, not wanting to be shown up, perhaps, also began giving financial help.

The World Monument Fund contributed, as did Venice in Peril. In time, the Stephen and Alida Brill Scheur Foundation stepped in and, through Save Venice, donated what was needed to see the project through to its completion. An Italian bank was publishing a hefty, two-volume work cataloguing the graves.

"I am free now," Cesare Vivanti said. "I can go back to my study of my family's history."

I DID GO TO SEE PAOLO GNIGNATI, the president of the Jewish community. A lawyer in his thirties, he seemed both outward looking and watchful.

"If I want to be buried on the Lido," I asked him, "how do I arrange it?"

"First of all," he replied, "you must prove you are a Jew."

There was no second of all.

23

Repeat Offenders

Carole Rifkind's invitation to join her when she gave her paper at Guggenheim Public was genuine as well as generous. A few days before it was scheduled she telephoned.

"Let's meet on the terrace a little after eight," she suggested.

When I got to the Palazzo Venier dei Leoni, Carole was already there with Dick. We went to the bar for a Prosecco and then I was introduced to Anita Sieff.

Short and round, with unruly black hair and thin black lines drawn above her hazel eyes, Anita, who runs GP, is one of Nature's embracers. Tilting her head and smiling broadly, she made me feel welcome immediately. I was introduced to the men and women standing in the small room which houses the bar.

Next I was filled in on the procedure. After a drink, milling around and chatting, a buffet would appear. We were expected to help ourselves and then take seats at the tables which had all been pushed into a big U in the backroom. It was too cold to eat outside, though in spring that's what everyone did. After dinner, we would walk across the garden to the library in the basement of the palace and listen to the speaker.

Dinner was good. There was pasticcio with mushrooms and lots of green beans. Bottles of red and white wine along with mineral water were on the tables. The next course was in the library, which had been a storage space when Peggy Guggenheim lived here. Now a long table took up most of the room. Everyone who could, sat around it. The people who had been slower coming over took seats along the walls. White china platters with plates of biscotti had been set out. On a small table in the back were thermoses of coffee and bottles of Prosecco and grappa.

Carole read her paper in Italian. I was impressed by her fluency and confidence. There was a set format. When the person Anita had invited to give a presentation was finished, someone else, who had previously been asked, would comment. After that, discussion was thrown open. Tonight Pucci Ricci gave her reaction to Carole's talk.

Pucci is a flamboyant, half South American, half Italian architect who, almost equally exotically, runs the University of Kentucky's Venice program. There was nothing about her, from the elaborate frames of her thick eyeglasses to the sequins on her T-shirt, to suggest Venetian sartorial restraint. And while socially she has Old World tact, verbally she can be a firecracker. Pucci is a sharp, funny and ferociously determined talker. Her response was a speech in itself.

I couldn't follow everything that was said by Carole, Pucci or in the discussion that followed, but it was exhilarating trying to keep up.

I thanked the Rifkinds again when the meeting ended. I told Anita I hoped to come back soon. In fact I became a regular at Guggenheim Public. But I never had another conversation with either Dick or Carole Rifkind.

Not long after this, the article I wrote about Peggy Guggenheim, in which I'd praised her accomplishments but not the PGC's decision to celebrate her life in the absence of the art she'd collected, was published. As I worked on it, I had the idea that maybe I should write a biography of the heiress. What was available was pretty poor and there was a lot of wonderful material. But I no longer had any desire to do so. The particular ways in which she'd been damaged by her mad and selfish family and spoiled by their wealth had made Peggy Guggenheim a repellent character—charming and entertaining for some, destructive and malicious to many others. With the publication of the piece in the *New York Times,* I felt I'd tidied up what I could of this unfinished business from my past. As it turned out, I did rather more housecleaning than I'd planned.

Thomas Krens, the director of Solomon's foundation, had told me he didn't care what was said about him as long as he got his column inches. And he didn't. But that wasn't true for the rest:

Philip Rylands was livid and refused to speak to me again. We had some funny nonencounters in the narrow streets of Venice. Whenever Philip suddenly caught sight of me heading toward him, he would twist his neck like a nervous duck and pretend he wasn't there.

Beate was instructed by her boss to remove my name from the PGC's press list. She didn't. I was surprised and naturally pleased by her independence. Before I'd been fond of her; now I admired her as well.

Jane also stopped speaking to me. Obviously Henry and I would never again be invited to Palazzo Caotorta. H., who enjoyed talking to Jane, was regretful but philosophical. Dick Rifkind's view appeared to be that I was wrongheaded. I had failed to make use of a crucial point he had passed on to me: Curatorial decisions, among them the choice of what objects are to be included in or left out of a show, must be left to curators. It seemed to me, if not to him, that while this may be a sensible attitude for a trustee, it is a poor one for a critic.

The Rifkinds were back in New York, however. And Philip Rylands didn't go to Guggenheim Public meetings, where happily I was not persona non grata.

When Wednesday night came around, I would set off for Palazzo Venier dei Leoni. The food was never as good as the first time when the Rifkinds had been present. In fact it was usually dismal—frozen cubes of carrots and peas, cold tasteless meats and fruit *"fuori stagioni,"* as one Venetian said sticking up her nose at watermelon that, being out of season, was sour. Yet, in spite of protests and practical suggestions, nothing improved. Nevertheless, the dinners were genial, so genial in fact that a few people never made it across the garden to the next stage of the gathering. In time I came to sympathize.

I found the presentations in the library difficult. It was hard following the Italian but the often alien nature of the content made things worse. Presentations were so abstract and convoluted that I had no idea what people were trying to communicate. On those nights when a talk was translated into English, which happened occasionally when a number of Americans turned up, the individual words were understandable but strung together they seemed like gibberish.

Once in a while a visiting American gave the presentation. It might be an artist or writer; twice we had self-proclaimed shamans and healers, for which trades Anita has a weakness. And, as the months went on, she became increasingly obsessed by love as the solution to, well, to everything. I felt as if I was trapped in a 1970s time warp.

One way and another I failed to be awed. The great days of GP clearly had ended before I ever got there. I began to be bored. What kept me going to Guggenheim Public was the cast of characters, the repeat offenders you could call them. Some were in their twenties, a few were well into their sixties at least, and a surprising number were captivating.

Besides Pucci, there was Luca, a painter who teaches at the Accademia. He is a tall fellow with a shaved head who wears black. He was not pretentious but *molto simpatico*. It was Luca who first got me past the "I can't speak Italian barrier." We both were frustrated by all we couldn't say yet we wanted to speak to one another. In an awful, fractured way we did. In his own language, Luca speaks with wonderful inventiveness. I knew just enough to appreciate that.

Aristocratic, impatient Francesca sometimes came with her towheaded, beautiful son. She seemed to know or have known practically everyone in Venice, including Fabrizio Hélion, Pegeen's son who died of an overdose.

"Peggy was a monster," Francesca said of Fabrizio's grandmother in whose palace we sat.

Antonio, the anthropologist, teaches at Padua and is a Tibetan Buddhist. His somewhat startled-looking pale and pretty girlfriend, about a third of his age, sometimes appeared also. Antonio was looked on as our multicultural expert, though in fact he said very little, always seemed preoccupied and had something about him that I felt might not be entirely benign.

Paolo, a sturdy blond and writer of poetry, is a lived-in sort of fellow. He'd spent time in New York, listened to a lot of jazz and seemed both jaded and kind. He lives holed up in the country outside Treviso with his books and his music and the birdsong in the hills. A wry man, he is easy to talk to and it was in our conversations that I approached the suburbs of fluency.

Giorgio, bearded and bespectacled, was described as a collector of collections. He has, it seems, amassed everything from 1920s menus to old newspapers, biscuit boxes, books and pictures, also advertising signs and, for all I know, embossed napkin rings. It was far too much to be kept in the house he shared with his wife. His friends, he told me, were his collection's outstations. Giorgio's mind also houses an incredible amount of stuff and he needs to share that also. Our collector had something to say on any topic and one thing would remind him of another. He spoke at length and in great detail, like an encyclopedia run amok.

"Giorgio! Giorgio!" Anita would cry. And Giorgio would continue until five or six others joined in the chorus. This did not so much convince him to shut up, as it drowned him out. In conversation, however, Giorgio was delightfully lucid, full of imagination and sharp. Nor was he a promiscuous collector, I learned eventually. He has a field, Modernism. Everything within it interested him—from Cartier to Bugattis, recipes and airplanes.

Claudio, the Talmudic scholar, is a masterly baroque cellist. He plays with such beauty, heart and understanding that you have to wonder why he isn't traveling the world as a soloist or in a chamber music ensemble. As I came to know him a little better, Claudio visited me at Ca' Donà. I said I would try to help him by putting him in touch with people in New York who have contacts in the music world. This appeared to be what he wanted. It was only afterward that I realized Claudio may be an unsung genius and cult figure by choice. Now that he's well into his forties, however, a degree of bitterness about the financial consequences of his choices is showing through. I ended up buying some of his self-produced CDs.

Fiora, ah Fiora. She is a natural beauty and her own creation. She wears her hair pulled severely back from her high-cheekboned, striking face. In her hair she sometimes tied strings of autumn leaves or roses or orange ribbons. Silver sparkles might teasingly dance under her eyes, while on another night her eyes would be ringed in purple. I always looked forward to seeing how she'd be done up. Once she arrived wrapped in a floor-length magenta cloak, another night she was lost in a swirling mist of scarves. Always there was something tied around her wrist or her neck that started out destined for another purpose. I visited her apartment at the top of a palace near the Rialto Bridge. From the twenty-five-foot ceiling of her kitchen, which she said had once been a chapel, to the little rococo chamber she had splattered with colored paints to the portego that was a gallery hung, top to bottom, with her drawings—her home is a vast Fiora experience. At Guggenheim Public she almost never spoke.

Susan, a poet, is an American who with her parents had gone to live in Paris as a girl and had grown up there. She became so smitten with France that she even writes in French. Her attitudes and the way that she sashays make her seem French, too. If you can imagine Grant Wood's farm woman being flirtatious, that will give you an idea of Susan. Thin, tanned, a lined face with straight graying hair tied in a bun, she has twinkling blue eyes, an elegant insouciance, a tremendous imagination and a past. Now living on her own and earning her way as a translator, she has had three husbands and three children. If, say, Luca complimented her on her dress, she might tell him she'd bought it at Standa. But on her finger she'd be wearing a large cabochon star sapphire ring. Apparently unambitious and devoutly unworldly, Susan was also competitive and determined, in the face of mountains of evidence to the contrary, on giving the best possible interpretation of people's actions. We became friends.

The meetings at Guggenheim Public didn't break up until midnight or later. At that hour, the interval between vaporettos was so great it wasn't worth waiting for one. The only company I had as I walked through the deserted streets of Venice was the sound of my footsteps on the pavement. Footsteps on stone are unnervingly loud when there is no other noise. In the beginning, I felt rather brave going back to Ca' Donà alone so late at night. The Prosecco helped.

One Wednesday, the meeting broke up suddenly. We were sitting in the library when at ten past eleven a siren screeched. Within three minutes, twenty men and women, who minutes before had been daydreaming, gossiping, holding forth philosophically and drinking grappa, had their coats on and were in the street. No one had anticipated acqua alta and everyone rushed to get home before water filled the streets and ruined their shoes.

In between floods, most people living in Venice do their best to ignore the whole business. Their attitude seems to be that it only lasts for a couple of hours. "Nessun problema."

And if you're in Venice for just a few days, acqua alta seems like another of the city's many charms. When the pavement of the piazza is flooded and the white stone buildings that flank it are reflected in the still water of its now liquid silvery floor, Piazza San Marco becomes an Italianismo Taj Mahal. Frolicking in king-sized puddles is also a treat. But I hadn't grown up with acqua alta, I wasn't just passing through and we were having a far-more-than-average number of floods; this incident at GP wasn't my introduction to acqua alta. That had come a week before and it had been a real pain.

I'D GONE TO PADUA FOR THE DAY. Venice might be heaven but sometimes I felt like getting out and Padua, twenty minutes away, was the Big City. It bustled, there was a venerable university and Giotto's great frescoes. Padua is also a terrific place to shop. Its two marvelous, arcaded market squares, the Piazza delle Erbe and the Piazza della Frutta, are crowded with stalls piled high with fresh, succulent peaches, artichokes, tomatoes. Under the colonnades are shops selling everything from wild mushrooms to salamis and pasta. One day I found myself in a fabulous bakery—everything in it was dusted with white flour: the floor, the shelves, the breads and the people behind the counter. On this particular sunny Saturday afternoon, I had come back from Padua, my arm muscles already aching from the weight of the heavy bags of groceries I carried. Arriving at the ferrovia in Venice, I noticed that some of the people climbing onto trains were wearing high rubber boots. When I walked outside I understood what was going on.

Since I'd left in the morning, there had been acqua alta. At the bottom of the station steps, passerelle had been set up along the pavement which was now under water.

Passerelle are wooden walkways about the width of two bodies, just broad enough to allow people coming from opposite directions to pass one another. Planks, five or six feet long, rest on tubular metal frames eighteen inches off the ground. Each of these segments is placed against the next, lengthwise, to create a continuous elevated boardwalk above the floodwater.

Every pontile in Venice has a map showing the passerelle routes. You can get off the vaporetto, and plan a path that will take you, dry-footed, to some point reasonably close to your destination. Of course the best way to cover a long distance without getting wet is to stay on a vaporetto until you're near where you want to go. That wasn't an option for me. The vaporettos between the railroad station and the Fondamenta Nuove had stopped running. The water in the Cannaregio Canal was so high that the boats couldn't pass underneath its bridges. There was no choice. I had to walk to Ca' Donà.

Up on the passerelle I climbed, joining the long, single-file line of people heading in the direction of the Rialto. We came to our first bridge across the wide Cannaregio Canal, il Ponte delle Guglie. From the passerelle I climbed onto the stone steps of the crowded, hump-backed bridge. I'd pick up the boardwalk again at the bottom step. I stopped to look down on the canal.

From the base of the buildings on my left to their cousins across the canal on my right there was only water. The broad fondamentas had been swamped. A few people were making their way along in thigh-high rubber waders. But if they didn't keep alert they might find them-selves nose deep in the canal.

As I descended I had a surprise. There was no boardwalk. Instead I found before me a lake the length of a football field. It stretched from the bottom of the bridge to where the passerelle began again. The water covering the Strada Nova looked about a foot deep. No wonder so many people were up on the bridge. They were stranded. And now I was, too.

I had no idea when the tide would go out, taking this lake with it, so I didn't know how long I would be marooned. But I could see from the depth of the water in front of me that it would be more than fifteen minutes.

I stood and looked toward the passerelle and wondered about the joker whose responsibility it was to make sure that the boardwalks are where they are supposed to be. I wondered if there was a number to call with complaints—though something told me accountability might not be a concept that applied in this situation, or in a number of others.

Then I had to smile. Good old Venetian entrepreneurial spirit. Straight ahead of me was a market stall piled high with rubber boots. And good old Venetian inefficiency. The stall set up in the middle of the Strada Nova was an island surrounded by the vast, foot-deep expanse of water. A person not already wearing boots wouldn't be able to get to it.

Venetians of course already have boots to wear if there's acqua alta. But even now, in early winter, there were plenty of day-trippers in town. How were they going to get back to their buses and trains? How was I going to get home?

An answer was heading toward me. Coming across the lake I saw people who had improvised with impressive results. Somehow they'd come into possession of large black garbage bags. They had placed each foot inside a bag and tied it above the knee to keep it in place. A person could then move through the water without getting soaked.

Some of my neighbors on the bridge were engaged in trying to talk the wearers of these makeshift boots out of their wonder-working sacks. Why shouldn't I? At first I had no luck. But was I glad that I'd been working on my Italian because, finally, a woman stopped to listen as I made my pitch.

I explained that from here there was an unbroken line of passerelle all the way to the station. Even without her bin bags, she would be able to keep her feet dry. At first the woman eyed me as if I were trying to con her. But she was kind enough to check my story with a man standing nearby. Then she stepped out of her garbage-bag boots and handed them to me.

I climbed into the sacks, tied them, hoisted up my groceries and waded out into the water.

Like everyone else, I walked slowly. The idea was to avoid making waves since that would only drive the water higher. Feeling like a buffalo trying to pass for a swan, I waddled and sloshed my way across to the passerelle and made my way to Ca' Donà.

The streets around our house were not covered with water. Fortunately they'd built the Fondamenta Nuove high. But when the next flood came I didn't have to walk far to see that solid metal barriers about eighteen inches high had been slipped into the ground-level frames outside many doors. These *paratias,* or bulkheads, are intended to keep water out and they seemed to be permanently fixed in place. The people in these houses, or in similarly barricaded shops, had to keep climbing over the things. My major adjustment to the threat of acqua alta was to carry my rubber boots in a shopping bag whenever I went out.

24

Higher Water

"Nessun problema" can wear a little thin when it floods day after day. This was a bad year for acqua alta and shopkeepers eventually got so fed up that one day a thousand of them gathered in Piazza San Marco. *"Basta,"* their placards read, enough.

Venice has always coexisted with acqua alta, but now was the water winning? Obviously some people thought so. And among them were those who believed that this was not evidence of nature's rapaciousness, but rather the result of mistakes made by men. Theirs was a disturbing story.

After the First World War, a huge petrochemical plant was built at Marghera which had previously been marshland. The hope was to bring prosperity to impoverished Venice, and thousands of jobs were indeed created. But Marghera also turned out to be an environmental disaster.

One misjudgment had followed another: The lagoon is only one or two meters deep in many places, yet a shipping channel, fifteen meters deep, was slashed across its floor. This achieved its goal. Thereafter, oil tankers could reach the new port. But it also meant that the equilibrium of the lagoon was compromised.

Petrochemical plants need water and it was duly pumped out from under the lagoon. That caused the islands on which Venice rests to sink.

Land reclamation, to make possible further industrial development, decreased the area of the lagoon and, thereby, the amount of water it could hold.

The muddy terrain on which the city was built, by its nature, tends to shift and sink. As a result, gradually, in the course of centuries, Venice got lower and water came into its streets more often. But the errors of the twentieth century had dangerously accelerated this. Then, too, because of global warming, the sea was rising. By the time they stopped pumping water from under the lagoon in the 1970s, the front of San Marco was six inches lower than it had been in 1900 and the base of the Campanile was lower by seven inches. The risk of acqua alta, of course, increased.

Everybody seemed to agree that something should be, and could be, done to reverse some of the damage caused by the creation of Marghera. But what?

On one side people said that "the MOSE" must be built. The other camp said it should not. The subject was sometimes calmly discussed. But often outrage smoldered and occasionally it erupted.

What was this MOSE? Why were people carrying on about it? Where did I stand on all of this? The answer to my first question, at least, wasn't hard.

MOSE is an acronym for the MOdulo Sperimentale Elettro-meccanico. This flood control barrier is a system of hinged, hollow metal flaps, one hundred feet high and sixty-five feet wide, to be placed on the floor of the lagoon where they will lie flat across each of its three openings to the Adriatic: San Nicolò/Lido, Malamocco and Chioggia. When an exceptional level of acqua alta is forecast, compressed air will be pumped in, pushing up the gates until they stand nearly vertical, their heads above water. In this position they will prevent the Adriatic from entering the lagoon, while water already there will be forced to remain. When the threat has passed, the air will be pumped out, the barriers returned to their former prone position and the tidal exchange between the sea and the lagoon resumed.

The pro-MOSE group believes the scheme will protect Venice from dangerously high water and that without it she will drown. But the flood barriers are intended to come into use only a few times a year when there is the threat of exceptional acqua alta. Garden-variety flooding in Venice, therefore, would continue unless other methods were employed to reduce it.

I couldn't understand this last part. Since the MOSE will cost so much, why not use it more often? The answer, it seems, is that it would be disastrous for Venice to use the MOSE for ordinary floods because when the gates are up they turn the Lido and Pellestrina into a dike. With no tidal exchanges between the Adriatic and the lagoon and no sewage system in the city, the lagoon would become polluted. Furthermore, when the mouths of the lagoon are shut, the ships on which the city's economy depends, can neither enter nor leave.

Even advocates of the MOSE don't want to cut Venice off from the sea and, thereby, turn the lagoon into a lake. This is seen only as a last resort should global warming eventually cause the Adriatic to rise so high that Venice will otherwise be underwater.

The anti-MOSE faction asserts that there's no need yet for a construction project costing more than $300 billion, and millions more each year to maintain, when Venice can be protected without it. They are not against meddling with the lagoon on principle. They know that for centuries the Serenissima had done exactly that and Venice was better off for it.

The powerful office of Magistrato alle Acqua was created in 1501 to manage the lagoon, which, with its channels and ports, was far too important to be left to nature. It performed amazing feats. For example, in an enormous engineering project requiring a system of dikes and canals, the Republic changed the course of the Piave, Brenta and Sile so that these rivers would no longer flow into the lagoon. This was done to stop the lagoon from silting up and to keep its water brackish. Too much fresh water would provide the sort of environment in which malarial mosquitos breed. Those potentially deadly pests had already wiped out the once large and thriving settlement at Torcello.

In 1744, the Republic undertook the last of its colossal engineering feats. The murazzi, a chain of monumental sea walls, was built on the Adriatic side of the Lido and Pellestrina. Made of vast chunks of Istrian stone with a base fourteen meters thick, they took almost forty years to complete.

The Serenissima's interventions had greatly helped Venice prosper. After the fall of the Republic, however, they slowly but inexorably were undermined by neglect. And then came Marghera. However welcome the increased prosperity, the effect on the lagoon was catastrophic. Well, given this long tradition of intervention, why are Venetians against the MOSE? The answer isn't money. The Italian government has already promised the funds needed to build the barriers. Why does opposition continue?

The damage done to the lagoon in pursuit of material progress is one reason local people are cautious. Great claims were made once before, but look what happened, they say. Cynicism may explain more, because a conflict of interest seems built into the MOSE plan.

In 1984, the central government set up the Consorzio Venezia Nuova. The Consorzio, a collection of big private firms including Fiat, was told to investigate the problem of acqua alta, to come up with a scheme to solve it, and then to build whatever was needed.

The Consorzio came up with the enormous, expensive MOSE. Their opponents say that for now Venice can be protected by a series of smaller, cheaper interventions including the Insulae Project. In fact, this is already underway.

The walls along the fondamentas are being raised and while the results are not always lovely, they will help keep high water in the canals and out of the calles. The murazzi have been repaired. The banks in front of the Palazzo Ducale are being made higher. There is also a proposal to raise the level of Piazza San Marco by fourteen inches, which will cost $60 million or more.

Will this be enough? Predictably, those in favor of building the MOSE say absolutely not.

I was confused and the more I listened the less clear I felt about which side was right. So many people in both camps seemed intelligent, well-informed and convinced. I visited the office of the Consorzio, which was filled with people in their twenties and thirties who were excited about what the project could achieve. I read their lengthy, detailed documents and, if anything, felt more puzzled.

I went to talk to Paolo Rosa Salva, an architect and environmentalist, one of the people John Millerchip recommended that I see. Rosa Salva is anti-MOSE. We met at his brick-walled office, downstairs in the house where he lives alongside a canal in Castello.

Rosa Salva talked for a long time and with much feeling about the Venetian lagoon. He showed me maps of its channels and described the ways in which it has been damaged. He also talked about how it can and should be improved. There was no question in his mind that the small interventions would work.

We talked, too, about acqua alta. I told him about my own introduction to flooding in Venice.

Paolo Rosa Salva laughed.

"They expect to be able to manage the raising and lowering of the MOSE barriers when they can't even manage the passerelle."

And I suppose it was this, above all, that made me remain wary. The MOSE will be operated by people, and human error is a lot more common than exceptionally high water. Nature, being famously capricious, does not always give advance warning of acqua alta. One recent winter day, 90 percent of Venice was covered by water that rushed in so quickly there wouldn't have been time to raise the MOSE, if it existed.

While I couldn't make up my mind about the MOSE, quite a number of other foreigners in Venice were sure that it was a good thing. Many of them, including Venice in Peril, were so certain that the MOSE must be built that they pressed, even tried to coerce, the city and the Italian government to get moving. They appeared to be a pressure group with first-rate journalistic contacts.

The *New York Times,* the *European,* and the *Art Newspaper* all published pro-MOSE articles and editorials. The following is representative of the tone: "Save Venice from the sea?" one English journalist began, "first save Venice from the Venetians. And from the Italians. . . ." In the *Times* of London I read that "the whirling tides of Italian politics have claimed a new victim: Venice. . . . Unless a decision is taken soon to build the proposed mobile barrage, Venice risks being consigned to a watery grave."

At one point, the charismatic philosopher-politician Massimo Cacciari got so fed up with the implied "I know best" attitude of bossy outsiders that he accused "the Anglo-Saxon press" of creating the idea that "one project will provide salvation. It is an infantile, Hollywoodesque approach."

I felt sympathetic. Toward the end of the nineteenth century, the *Times* of London had told its readers that "Venice belongs to the world." One hundred years later, John Julius Norwich, in his foreword to Venice in Peril's Silver Jubilee pamphlet, was speaking for many when he wrote, ". . . Venice is not just an Italian responsibility; she belongs to Europe and the world." But there are no more empires. Colonialism is supposed to be dead.

Poor Venice. A thousand-year history of independence and she is talked about like this.

One wealthy American, a big contributor to restoration work in Venice, actually said to me, "If they don't build that MOSE, I am going to stop giving money." He was not the only person I heard say such a thing. It would be a pity if these people acted on their threats, of course. But how shamelessly self-important and embarrassingly ill-informed they sound. Ninety percent of the money for restoration work in Venice is provided by the government. The city won't go to ruin if foreigners stop writing checks.

THE MOSE IS A VAST AND COSTLY PROJECT that its backers say will solve a grave problem. But, in fact, it is only one of the many schemes that are proposed and argued about in Venice. Whether it's flood control or rebuilding the Fenice or ideas about how to stop the exodus of Venetians from their city, there is always this mixture of cynicism and hope for the future, a desire to preserve Venice as she is, and a demand that she should modernize. Politicians seem unable to resist the chance to get their hands on corporate or European Union money for showy and questionable new projects, whether it's "improvements" to the Rialto market, a conference center in the Arsenale or a subway under the lagoon connecting Venice to the mainland. Possessive foreigners think they know what's best for her, while tired, bewildered and dazzled tourists tramp along, indifferent to everything but their aching feet and the beauty of Venice.

I followed as many of these stories as I could in my attempt to understand the city. But my emotions were not often caught up in these battles. My emotions, alas, had a perpetual previous engagement.

*   *   *

HENRY AND I SAW A POSTER for an exhibition in Ferrara and decided to go. Since we were taking an early train, we went to bed at eleven o'clock.

In the middle of the night I was woken up.

"Don't you hear the dripping?" H. demanded accusingly, as if my being asleep at three in the morning proved I was being willfully negligent.

Had a tap been left on in the bathroom? In the kitchen? It turned out that Henry had already patrolled the stucchi in search of the source of the drip. Now he wasn't going to let me go back to sleep. I, too, had to get out of bed to see what he'd discovered.

This time the rain had elected to enter the stucchi from a new place. A stream of water was coming in from the top of the window nearest the wall of closets. It did not follow the window frame down toward the floor, but flowed out into the room, along one of the thick beams that cross the ceiling. It seemed to reach a dam when it got halfway across and there the rivulet ended its horizontal course and began its dripping descent. The drips had already created a nice sized pond on the eighteenth-century pastellon.

Exhausted, disheartened and annoyed though I was, I couldn't help thinking about Françoise's "new contract." On signing it, I was to become responsible for this historic and lovely floor. Nor could I fail to see that bubbles were erupting on the bottom of the ceiling beam. This was the very place from which strips of paint already curled down. Here, too, was a problem with the past.

"What are you going to do about it?" Henry asked.

"I'm going back to sleep," I told him.

This wasn't a gambit. I didn't expect him to get the mop. While it disturbed me to think of the floor and ceiling being soaked, the paddling pool would have to stay until morning. I had not agreed to be a flood control officer when I'd rented the stucchi.

"What if the rain had poured in tomorrow and we were in Ferrara?" I said to Henry as I pulled up the quilt.

If that had happened, the mopping would have had to wait until we were back home. It could wait now.

We went to sleep. During what was left of the night, the rain stopped. By morning, much of the floor was dry. I quickly moved the furniture away from under the slow drips that were still plopping onto the floor and put a bucket under them. A reservoir must have formed up between the beams, under the plaster.

I had learned an idiom Venetians use when they are having troubles. *"Sono in acqua alta,"* they say.

One way and another, I was in acqua alta at Ca' Donà. Only for me there was no MOSE. And if there were "small interventions" that might do the trick, I didn't know what they were.

FANS
IN
FEBRUARY

25

Happy Christmas

Any night that we didn't go out, we would sit down on the green velvet sofa in the salone at seven o'clock and turn on the RAI3 news. This was our ritual Italian lesson. It was, of course, a culture lesson, too. The sound bite, for example, has not arrived in Italy. Whether it's a politician or a policeman, a theater director or the victim of a crime, people speak at length.

The first half hour of the news was given over to national reporting, along with any international items considered of great importance. Then, before the local news, which usually opened with a tally of the previous night's fatal car crashes, we would get the *meteo regionale,* the local weather report.

Once the mosquitoes left town and the gorgeous fur coats came back out of storage, it was officially winter. But now it was much colder. Night after night came the bad news: The north of Italy was gripped by an unusually bitter winter. The Venice airport was shut again for more than an hour due to fog. Tomorrow would be worse. On my computer's weather page, "One hundred percent humidity" was often the message.

In Venice, as in London, the subject of weather unleashes grumbling. And, from my experience in England where heat waves and droughts are always called "unprecedented," I had an idea that every year, when winter comes to Venice, the weather is very cold and very foggy. For some time, I was going to be stuck with a frosty reality.

You can't just jump into a cab if you have a distance to go and the wind is giving you hard slaps across the face. You have to trek to the pontile. The vaporetto, when it arrives, has no other source of heat than that which you and the other bodies give out. Of course you can always walk to where you want to go. It's often quicker. And walking fast does warm a person up. But not enough.

I longed for a fur coat, fur shoes, a fur face mask, fur leggings. And not only when I was outdoors. I have been centrally heated since birth. I expected to be warm. You could say I required it. Instead I froze and paid a colossal heating bill for the privilege.

Things weren't impossible until the temperature fell below freezing. But after that . . . The fireplace in the salone was unusable. Every radiator in the stucchi was an underachiever. The bedroom, which had three of them, remained tepid. The study, with only one, was unendurably cold and drafty. Sometimes I turned on the oven and sat in the kitchen with my computer. I wore layers of heavy sweaters. This helped, but sitting for hours reading or writing was impossible. I kept getting up to march around the room in order to warm myself. I felt like a prisoner of the cold and I worried, because soon we were having company and they would freeze too.

OUR FRIENDS, BENOIT AND BRIGITTE, and their two grown daughters were coming from Paris to spend Christmas with us. I was looking forward to it. Not only because I liked them all but because in the past they had been so hospitable and now I hoped we might be able to give them a treat in return: a holiday in a wonderful Venetian palace. The guest room/study, however, was as cozy as the windswept Russian steppes.

I borrowed an electric radiator from Francesco and put it in the studio. I prayed this would help. I instructed myself not to worry about how much the heat was costing. I tried not to think about the subject at all since there was nothing more I could do. And, in fact, when I wasn't shivering, I was enjoying winter in Venice.

The city was unusually peaceful. Tourists stayed home or traveled to warmer climates. For the first time it was easy to get a table in our favorite restaurants at short notice or even with none, and that included the otherwise almost impossible Da Fiore. A visit to the basilica or the museums didn't bring on motion sickness; there were no crowds passing between my eyes and what I was trying to see. And the silence of the empty streets, whether in the gray blurry light of day or the crisp, star-sprinkled nights, made Venice seem even more touchingly beautiful.

As Christmas approached, the city emptied of the few tourists adventurous enough to come in December. It was a marvelous, unexpected present. For a while, I had no idea how long, the town would belong to people going about their daily lives. And me.

Selfish and grouchy as I must sound, all I can say is it wasn't anything personal. Ten million or more strangers piling into a small city is overwhelming. Most of the year you don't just go to the fish seller in the Rialto market to buy sole. Oh no. Half a dozen people stand between you and the stall, all of them oohing and aahing about how picturesque it is. Right away you become an extra in someone's home movies. More than once, I was snapped or digitalized and turned into "a genuine Venetian" in some photograph album in Dallas or Osaka.

It's true that I'd taken pictures of people shopping in the Rialto market myself and had been terrifically pleased if I caught sight of a Venetian, a real Venetian, leaning out a window watering her geraniums. But that was before; this was after. The longer I stayed in Venice the more obvious it was that the balance is all wrong. There are too many people ogling; too few buying fish.

Venetians are becoming like pandas. The pleasure we find in just looking at them is helping to make them into an endangered species.

I was surprised to find that Venice does not dress herself up for Christmas. I'd expected tinsel and bells everywhere. Eventually a large tree did appear in the middle of the piazza; a few days later it was hung with giant red balls. But in the rest of the city, where were the decorations? Apart from a few plastic figures for a crèche on sale at Standa, I couldn't find anything to buy. So I trooped out to Panorama. There I found what I wanted. I bought boxes of gold bulbs to dangle from the red roses in the blue-and-white Chinese vases, our Christmas trees. I also picked up swags of silver paper chains to drape over the salone's round tables. I negotiated my return on the bus holding two hefty *stelle di natale,* Christmas stars, poinsettias, their pots wrapped in scarlet foil on which was written *Buon Natale,* Happy Christmas. Admittedly I could have bought the plants down the street from Ca' Donà; but they were half the price in the supermarket and who am I to pass up a bargain.

Early one evening on my way home, I did find Christmas in one corner of Venice. I came upon a charming Mercatino di Natale in Campo San Polo. San Polo is ringed with fine buildings, among them a grand double palace. Now, making a second square within it, were rows of small white tents. The lights from each of these makeshift shops shone in the soft charcoal darkness. Strings of looping lights connected the bare trees.

Some stalls in the Christmas market sold handmade candles, others painted masks. One tent was piled with the sweets from a local confectionery shop. In a double-sized booth, ruddy-cheeked, robust men and women had come down from Cadore to sell their local grappa, jams, and salami. (Titian, who was born in Cadore, could see his birthplace in the hills across the lagoon from his house in Venice. That house is in a street behind Ca' Donà, which has cut off its view.)

The atmosphere in the Mercatino was gentle, not bustling. There didn't seem to be any frantic gift buying. It was only in food shops that I saw acquisitive mobs. I realized I'd better get busy joining them. But for how many days did I need to stock up?

In New York I wouldn't have even thought about this. In a pinch you can shop on Christmas Day. In London, the whole city shuts down for what feels like forever: from the afternoon of Christmas Eve until the twenty-seventh, at least, and advance planning is essential. What happened over the holidays in Venice? How long were our friends staying? Were both daughters coming or only one?

All I could do was buy as much as I could store without it spoiling or turning to ice.

For Christmas dinner, I decided on lamb.

I asked Vivian Vianello's advice and she gave me the name of a butcher in the Rialto market. I joined the crowd there and when I finally declared, *"Tocca a me,"* it's my turn, I ordered a leg of lamb. It was incredibly expensive. But I was assured it was the finest: *"Da Sardegna."* I was to collect this Sardinian jewel on the morning of Christmas Eve.

Debby, my garden designer friend, once managed to get a place on Marcella Hazan's very exclusive, very expensive five-day cookery course in Venice. Apart from the best way to peel a tomato, what I learned from her adventure was that there's a grocery off the Rialto market that sells the best mustard fruits in town. These whole candied pears, peaches and cherries are set in a thick syrup to which mustard powder has been added. Debby reported that the mustard used was so potent, it's sold only by prescription. *Mostarda* is a traditional Christmas condiment and I went to get some.

The woman behind the counter in the packed store scooped out the fruits from a large vat sitting on a broad marble shelf behind her. She didn't empty the ladle into a jar or a tub; everything was poured onto a big sheet of coated paper which she then rolled up. It didn't leak.

Henry and I bought plenty of Venegazzu, the one red wine from this part of the world I really liked. For dolce we'd have Didovich pastries, of course. But I also went out to Rizzo's because they bake the best olive bread in Venice. And I got a traditional Christmas pan d'Oro, the mountainous sponge cake, from them too.

Rizzo was a lucky discovery and an early one. Probably six bakeries in Venice have that same name. Maybe more. But the shops appear to function independently of each other and only one of them makes the moist bread rich in green and black olives that I fancied. I first tasted it at a lunch during the Biennale. As soon as I took a bite, I asked where it came from.

"Rizzo, in the Via Garibaldi," the hostess said.

I quickly found it. Rizzo has a wide, brown-and-white–striped awning over a window, a third of which is almost always piled with flat rectangles of olive bread. Inside, next to the counter is a hand-lettered sign, which, translated says, "Watch out for the olive pits." They don't worry about liability lawyers in Venice. I often went to Rizzo's after that.

Our friends were going to drive down from Paris. They telephoned to say they would be arriving Christmas Eve. One daughter would come directly by plane, the other was staying in Paris with her boyfriend. They were bringing a case of champagne.

Feeling like I was back in the Brownies, I warned them it was a schlepp from Piazzale Roma where they'd have to leave the car. I told them there were many steps before they would arrive at our door, but they insisted. A case of champagne would come. What heavenly guests.

Inspired by Benoit and Brigitte, I thought we should have a party over Christmas. I had to do a lot of shopping, why not a little more? Boxing Day, the twenty-sixth, is a holiday in England, why not have a Boxing Day party here in Venice?

I started phoning around.

Some people were going away for Christmas. Others already had plans for the day. When I called Sally Spector, she told me the twenty-sixth is a holiday in Italy, too. It's Santo Stefano's day. I did not ask for details. I was pleased to hear she and her Venetian boyfriend Franco could come. We'd met him before and both Henry and I liked him. Then Sally asked if she could bring Barbara and Adam. Barbara, she explained, was the daughter of Carole and Dick Rifkind. (Evidently I had not been sacked by the entire family.)

"Sure," I said.

Faith and Eve would come. Vivian, also. And Michele and Daniele.

We bought a case of Prosecco. The champagne would be for in-house use. I rushed over to Sandro e Nives. I'd already ordered a massive pasticcio. Now dozens of olive ascolane and a mound of baccalà were added to the list of what I would pick up on the morning of Christmas Eve.

When I got back to Ca' Donà, two figures were standing near the far end of the androne. They were Gaia and her mother.

We wished each other a happy holiday. I turned to climb the stairs.

"Francesco and I must meet with you and sign the contract," Françoise announced.

Merry Christmas.

Like a wet dog, I tried to shake off the gloom as I climbed up to the stucchi. Anyway, I'd managed to put off the meeting until the evening of the twenty-seventh.

Christmas was grand. Our friends arrived during the afternoon of Christmas Eve. They loved the stucchi.

Benoit and Brigitte unpacked their bags in the guest room where I had already turned on the electric radiator. The caldaia was going day and night. The place was not toasty. I just hoped it would be warm enough.

Pert Julie, with her head of long black curls and her feet in sky-scraper heels, appeared. (God may not have made her tall; she did not have to settle for short.) Now we had to work out where she would sleep. None of the choices was sensational. There was the couch or a mattress on the floor of the salone or the bed in the little room with a sloping roof I discovered up in the hunting lodge. I'd given this cranky, long-unused chamber a good cleaning and turned on its radiator. It proved to be the only efficient one in the house. The room was hot. And it had a derelict charm if a person wasn't put off by walls which had paper falling off them. However, the plumbing in the bathroom next to it was kaput. If Julie stayed upstairs, she'd have to trek back and forth to our bath and WC.

Julie chose the attic, though I don't know how much time she spent there. The stairs to her quarters were in the foyer and I seldom saw her. This good-looking, clever, full-time muncher of men's hearts happened to meet a Venetian in Paris not long before Christmas. He'd given her his number and no doubt casually said, "Get in touch if you're in town." I reckoned Julie met half the people her age in Venice within forty-eight hours. She'd be spending the New Year in Venice, too, though she would have to fly to Paris in between.

After our Christmas Eve meal, Benoit, Brigitte and I walked to San Marco for Midnight Mass. Julie had other plans and Henry was taking a rest from churches. The three of us raced to get to the basilica early enough to find seats but I blundered and chose the wrong bridge out of Campo Santa Maria Formosa. At least we found places to stand. The church was jammed.

I'd listened as Venetians argued about whether spotlights should ever have been installed in the basilica. Purists say that the men who built and decorated Byzantine churches like San Marco, with all those mosaics and gold, meant their work to be seen by candlelight, which obviously is true. But the new lighting does make it much easier to make out the imagery on San Marco's ceiling and walls: the beasts and angels, the apostles and plants and trees, all set off by gold-backed, translucent glass tesserae. This Christmas Eve it was our good luck to see the interior of the basilica both ways because at a certain point during the service, every electric light was turned off. For the first time I saw the church lit only by candles. San Marco was transformed into the celestial grotto I'd read about.

On the far right there was a swath of wall that looked like thick, shimmering, intricately patterned silk damask shot with golden threads; to the left of the altar, under one of the many arches in the church, the curved gold ceiling sparkled as if handfuls of tiny yellow diamond chips had been hurled at the wall.

The air was smoky with incense. There was much chanting.

The three of us walked back to Ca' Donà in the clear, black night, silent and content.

What with the champagne and wine, we managed to keep reasonably warm. Christmas dinner was tasty, thank goodness, but the portions of our main course were rather more modest than I had intended. The lamb from Sardinia was exquisitely tender, even luscious, but he'd been a lean little thing—all bone very nearly.

Still, there was lots of other food. Or so I consoled myself.

Michela was first to arrive for our Santo Stefano/Boxing Day party. A few minutes later Daniele appeared. He handed me a present: a large, flat, rectangular package.

When I got it open, I found inside a black-and-white photograph. It was a view of the Grand Canal in the nineteenth century. The image was sharp; the water was dead still. Daniele told me that it had been printed from a glass plate. He started explaining why the Grand Canal itself looked like glass. I couldn't follow much of his technical talk but I was delighted by the result.

I gave him a big kiss. It was so kind of him. I was moved.

Everyone got on unexpectedly well. Daniele and Benoit babbled away in French. They both are keen sailors. Benoit thought maybe we could take a trip around the lagoon.

"*Ma il tempo e brutto,*" I heard Daniele say as I joined them. And certainly the weather was lousy.

"*Si, ma con champagne. . . .*" I piped up. Daniele smiled. Yes, he could see champagne would help.

I imagined this winter adventure as a waterborne version of a ride across snowy Russia in a horse-drawn sleigh. All of us would huddle together, well wrapped up, our insides warmed by bubbly instead of vodka.

Unfortunately it turned out that Daniele's friend with the boat had already left to see his in-laws in Bologna and wouldn't be back until New Year's Day. By then, Benoit would be gone. Brigitte was staying with us, but he was going skiing.

Daniele's eyes lit up at being introduced to "the famous Sally Spector." She, in turn, quite naturally, was pleased to be a star.

Vivian and Faith talked about real estate.

I talked to Franco about his book on Murano glass, on which subject he is an expert. Then Adam and Barbara noticed the large embroidery of the white poodle. Immediately we were deep into poodle talk. They wanted to get a standard poodle puppy. I, who raised three, encouraged them.

Michele and Henry, I could hear, were exercising his Italian.

Eve drifted around looking beautiful. She was friendly and spoke in any language that was in use.

When I found out that Adam teaches at the Harvard Business School, I mentioned that Benoit was a graduate.

Barbara called him over right away.

Benoit's first words on hearing about Adam's job were, "Are you rich?" I laughed and left them to it. I was only sorry Benoit couldn't negotiate with Françoise on my behalf.

I am not always such a happy hostess, nor is there always so much to be happy about. But on Santo Stefano's day in Venice, I felt that the stucchi had brought everyone together and we were all at home in Venice.

THE FOLLOWING NIGHT B&B were taking us to dinner. I'd booked a table at Da Ivo, although I felt sheepish about it, as it's expensive and not worth the money. However it was the only place I could find that was open and not a dive. Julie was coming, too. I was looking forward to that because I'd hardly had a chance to talk to her. But as soon as the champagne bottle came out of the refrigerator for a pre-dinner drink, I had to leave them. I was due next door for my showdown with the poisoner and her apprentice.

I rang Francesco's bell. Françoise answered. I followed her inside. The only light in the whole of this huge room came from a solitary small lamp on a table in the far corner. The place was dark and icy cold. They didn't bother trying to heat it.

"It would cost too much money," Françoise explained.

I did not laugh bitterly.

"Come into the kitchen," she said.

There was no sign of Francesco. Françoise and I sat at the large table. Above us a single yellow light bulb hung down.

Here we were, a countess and her tenant, huddled in a barely lit kitchen surrounded by the vast almost completely dark apartment at the top of the palace that would one day be the pride and burden of her son. We sat together in the only warm spot in her Venetian domain; the only room in the apartment where, if your eyesight was good, you could see a piece of paper well enough to read what was written on it.

I felt as if I was in a Chekhov story.

We wished each other a happy holiday.

I straightened my shoulders preparing for combat.

I sat. I waited.

Françoise began to speak. "We have decided to continue as before," she told me.

Stunned, I didn't say a thing.

So. There would be no new contract. The paintings and furniture were not going to be taken away.

Well, in that case we had no further business to discuss. I stood up, said goodbye, and left.

I rushed into the stucchi. For the first time since we had moved back to Ca' Donà, I felt free.

"It's over," I said with a big smile, picking up a glass of champagne.

"*Salute,*" I belted out. And then, as if Françoise might hear me, I added in a whisper, "I'll tell you all about it over dinner."

26

Carmen Miranda and Friends

I'd always wanted to have a look around the Fortuny palace, but it was closed for restoration. Then, at last, its piano nobile was finished. I had my chance to get inside when an invitation arrived for the opening of an exhibition to be held there. It was doubly alluring because the show was devoted to Mariano Fortuny. Apart from the fantastic gowns he designed—columns of the tiniest silk pleats, their seams hung with looping threads strung with minuscule glass beads—I knew almost nothing about the man and I was curious. Those gowns had been sought after by some of the richest and most daring women of the early twentieth century, Peggy Guggenheim among them.

On the evening of the show, Henry and I set out through the cold dark streets. We were only halfway to the Miracoli when, from the corner of a campiello, three women right out of the eighteenth century suddenly materialized. The fact that the three men who came up behind them were outfitted in ordinary dark suits and that the couples talked away as any Italians would on their way to drinks or dinner did not make the vision any the less startling. From shoulder to toe the women wore brocade. Their skirts were wide, their waists narrow, their bodices tightly laced. And they carried fans. Fans in February.

Carnival hadn't yet begun. Well, maybe people didn't bother waiting for its official launch. The fact is, I knew almost as little about Carnival as I knew about Fortuny. Once it had been a fabulous nearly perpetual party and then, with the fall of the Republic, Venetians went into mourning and it stopped.

And now? Obviously we were starting to find out.

Henry led us through the maze of alleys off Campo Manin, straight to the heavy, wooden door of the palace. We entered a dramatically planted courtyard where, hugging the wall on the left, an external stairway led up to a colonnade. When we got to the top we looked down and watched the next group of people arriving. After a few minutes we walked along the open corridor to the piano nobile.

Just inside its entrance there were many panels printed with masses of information, most of which we left for later, if ever. Though I did take in the fact that Fortuny, born in Granada in 1871, had bought and carefully restored the fifteenth-century Ca' Pesaro when he adopted Venice as his home. His widow gave it to the city and the palace now takes his name. But who wanted to read when there was so much compelling stuff to see? Mariano Fortuny must have been intoxicated by the visual extravagance he saw all around him in Venice, and goaded on by it too.

For this exhibition, the walls of the piano nobile were hung with velvet fabrics. Tables were piled with Fortuny's amethyst and emerald velvet cushions edged in thick gold braid, his pale silk, gold-painted lamps hung down from the beams, and in the center of the long portego were mannequins draped in Fortuny-designed clothes.

In some ways Fortuny was a Mediterranean William Morris. Both men had looked to the past for inspiration and turned their minds to making furnishings of many kinds. But what different results were produced by them. Neither sumptuous nor sensual are words you associate with the earthbound, worthy Mr. Morris, whereas Fortuny's world is heady with perfume and wrapped in luxury. Yet he had a social impact too. In the early twentieth century, women's clothes constrained them. When they put on a Fortuny silk column they were freed.

Exhibition invitations sent by the comune of Venice have a tilted martini glass stamped near the bottom if there are going to be refreshments. No such device was on the announcement for this show. Evidently this hadn't kept anyone away; the place was crowded. Venetians, as I've said, support cultural events. And they do it without seeming smug about it. The men and women walking around the palace looked no more diligent, and spoke no more nor less knowingly, than they would have if they'd been riding the vaporetto talking to their neighbors.

As always, people looked smart. In winter, Venetians prefer sober tweeds and thick, soft cashmere along with well made, sturdy shoes. This is a city of walkers, after all. There was a fondness for anything Burberry, too—from plaid umbrellas to mufflers and raincoats. But tonight there were some striking departures.

Four eighteenth-century gentlemen came through into the piano nobile from the corridor outside. They entered one by one. Though they didn't seem to know one another, each was outfitted in much the same way: a ruffled vest worn under a frock coat and a curly, powdered wig topped by a black tricorne hat. One of the men boldly mixed his fashion metaphors: a pale brown mink coat—circa 1950—swung from his shoulders. These outfits made the dresses of Mariano Fortuny look even more modern than they must have in 1910.

So, the famous Carnival in Venice was beginning. And it wasn't only for tourists. I started wondering to what degree the local people would get involved. Would the men I buy fish from in the Rialto market be wearing masks the next time I asked for shrimp? Would the shoppers and clerks in the stores wear three-cornered hats and beauty marks? Would I get an invitation to a ball? What would I wear? Should I get busy working on some sort of everyday disguise?

The excitement I was beginning to feel and my uncertainty belonged to Carnival, too. But on the way home, passing through Campo Sant'Angelo, I was taken aback.

I'd read in the *Gazzetino* that stages were to be set up in several campos across the city for musical performances during Carnival. One campo would specialize in pop music, another in classics. So I knew that there would be a stage in Campo Sant' Angelo. What staggered me was the performer on it.

Standing in the middle of the platform all by itself in the Venetian night was a shiny yellow, brand-new car. Volkswagen was sponsoring Carnival this year. In carless Venice. Feeling more bemused than usual, we carried on home.

Masks outlined in fairy lights had been strung across the calle leading north from Campo Manin. Even before Carnival got going, Venice
was looking more festive than it had over Christmas. And this was true
in the restaurants, too. As we walked along we saw that many of them
had hung crinkled paper chains from their ceilings. There was even
confetti in the streets.

In 1645, John Evelyn traveled to Venice to "see the folly and madness
of the Carnival; the women, men, and persons of all conditions disguis-
ing themselves in antique dresses, with extravagant music and a thousand
gambols, traversing the streets from house to house. . . ." People flung
eggs at one another, he says, which were "fill'd with sweete water . . ."
And they "hunted bulls in the narrow calles. . . ." Venezia as Pamplona.

By the eighteenth century, Carnival lasted half the year. Then, with
the fall, Carnival ended.

Its revival was relatively recent.

"It was invented from nothing, all invented," Angelo Goldman, an
Italian who has lived in Venice for thirty years, told me. "When I came
here, we would all go in our masks on the boat out to Burano."

John Millerchip had said much the same thing. He and Chris and
their four girls went to the Fondamenta Nuove, took the vaporetto
across the lagoon to Burano with its prettily painted houses, and joined
the small celebration there.

And Angelo Goldman had told me something as hard to believe as
Evelyn's account of bulls in the calles. "There were no mask shops
twenty years ago," he said.

These days every other shop in the city seems to sell masks. And people now come from all over the world for the party. Tens of thousands
of them.

The week-long Carnival didn't merely inject tourism's deadest
month—dark, cold, foggy February—with vitality, it turned Venice
manic. An awful lot of people want to dress up and show off their costumes and an awful lot more want to watch them.

In THE END, I did not go to a Carnival ball. There are several reasons,
the chief one being no one sent me an invitation. But there was another.

Ten days before the Fortuny opening, Henry flew to London for a week.

At the airport, waiting for his return flight, he picked up a copy of a travel magazine. The Venetian Carnival was featured. Everyone dreams of being in Venice for the Carnival, of going to a masked ball. And the magazine was going to tell its readers how to do it.

It's not complicated. What you do is buy a ticket. Evidently, they even hand out brochures at the ferrovia listing all the palaces giving balls and their phone numbers. Pick your palace; it was only a matter of money. Some tickets sold for $500. One or two might have been more, others less.

The charity dinner at Palazzo Ducale had seemed glamorous to me and romantic. But to stand around in a ballroom wearing a big-skirted gown with my waist pinched, milling about with a bunch of strangers, all of whom paid a lot of money to have a good time, seemed even less appealing than going to Times Square at midnight to celebrate New Year's Eve.

Nobody we knew seemed to be going to a ball or even sounded interested in the idea, though it turned out that Francesco did go to one given by somebody he knew.

"It was beautiful," he told me when we talked about it in the androne afterward. But it hadn't been fun. He said that the small group of friends he'd gone with stood around huddled together. They didn't talk to anyone else, and no one else talked to them.

The fact that I wasn't going to a ball didn't make me feel deprived because there was always so much to see. Everywhere people were in costume. My very favorite was a woman I saw in Piazza San Marco one gray afternoon. She had done herself up as a Christmas tree or, rather, she had created the impression that she was one by bunching yards of green tulle around her body and then dangling Christmas balls inside the folds. On top of her head she wore a long, thin red glass ornament. It was lighthearted, ingenious and effective. It cheered me up. But there was also plenty that was store-bought—or rented—that was a pleasure to look at, too.

There were hundreds of people around the city wearing elaborate costumes rich in gold and heavy with velvet. Their faces were painted with beauty marks, their toes pushed into long, pointy shoes. And you never knew who you were going to come upon or when.

One day I decided to read in the Biblioteca Marciana. While I thought the piazza might be crowded, I needed to look something up so I went ahead.

The streets near Ca' Donà were empty as usual. There was no sign of the claustrophobic mobs I'd been warned about. As I approached the Miracoli, I was overtaken by a tall fellow. From his gait and posture, I supposed he was about thirty. He had on a light brown corduroy suit. But the reason I noticed him was his hat. An enormous bowl filled with bananas was perched on his head.

Because he was now ahead of me, I couldn't see his face but I certainly saw the look on the faces of people heading toward us. Not one of them was smiling. Venetians really have seen everything, it seems. Not me. Behind my Ray-Bans, I was beaming at this Chiquita Banana in corduroys.

At the Miracoli all hell had broken loose, costumewise. A quartet of masked beauties was wafting about. If Bergdorf Goodman had a Carnival theme, these creatures with their lavish dresses and gold makeup would have been perfect for its windows. There was something contrived, a little too polished about the result, I thought. Though my confusion about their gender did add to the dramatic effect.

I made for the bridge over the canal at the back of the church. Tied up below I saw two confetti-sprinkled gondolas. The gondoliers were waiting for the four beauties to stop parading about and get on with their circuit around Venice. The whole town would see this performance.

Inconveniently for me, the lovelies decided to pose on the bridge I wanted to cross. I waited on the fondamenta. Photographers materialized.

Snap snap. "Raise your right arm," one of them called out to the creatures on the bridge.

Snap. Snap. "Turn this way."

Finally it was over. The photographers were satisfied and the foursome got into their boats. I made for the bridge.

Just as I was about to step onto it, a vision in white started coming toward me. Half a dozen visions in fact. Each figure was dressed in a flowing white robe and clouds of filmy white organza. They didn't wear masks; instead their faces were covered in white powder. The leader carried a shiny silver ball and wore eyeglasses. I looked down. All of them had on everyday dark shoes.

The leader had a gentle, intelligent face, he could have been a professor or a doctor. As he entered the campo he turned to an old lady, whose skin and hair were as beige as her clothes, and spoke reassuringly. "We're from the sky," he said.

I loved it.

The sky folk processed across the square. As they passed me, I noticed one of them was crowned with a circlet of butterflies, en tremblant. In their solar system, *farfalle* were the stars.

I felt as if I'd been sprinkled by fairy dust myself when I was finally able to go on my way.

The piazza was full of people doing their best to make merry. Many of them had children. One giant dalmatian had come with a litter of dalmatian puppy/toddlers.

I went into the library and settled down with my book. It was four hours before I finished. In that time I hadn't thought about Carnival, I'd been too busy looking up words in the dictionary.

As I left the Marciana, my eyes had to adjust to the fierce winter light. The piazzetta was packed now. There were thousands of costumed people, photographers and milling youths. Swarms of teenagers loafed around in the tall, multicolored velvet hats from which jingle bells dangle that are sold by souvenir hawkers. The place had the atmosphere of a giant funfair. In the piazza, under the colonnades of the Procuratie Vecchie, men and women in costume were having their faces painted. I watched for a while and then headed for Santa Maria Formosa and home.

When I got to the campo, a ballo was taking place. On the bandstand opposite the church a group, complete with heavily amplified guitar and conga drums, was playing that old Venetian favorite, "(I Can't Get No) Satisfaction." Below the stage, a boy in a teddy bear outfit danced with a pint-sized Minnie Mouse and other children flung one another around. There were quite a few fairies—most of them without their magic wands. Their older brothers and sisters were also busy doing some sort of rambunctious cavorting. And there were maybe fifteen rather senior-looking men and women. They were all in eighteenth-century outfits, though none wore masks. They, too, were bopping away.

One of the men was dressed completely in black and white topped by a tricorne hat from which three immense fluffy plumes were swaying. His face was painted white and there were rouged circles on his cheeks. I guessed he was in his eighties. I was sure this was the Émile Faith had told us about.

Émile, an aristocratic Frenchman, had made his home in Venice for many years. He lived in a palace near the hospital along with his Ethiopian manservant. Émile, Faith said, spent the whole year working on his costumes for Carnival. When it came, he was out and about all day, every day, going home only to change outfits. Watching him boogie with a woman in top-to-toe gold, it was clear the Carnival rejuvenated him.

I was tempted to join in, but I had no costume and I felt too shy. Next time.

For who knows what reason, I decided to choose a different route from the one I usually took. It meant a very short backtrack toward San Marco. Soon after I had left the campo, I found myself surrounded by a mob. Police were telling me to follow the one-way system.

Police? I'd never seen a policeman on the streets of the city. And pedestrian one-way traffic? In Venice? What was going on?

Carnival was going on and Venice had too many people, so many, in fact, they'd closed the causeway connecting the city to the mainland. Not another car or bus could fit in Tronchetto or Piazzale Roma.

Ahead of me, as far as I could see, people filled the calle. I turned around. The same was happening behind me. Most of the shops had their metal shutters rolled down. If the crowd got agitated, not to say out of control, there was almost no place into which a person could escape. I did not like this. But everyone was calm. I breathed in and out slowly. Putting one foot in front of the other, I inched forward. Finally I was able to turn off and get to our neighborhood where the streets were practically empty. Until Carnival was over, I wouldn't go near San Marco again.

The next night fireworks were set off from the Cannaregio Canal. Along one side of the fondamenta, tables had been set up. Baccalà and spaghetti were being given out to everyone. The food and the mood were much as you might imagine—the former so-so, the latter terrific. The special sweet for Carnival is *frittelle,* deep-fried donuts. The best of these are the lightest ones but you can also get them filled with custard and candied fruit. The idea was to drink fragolino rosso with them. I managed this, too. Lent, and I suppose dieting, would follow.

On Martedì grasso, the last day of Carnival, I saw an announcement in the *Tacuino* that in the afternoon a ceremony marking *la chiusura del carnevale* would take place in front of the church of San Francesco della Vigne. It was less than a ten-minute walk from Ca' Donà.

When Henry and I got to the campo it was deserted. Then a couple appeared. He was reading a map. She carried a camera. They, too, were in pursuit of the ceremony.

Banners were strung across the district's small calles. But where was the Fat Tuesday celebration of Carnival's closure? It was very cold. We kept walking. Then I saw a woman with a little boy dressed as Zorro.

You didn't have to be Sherlock Holmes to work out what to do next.

Trailing behind Zorro, we arrived at a wider street in which a large square area had been marked off with ribbons. Many children were gathering. Soon there were at least forty of them. There were exactly forty of them as a matter of fact.

This was to be a costume competition. I knew precisely how many contestants there were because each child was given a number in order that the judge—a blonde in a ponytail wearing a long skirt and wrapped in a black shawl—wouldn't make any mistakes. She noted down every child's name and then pinned a numbered card on each little chest.

There were three Zorros and a bevy of princesses, all in commercially manufactured outfits. The equally large representation of Minnie Mouses, however—ranging from toddlers to six year olds—wore a combination of the homemade, the hand-me-down and the purchased.

There were babies dressed as bunnies and dalmatians. A tall boy was outfitted as an executioner with a gray felt hood over his face. I didn't know what to think of that.

I was drawn to a girl, about five, pale, with just barely rouged lips and a faraway expression. Most of the other girls seemed confident behind faces thick with lipstick and rouge. This one looked skittish and lost.

The charmer wore a knitted green cap which came down over her ears; on it were appliquéd felt flowers. Sewn to the sides of the cap were large dangling gold earrings. Her long skirt was made of flower-printed cotton, a fringed shawl was around her shoulders, and a petite straw basket rested on her arm. This was a vecchia Veneziana, circa, say, 1830. Delightful. But she looked frightened at the sight of so many swashbucklers and fairies. I was afraid she was going to run home before the judging began.

The judge, too, had noticed this shy Venetian with a basket. She led the little girl to a group of other children. There, this bashful jittery thing was given the hand of a miniature Russian aristocrat wearing a red satin gown, its jacket trimmed in white fur with a red-and-white fur hat to match. The peasant didn't flee; the regal one didn't act haughty.

No one was in a hurry to get to the judging. I began to grasp that the contest, while very important to its participants, was not the sole object of the get-together. I watched as the ragazzi were taught a dance. Once they had the hang of it, more or less, they were led off by the judge, who was clearly also a local schoolteacher.

A chain of forty small persons in fancy dress, all holding hands, now began to dance through the streets of Castello. Then they disappeared from sight. And they were away for a very long time. The mamas, left behind, started joking that their children must be dancing all the way to San Marco. Then they stopped because it was too cold to laugh.

I was freezing. After a while a stand with drinks was set up. Before there was time for them to serve anything, people had taken it down again and put the bottles away. Obviously no one had a fixed plan, never mind a timetable. When were the children coming back? Henry and I decided we would hold out for another five minutes. If the dancers didn't show up, we'd go home.

Just as we were about to leave, the children came into sight. The group straggled toward the judging ring. As soon as they stood still, many of the ragazzi started yawning. But in two minutes they were all keyed up again. It was time for the contest to start. I realized that with forty children involved, it was going to take a very, very long time. My feet were numb. Though I longed to wait, in the hope my favorite would win, I couldn't bear the cold anymore. We left and went back to our own beautiful icebox. I turned on the oven and stood in front of it waiting to warm up.

The next day's *Gazzetino* reported the results of the costume competition. The winner was a little girl of four. I remembered her in her lime-and-fuchsia skirt made of tiers of ruffles. Her face was brown with foundation, her eyes circled in pale blue shadow. She had a Carmen Miranda hat, complete with hanging plastic cherries. This ragazza had a saucy look but not a hard one. And she was adorable. She hadn't been my first choice but I didn't begrudge her—or her mother—first prize.

About a week after Carnival I was over at UNESCO talking to John Millerchip. We got to gabbing about the festivities. John told me that the people who had set up as face painters in the colonnades surrounding the piazza were art students at the university hired by the city to jolly things up. And the comune also employed quite a few men and women whose job it was to dress in elaborate costumes and stroll around town, patiently posing for photographers and generally giving Carnival an air of authenticity.

I was stunned.

So. Even in fairyland there is no Santa Claus.

27

Making Waves

Whenever I turned into ramo Donà and approached our garden gate, I felt as if I were about to enter a dark and secret world. Whether it was twelve noon or midnight, winter or spring, whether I welcomed the cool dampness or dreaded the ominous preview it gave of the cold that stalked the stucchi upstairs, I always had the sensation that marvels were waiting on the other side of the door to the cavernous hall.

My eyes would adjust to the dim light, and boats, ancient ships' lanterns, faded gold embroidered battle banners took shape in front of me.

If I hadn't already done it, I would stop to check our mail in the room beyond the stairs. A former *magazzino* or storeroom, its eight-foot wooden doors held an enormous iron bolt. It was never shut. A worn carpet covered the stone floor. I would push the plastic light switch and a fluorescent bulb would start flickering. A terrace of brass mailboxes hung from the right wall. Ours was the last one in the row.

I was reluctant to linger in the androne. I suppose I didn't want other people to see that what they took for granted was Aladdin's cave to me. But once in a while, I stuck around. I could hear the canal outside slapping against the watergate as I studied one or another of the boats.

They were all made of wood. None of them was new but each shone. One, sleek, slender and black, was positively elegant. A painted notice resting on one of its small, wooden seats read: "Restored by Save Venice, Inc. 1995." I found this puzzling. Why was such a label on an object in a private house?

When I stood still in the androne and stared, I fell into a kind of boat reverie. Thoughts about the Serenissima's great maritime past slid together with images of the water life I saw around me every day. I had watched so many people getting into and out of boats and was impressed by their grace. It didn't matter whether the boats were lithe, racing puparini or hulking motorized cargo barges; it didn't matter how old the people were or what their sex, Venetians on their boats are as agile as mountain goats.

Great leaps are taken between deck and fondamenta, routinely. And since there is often triple parking of boats in busy canals, people spring from one boat onto the next and then onto land without any hesitation and certainly without tripping. Many of them carry awkward or heavy loads as they do so. There were times when I stood transfixed as a man, having tied his boat fast to a wooden pole in a canal, then made his way to the nearest fondamenta by creeping sideways along the flat, stone wall of a house as if he were a human fly. It was a while before I noticed that small metal rods were nailed into these waterside walls, though never many.

It was an even longer time before I discovered that most of the boats in the androne also had a modern story to tell. I only found out about that when Michela gave herself a birthday party on April First and I was introduced to Arzanà.

IN ITALY THEY SAY *PESCE D'APRILE,* April Fish not April Fool. Michela told us that she was always getting presents of fish kites, fish plates or fish-shaped pot holders for her birthday. From the expression on her face I got the message. I looked for a present that was scaleless.

In the end I didn't manage to avoid the animal kingdom, but at least I went in the opposite direction. Our gift to Michela was a large cake in the shape of a bird.

Having a big spirit and being a generous hostess as well as a good cook, Michela's party was bountifully provided with food and drink. In

Venice, you can buy cellophane-wrapped loaves of white bread, crusts removed and cut horizontally. It's a standard item. Michela had taken these long, thin slices and smeared some with tapenade, some with Gorgonzola, others with anchovy paste. Each was then rolled up and sliced into bite-sized swirls. She'd made little envelopes of ham which she stuffed with ricotta. And friends came out of her kitchen carrying platters of little pizzas and other hot treats. There were dishes of olives and nuts and bowls filled with some experiments—Middle Eastern concoctions she'd been wanting to try. A mound of crudités was on the table and there was plenty of Prosecco and white wine. "From Treviso," Daniele told me by way of recommendation. Nearby Treviso is Michela's hometown.

I'd guess there were about fifty people at the party. Beate from the Guggenheim was there. As always, she was affectionate and worried. This time she was anxious because we had not yet been to her house, the house where Ezra Pound had lived with Olga Rudge. We agreed that we would visit soon. Francesco was talking with evident interest to some tall, deeply tanned, dark-haired man wearing eyeglasses whom I didn't know. Manuel, the lawyer-turned–tour guide, remembered us. Quickly we were babbling away. Still in English, alas. A woman in a bright red suit joined us. She had swinging dark hair and large brown eyes.

"I'm Rosalie Caniato," she said. She came over because we were speaking English, she told us.

"I'm from Canada," she explained.

I was surprised. I'd assumed she was a local. And in a way she was. She'd married a Venetian and had been living in the city for twelve years. Her husband was the man talking with Francesco.

"How do you know Michela and Daniele?" Rosalie asked.

I explained that we were neighbors and returned the question.

"We haven't known them long, but my husband and Daniele belong to the same rowing club." Rosalie said that her husband knew quite a lot about the boats in the androne. As soon as I heard that I insisted that she introduce me to him.

With dimpled cheeks, a muscular build and very short black hair in which some gray was sprouting, Giovanni Caniato would seem movie actor handsome except for the gravity of his expression. He's a historian who works for the State Archives.

I told Giovanni that I was curious about the boats downstairs and that Rosalie said he knew all about them.

"Most of them belong to Arzanà," he said.

That is how I learned that not all the boats in the androne were "ours." But who or what was Arzanà?

Giovanni explained that it is an association made up of about a dozen people. All of them are fanciers of the old rowing and sailing boats of Venice and the northern Adriatic. Ten years earlier, they'd banded together to try to save what was left of these boats, abandoned as motorized transport took over. Their interest was in both the boats and in the history and traditions they embody. Even the name they chose for their association honors the glorious maritime past. Arzanà is another way of saying Arsenale, the enormous shipyard in eastern Castello that was built in the twelfth century. According to maritime scholar Frederick C. Lane, by the sixteenth century the Arsenale had become "the biggest industrial establishment in all Christendom, perhaps the biggest in the world."

When Giovanni and his friends formed Arzanà, they found that it was too late to save many of the boats that had been left to rot. Nevertheless they had already managed to acquire and restore forty-five of these venerable craft. He explained that while, on paper, fifteen or twenty people were part of the group, "only a handful of us are actively involved."

"If you'd like to find out more, why don't you come to the *squero*?" he proposed.

"Yes, thank you, I would like to," I replied.

I knew that a squero was a boatyard and that a few still survive in Venice. The most picturesque, and therefore most often photographed, is near San Trovaso just in from the Zattere.

Giovanni explained that their squero wasn't large enough to house more than a few of the boats they'd salvaged. That's why Francesco was keeping some of them downstairs. Other members of the association stored what they could, and some of the boats were being garaged in one of the sheds at the Arsenale.

Their plan was to turn their squero into a museum of boat-making techniques, while their museum of historic rowing boats would be in the Arsenale itself. "To live, boats must be in the water," Giovanni said. He gave me Arzanà's phone number. I said I'd call and come over the following week. He then drew me a little map on a yellow Post-it. The squero was around the corner from Sandro e Nives'. That made me feel good. It was on my beat.

Francesco joined us. I told him I'd seen him a few days before in the canal outside the house rowing one of the boats from the androne.

"I have to get in shape for the *Vogalonga,*" he said.

In May, he and Daniele were going to take out one of the boats and join the long row. Giovanni Caniato would be rowing in another. But before I could find out more about that, the two of them were busy trying to enlist me in the campaign to stop *moto ondoso.*

According to Giovanni and Francesco (and quite a few other Venetians I soon discovered), the most serious danger to Venice is not from acqua alta but from moto ondoso, the waves produced by the wash of motorboats. The faster a boat travels through the canals, the greater the velocity of the waves that smash against the foundations of Venice's beautiful, old buildings. No one disputes the fact that this causes severe damage. But there was very little being done to stop or even reduce it. "Well," I said, "at least the problem of moto ondoso can be solved more easily—and cheaply—than acqua alta. All the comune has to do is set a suitable speed limit and enforce it."

I ought to have known better by this time. "Molto Barocco" is the unofficial motto of Venice.

First, there was the matter of ambulances, fireboats and police. It is understood that when there is an emergency, these boats have to travel on the water at high speed. Second was the problem of everybody else. It turns out that in Venice there are different speed limits for different kinds of water traffic—boats carrying merchandise, for instance, private pleasure boats, taxis. Each type of transport is controlled by a different government agency.

In order to fix a single speed limit for the canals and lagoon and make it work, these agencies would have to cooperate. Or give up their power to a single responsible body. There has been no rush in that direction.

In fact, neither Giovanni nor Francesco believed that a solution to moto ondoso has to involve all these different agencies. To them the overriding source of damage to the stones of Venice came from one source only: taxis. One in four boats traveling on the Grand Canal is a taxi and they routinely break the speed limit as they whiz back and forth through the canals all day and into the night. Control taxis and you've got moto ondoso licked.

So why aren't they more law-abiding?

Because they've got political clout. Or, in the words actually used, "they're a Mafia."

As we talked on, I saw that Giovanni really wasn't very interested in the subject of speed limits. Except in the broadest sense.

"We should get rid of motorboats altogether," he told me. "Tourists can ride in gondolas from the railway station the way they did in the past."

"But who will row all those gondolas?" I asked.

"In the Republic they used slaves," Giovanni answered. "Now they can use the illegal immigrants."

I had the feeling he might not be kidding.

ONLY DAYS LATER the following headline appeared in the *Gazzetino*: "*Fuori i motori dal Canal Grande!*" The newspaper was running a campaign against moto ondoso. One of its proposals was to stop all motor traffic in the Grand Canal and replace motor taxis with a *servizio taxi a remi*—gondolas. Furthermore, to promote the scheme, gondolas were meeting tourists at the railway station and offering to take them to their hotels, for free.

Something for nothing in Venice? The new arrivals were suspicious, they thought there must be a catch. They had to be cajoled into accepting the offer. But according to many accounts, they enjoyed their ride.

The paper was sponsoring a public meeting about moto ondoso at the Ateneo Veneto. Henry and I, newly alerted to the importance of the subject, decided to go.

When we arrived at the hall near the Fenice, the big room downstairs was fairly empty. But by the time the speakers got going, all the folding chairs were occupied, as well the marble benches built into the sides of the room. It was a standing-room-only crowd. And an emotional one.

The Ateneo was filled with Venetians who were passionate about their lagoon, their buildings and the destruction to both caused by motorboats.

A man in the audience introduced himself as Stefano Boato, a member of the Green party. He stood up and declared: "No city is more delicate than Venice; no city is less controlled."

Everyone in the crowd applauded.

Paolo Lanapoppi, president of Pax in Acqua, the organization representing rowing and sailing clubs and gondoliers, spoke eloquently and then got to his main point: "For decades," he said, "since the inauguration of the Special Law for Venice, nothing has happened. *Parole vuote!*" Empty words. That's all they'd heard since. "Act now," he said. "Within the next sixty days. No more studies; no more plans. How much more time has to pass?"

People cheered.

The beleaguered-looking mayor said he would look into it.

NOT LONG AFTER MICHELA'S BIRTHDAY PARTY I ran into Rosella. I was full of enthusiasm about Arzanà and told her about meeting Giovanni Caniato.

"A good-looking man?" she asked.

I suspected that with my rotten pronunciation Rosella wasn't sure she knew who I was talking about and that she was tactfully probing.

I nodded, yes.

"What a beautiful baby he was," she said. "A really beautiful baby."

In Venice, *"che bello"* is a standard remark on looking into a baby carriage even if the creature inside is a thumb-sucking troll. But a "really beautiful baby" meant he really had been bello.

Giovanni's parents, it now turned out, were old friends of Rosella and Marino's. They'd known him before he was born.

I smiled as I imagined Giovanni as a bellisimo bambino. The image came along with me when I went to meet him at the squero.

I knew from books, and from what I'd been able to see in my walks around town, that these old-fashioned boatyards are sheds set back from the edge of a canal. The space between shed and water is an outdoor workshop. A ramp slopes down into the water and sometimes, at the water's edge, there's a winch for lifting boats out of the canal and swinging them indoors for repairs. Gondolas are built in squeros.

I studied the little map Giovanni had given me. There was only one way to approach his squero by land because the calle leading to it is a dead end with no cross streets. I walked along the Strada Nova until I came to the defunct Cinema Italia and then, having passed its door, I turned right.

I followed the dark alley along the side of the movie theater. Its doors were open and inside teenagers, sitting in the old seats, were taking exams. Farther along I saw a brass plaque engraved with the word "Arzanà." I pushed the bell and Giovanni let me in.

I entered a long narrow room; it was the back end of the squero. The only natural light came from a rectangular window with frosted glass overlooking the dingy calle. This was Arzanà's office. There was a fax machine and telephone; there were stacks of posters illustrating types of rowing boats and pamphlets about the organization. Along the walls were shelves on which lumps of red rope were piled up next to duck decoys; a stack of rotted reed baskets leaned up against a row of oil lamps.

What appeared to be a large black hutch was sitting on the floor in the middle of the room. It was one of those gondola covers you see in old paintings and engravings of Venice.

"That's a *felze*," Giovanni told me. Passengers sat inside the felze while the gondolier rowed.

Now when it rains on their gondola, tourists unfurl their umbrellas. And should a couple want to smooch as they glide along, they no longer feel the need to hide. You never see a gondola topped by a felze anymore unless it's being rented for a movie, as indeed according to Giovanni, this one sometimes is.

We walked through into the main room of the squero; a workshop-cum-storeroom. It had a high, peaked ceiling and exposed wooden rafters. Fat cross beams ran from side to side. At the far end there was no door. A weathered wooden gate stood wide open. I could see the canal beyond. All that protected us from the wind were two enormous sailcloth curtains that snapped loudly as they were blown in and out.

Everywhere I looked there were piles of objects—masts, oars and tools. One wall was hung with some fifty carved pieces of wood, each one about a foot high and a few inches across.

"That's a *forcola,*" Giovanni explained. The single oar used by a Venetian rower rests on one of these hand-carved pieces of wood, no two of which are alike. In Venice they do not use oarlocks.

The most beautiful object in the room was a handsome black boat.

"It's a gondola *da fresco,*" Giovanni told me. Built in 1880, it was called "da fresco" because on a hot, still summer's evening people had themselves rowed into the lagoon in search of fresh air. It looked huge to me, but Giovanni immediately set me straight.

"It is only thirty feet long," he said. "Today's gondolas are more like forty. And it's much lighter than the boats we see on the Grand Canal today. It was constructed from wood no thicker than one centimeter."

The boat was finely crafted and graceful. A curved piece of shiny metal with a series of notches cut into it stood in front. I'd seen lots of these; I think every gondola in Venice has one.

"That's a *ferro,*" Giovanni explained. Its six notches, he told me, represent the sestiere, while the bit of metal sticking out on the opposite side stands for the Giudecca. The ferro's rounded top is in the shape of a *corno,* the doge's cap.

"Fifty years ago, these boats were still in use," he said. "Now this is the last gondola of its type in existence."

Giovanni added that, "every gondola is made by hand and built by eye." I found this extraordinary. The standard gondola is a boat twelve meters long, made from twelve different types of wood. Hundreds of pieces of wood must be fitted together to make one gondola, yet all of it is done according to a plan that exists only in the boatbuilder's head.

All of these things—from the design of gondolas, to the shape of a forcola—as well as the tradition of a rower standing at the back of his boat facing the direction of travel and using only a single oar, were Venetian solutions to the problem of how to navigate through the many narrow, twisting and very shallow rios of their city.

In a small room off to the side, I discovered the entire contents of an oar maker's studio. It had been donated to Arzanà by the craftman's widow. Now that all Venice's boats have motors, with the exception of those used for sport, there is much less call for oars, masts and such. People see a forcola and buy it to display as a piece of sculpture. Arzanà intends to make the squero into a museum of the long-lived maritime traditions and crafts that only recently died.

When we left the squero and walked to the Strada Nova, Giovanni invited me to join him for a drink at a nearby bar. We each had a spritzer Aperol, white wine mixed with a wonderfully lurid red aperitif.

"Today is my fortieth birthday," the bellisimo bambino told me.

I wished him *Buon compleanno*.

Beguiled and enthusiastic, I made my way home. I felt quite relieved. Ever since I'd come to live in Venice I'd been hearing expatriates complain that the local people are hopeless.

"Sponges," one Austrian woman who'd been living in Venice for decades called them. An American who has given tens of thousands toward the restoration of buildings in the city said despairingly, "No matter how much you try to do, the Venetians won't do anything to help themselves." I was as shocked as if he'd come right out and called them shiftless.

I dismissed what these expatriates said. Or, rather, I thought I did. Only after I visited Arzanà and saw the proof that such critics were wrong, did I realize that doubt had wormed its way in. Now it was gone. Venetian men were saving important evidence of the nautical history of the city and its traditions, and they were spending their own time, energy and money doing it. They had formed Arzanà because they love old boats, but also because they love their city. And for the same reasons, they took part in the Vogalonga.

The Vogalonga, or long row, was conceived in the 1970s as a celebration of rowing—and a protest against moto ondoso.

AT FIRST, only Venetians entered the Vogalonga. But by now, it has become an international sporting event with Americans, Russians, Swedes and Chinese paddling away in hundreds of craft, from canoes to kayaks. There is some muttering among local rowers that even their protests are being overrun by tourists. And it's true that a lot of the outsiders who take part in the long row know nothing about moto ondoso and aren't aware that their strenuous day out in the lagoon is part of a protest movement. But for Venetians, the need to call attention to the damage done by motorboats seems even more urgent now than it did when the Vogalonga began. Not least of all because little or nothing has been done to control it in all this time.

The Vogalonga is a rowing marathon. The thirty-two-kilometer journey follows a course from San Marco out through the northern lagoon. The finish line is in the Cannaregio Canal near the Ponte delle Guglie. But the long row is not a race. Everybody who finishes is a winner.

"The best place to watch is along the Cannaregio Canal," Francesco advised me. "It is a people's neighborhood."

On the May morning of the long row, I got out of bed promptly when the alarm rang at eight. Francesco had told me that the boats gather in the bacino at nine.

"We try to get there early," he'd said. I would too.

When I got downstairs I saw that two boats from the androne were gone.

The day was overcast and chilly. I pushed myself to walk as fast as I could. I didn't want to miss the sight of the rowers just beyond the Palazzo Ducale, massed and ready to set off. The streets were deserted and the city was unusually quiet. Of course, there were no motorboats. Traffic had been stopped and would be until the Vogalonga was well under way.

At San Marco there was a crowd, but it was breaking up. The street sweepers were busy cleaning away the debris. Out toward the Public Gardens and heading east, I could just make out a vast swarm of boats—like a cloud of dragonflies hovering over the lagoon. I had clearly misunderstood when the Vogalonga was to begin.

Well, at least I got a good look at a couple of the very biggest of the boats—they must have had twenty or even thirty people rowing them. Behind each boat flapped the orange-and-red flag of the lion of San Marco.

I went home, this time walking slowly. Henry and I had breakfast. Two hours later, we set off for the Cannaregio Canal to watch the boats come in. The sun had done its work: It was now a bright blue and golden morning, a "typical" picture-postcard Venetian day.

On both sides of the canal, spectators stood in rows four and five feet deep. In the stretch between Tre Archi and the Guglie, we managed to wriggle through the crowd to the edge of the fondamenta. A Venetian standing nearby warned me to be careful lest I fall into the water while taking photographs. I thanked him and watched where I put my feet.

Boats began to arrive. There was hearty applause from the crowd as each one passed the finish line. The applause was loudest for boats with a single rower. And there were lots of cries of Bravo!—loudest when the rowers were local. Officials were standing on the pontile at the Guglie vaporetto stop. They checked off each boat as it passed. If Venetians were rowing, they lifted their oars out of the water at this point and raised them vertically toward the sky. I'd seen it before, this traditional way of finishing a regatta. For a moment your heart lifts too and you share the rower's joy.

Henry got tired of being jammed in with other people. We made a plan to meet up later and he disappeared. I was getting restless myself. Where was our boat?

I decided to move onto the bridge. From there it might be easier to see who was rowing.

I climbed the stone steps to the top of the Guglie and looked down. The boats were heading straight toward me now.

Could it be? Could that be Francesco standing up at the back of the boat now approaching? Yes, it was. And there was Daniele at the front. I pressed through the crowd and leaned on the parapet.

" Bravi!" I shouted. "Bravi! Bravi!"

Just before the boat glided under the bridge, Francesco looked up. He saw me, smiled and waved.

28

Fireworks

It was hot, humid and still. The paper napkin on the table in front of the open window didn't move. I sat and sweated and waited for the breeze that I hoped would eventually return. But when? The worst of summer had come prematurely and everyone was limp, sleepless, dazed.

I stared out at the lagoon. I wasn't focused on anything special until I saw a flock of silver birds.

They were shaped like swallows. In recent days there had been many of them swooping over the water, giving out their high-pitched cry. Morning and evening, all over the city, swallows gorged themselves on the insects that had suddenly materialized in this unseasonable heat wave. But the silver birdies I was watching seemed smaller than swallows and they flew in tighter formation than the others I'd seen.

They surged forward and then, as if blown back by a strong gusting wind, the shimmering creatures retreated. Instantly they would gather strength and lunge forward once more. This was repeated over and over again, the silvery feathered things never managing to fly out of sight.

The fact is, they never flew anywhere. They weren't birds. I'd been staring at an avian mirage.

I pulled myself together and went down to pay the June rent.

Francesco and I sat just inside the door to the amministrazione, where the cool air of the androne could reach us.

"I saw you the other night at the theater," I told him. "But it was so crowded I couldn't make my way over to say hello."

It had been a fabulous, gala night: the first performance in modern times of *Il re alla Caccia,* which had its premiere in Venice in 1763. The authors were two local boys: Carlo Goldoni, who wrote the words, and Burano's Baldassare Galuppi, the composer. (There's a statue of him in the island's main square.)

The audience of invited guests filled the theater. On the program, the list of sponsors included Nicolò and Giuliana Donà dalle Rose. Both of them were there. So was Gaia accompanied by Giovanni. We said hello as we passed them in the lobby before the performance began. Gaia was a beauty that night, wrapped in a black, fur-trimmed, Chinese-embroidered cloak. She did not sit with her brother, her father and his second wife. In fact I didn't see her again all evening.

The play with music was a transition from *commedia dell'arte* to the opera we know, where music and action are integrated. But this was not an educational experience. *Il re* was lively and amusing, the staging pretty. The atmosphere was so festive and il conte looked so happy, I felt that this event must also be a kind of an announcement to his friends and neighbors that fortune was favoring the house of Nicolò Donà once again. The lawsuit, at last, must be coming to the conclusion they were hoping for.

Now as Francesco and I talked, he suggested that this indeed was happening. The court case was going well. Also, he would be finished with university, soon. He could begin to relax. His mind was turning toward the coming summer holiday.

"Every year," he told me, "if we have enough people, we take out one of the largest boats for Redentore. We decorate it, provide food and drink. People pay to spend the evening on the boat. The money goes to Arzanà. Would you and Henry like to join us if we do it again next month?"

What a memorable, magical evening that would be: We would row into the bacino on an old Venetian boat that had been rescued and restored. All around us would be hundreds of other boats, maybe thousands, lots of them decorated with colored lanterns. Everywhere Venetians out together for a night on the lagoon would be laughing and eating and drinking. Later the fireworks would start. On and on they would go, the noise like cannon fire careering across the black water.

On every side, people would be oohing and aahing as the great spectacle went on. Above our heads the exploding stars and comets would multiply. And as we gently bobbed up and down in the water, bits of colored light would rain down on us like handfuls of emeralds, sapphires, topaz and rubies. In a flash I was seeing myself as Tiepolo's portrait of Venice looking on as Neptune emptied his cornucopia of jeweled treasures at her feet. Never mind that this painting in the Doge's Palace shows Venice as a blond beauty in a sensational eighteenth-century gown, and rather younger, too.

The eve of the Feast of the Redeemer would be a glorious party on the water. And for me, it would be the celebration of my dream come true. Our year at Ca' Donà was approaching its end. I would be celebrating with my Henry and members of the family of this house which I loved. Of course, we would be paying for the pleasure, just as we paid to live in their palace. This made me no less enthusiastic about joining in.

"Yes I would like that very much," I told Francesco. "Don't forget to let me know if it goes ahead. I'm sure we'll want to come along."

Our first Redentore had been special and exciting. Rosella had invited us to the Marciana for the fireworks again, but I felt she and Marino would understand if we went out on Arzanà's boat instead.

I had avoided thinking about what was ahead. There was so much I had to do before our stay was over: pack our books, papers, glassware we'd bought for Prosecco as well as a set of small, stemmed glasses with grapes etched on them from which we drank Vin Santo. On top of all that there was my Bread Museum.

How was I going to transport, intact, the collection of special holiday treats I'd assembled, cookies I'd discovered hidden in the pastry shops of Venice during the year? Among them were two dough Carnival masks to cover the eyes—one simple and masculine as I thought of it and the other more like Peggy Guggenheim's outlandish winged sunglasses. I'd found a plump white dove at Eastertime and before that a large, heavy square of bread with braided edges; a plaque on which was written "Buon Anno." I treasured my little gondola, its felze fringed with blue, red, and yellow M&Ms. Squiggles of green icing along the bottom represented the lagoon and VENEZIA was piped along the body of the cookie boat in chocolate icing. I even had a dough rendition of the church of San Pietro piped in pink. During Castello's spring festival it had appeared in the window of Rizzo. And I couldn't abandon San Martino, who had started me off on this collection and so much else. He must come with me too.

Above all, I didn't like to think ahead because I didn't want to leave this house and Venice. No, I wouldn't think about any of it yet. I knew it was going to be awful when we had to go. And we did have to go. The Donà wanted to use the stucchi for a few months; Chiara, the eldest child, was coming from Paris to work with Gaia on a textile design project they had already begun. And I never wanted to spend another winter being so terribly, terribly cold. I'd been leveled by flu three times before warm weather arrived.

But I didn't want to think about going away. Or for how long it might be. I wouldn't until I was forced to. Instead I began to plan a birthday trip.

We were in Italy. We should take advantage of it. My birthday is in the first week of July. "Let's follow the 'Piero trail,' " I proposed.

I had read that, after years of being *in restauro* ("in restoration"), the work on the great cycle of frescoes Piero della Francesca painted for the church of San Francesco in Arezzo was now finished. We would begin our trip there and then head east to see the Pieros at Monturchi and Sansepolcro and end with those in Urbino. How could it fail to be a memorable adventure?

Henry was not enthusiastic. He had done all this years before. The frescoes probably had been overcleaned. There would be too many tourists. The Madonna at Monturchi had been moved from the chapel out in the countryside where Piero had painted her and put into an ugly building in the village.

Then I, too, began to have reservations. When I telephoned the Arezzo tourist office to ask about hotels, I discovered that, contrary to the report I'd read, only half the frescoes in the church of San Francesco had been unwrapped. The rest were still curtained off behind scaffolding—still being restored.

"When will they be finished?" I asked.

The woman laughed. *"No lo so,"* she replied. I don't know. Maybe next year?

I wavered. But I felt so strongly that it was time I saw what I could of Piero's work, that I must go while we were relatively near. And Henry agreed.

There followed a tricky problem. How to get there? I am the sole driver in our household and I have altitude sickness, at least that's what I call my fear of precipices. I like it better than saying I have a phobia about heights. And besides it's not heights, it's drops straight down from high places that I can't cope with.

Mountain roads are not where I want to find myself driving. Oh I don't mind much if I am a passenger. In Morocco I managed to go across the High Atlas, the Middle Atlas, and the anti-Atlas ranges without getting palpitations. We'd made those journeys by bus. Though there was a ghastly moment when the old bus shook to a stop on a mountain pass not much wider than it was. If the driver had told us we had to get out and walk . . . Fortunately the old thing started up again.

If the roads across Tuscany into Umbria had steep drops, my birthday treat would be a nightmare.

I bought the Touring Club of Italy's detailed map and studied the route. There were certain telltale squiggles; green and yellow lines like pairs of coiled springs. Between Urbino and its Ducal Palace, in which hangs Piero della Francesca's "Flagellation," and the town of Sansepolcro, home of his "Resurrection" and "Madonna of the Misericordia," were the Apennine Mountains.

Some people who'd driven the road assured me the mountains were not precipitous. But when you aren't twitchy about such things, it's easy not to notice them. Inge was more direct. "Don't do it," she said. "You will not like it."

Inge, an art historian, and her husband Hans, a neuroradiologist, had become friends of ours early in the spring. Three days a week they lived in an apartment on the Zattere while Hans, who had recently retired as head of a Frankfurt hospital, set up a clinic at a hospital on the mainland.

We had met at Beate's little house near the Salute when we went there to dinner. The house had been stripped and modernized before it had been rented. There was no trace of what it had been like when Pound or even Olga Rudge had lived there. But the evening was a pleasure.

Hans, explaining how he'd come to know Beate, had joked, "I picked her up on the boat when I saw her reading *Frankfurter Allgemeine*."

Inge and I made a good contact right away—even before I found out that she'd liked my article about Peggy Guggenheim so much she'd cut it out of the *New York Times* and kept it.

We saw Hans and Inge several times after that. I found Inge quick-witted and lively. Hans was obviously intelligent and cultivated. But whenever we got together Hans would nod off before the end of the evening. Did he suffer from narcolepsy or a chronic lack of sleep? The subject was never discussed. It was clear we weren't supposed to notice, so we pretended we hadn't.

Now when I told Inge about my plan to visit the Pieros, she not only gave me advice about how to travel, she also said, "You must come and stay with us."

They had a house in Tuscany, not far from Arezzo. And they were going to be there in early July. Hans was looking forward to doing lots of work in his garden, about which he was passionate.

It was an unexpected but very welcome invitation. We might get to know them a little better and Tuscany, too. But because of their schedule we would have to change the direction of our journey, finishing rather than starting in Arezzo. Well that wasn't difficult. I hadn't made any bookings yet. Very soon everything was arranged.

Henry and I would take the train from Venice to Pesaro. From there we would take a bus to Urbino and spend two nights; one of them my birthday. We would then take the seven A.M.—and only— bus across the Apennines to Sansepolcro. We'd continue on from there to Monturchi and spend the night in Arezzo. Hans and Inge would meet us the next day at the church and, after we'd seen the frescoes, they would drive us to their house, south of Siena. After a few days, we would all head back to Venice together. They intended to drive to

Florence and leave their car there, so the last lap of the trip would be by train.

Urbino, in its landlocked way, is as much a fairy-tale town as Venice. It's at the top of a steep hill which sheers off on one side. The castle dominates both the town and the plain it overlooks. In the fifteenth century it was the domain of a remarkable man.

It's curious how the personality of a powerful ruler can continue to permeate his city hundreds of years after his death. At Mantua, a menacing, sulphurous cloud still seems to hang low over the Gonzagas' ducal palace. The last time we'd gone there, my best clothes were stolen from the hotel. I was outraged but not surprised. Mantua feels like a place were evil crouches ready to spring. The opposite was true of Urbino.

The big, beneficent spirit of the great humanist, the Duke of Montefeltro, forms a radiant halo over his city. Even today, Urbino bustles with invention and productivity of the most sympathetic kind. Along every narrow, tightly curling street there are workshops of craftsmen and artisans: picture framers, papermakers, bookbinders, people fashioning ancient instruments. These are working premises, not the Urbino equivalent of shops cranking out masks. If, as I packed to leave, I'd discovered a garland of gilded flowers tucked into my suitcase, it would have seemed in keeping.

I didn't find one. But I'd had an enchanted birthday. There'd been no special cake, either, for that matter. But how could I complain when I'd dined on truffled pasta at The Angel Divine.

The road to Sansepolcro over the Apennines looks like a paved mule track. It is one long series of hairpin turns. Thank heaven I did not have to drive it myself. Though when the exhausted-looking driver stopped for coffee before we began the ascent and I watched him pour a shot of Sambuca into his cup, I was not altogether comforted. It was a beautiful, if not relaxing, drive and a long one. It was eight hours before we arrived at Sansepolcro. We made it to Arezzo in time for a very late dinner.

The next morning, when we got to the church of San Francesco and met Inge and Hans, we found that the scaffolding was still up on both sides of the altar. But the situation wasn't as bad as it looked. On one side, the restoration really had been finished and we were allowed to climb up and look at the fresco almost nose to nose with Piero's painting.

Hans and Inge drove us to Siena and then on to their perfectly redone farmhouse. They were generous, considerate hosts. We ate our meals outside on the terrace under the trees. We drank the Chianti of a local farmer, who gave it to them in exchange for using their fields for hay.

While Hans puttered among his roses, Inge drove us to Monte Oliveto, a Benedictine monastery high up in pine forests where the monks still make all sorts of medicines and potions they sell in a little shop. Unfortunately, in the company of this pair of no-nonsense art lookers, I couldn't fit in both a visit to the frescoes in the libraries and a nip into the shop. Another day we visited a spa and the striking Renaissance hill town of Pienza. On our last night we took them to dinner in nearby Montalcino, a town on top of a hill that had been very poor until it began producing and promoting the now coveted Brunello.

It was an idyllic holiday.

On our last morning, Hans, shirtless and wearing long khaki shorts, worked away harvesting his lavender. There was a vast amount of it which he set out to dry in a long stone room at the bottom of the house. Inge sent Henry and me out into their large vegetable garden. "Take as much as you want," she said. "By the time we come back it will be rotten."

The plan had changed. That afternoon the four of us were going to drive all the way to Venice. They'd remembered that they had to take the car to Frankfurt for its yearly inspection.

They had other cars. Indeed they owned other houses—five altogether, I believe. But Hans told us that he was especially fond of this tank of a Mercedes station wagon. He looked after it devotedly.

"It is old," he acknowledged, "but it's been fitted with every modern safety device. Even new steering." Clearly it was his pet.

Inge began making preparations for lunch. Henry and I already felt overfed. She had made us lovely meals, we'd had a big dinner the night before. It was very hot and getting hotter, and there was a long drive ahead.

"Why don't we skip lunch?" I suggested. "We can get a snack on the road."

"But I have these steaks," Inge responded. "It will be a simple meal."

I felt I didn't know her well enough to argue. They were formal people. We were their guests. And I'd already seen how much attention Inge gave to being a flawless hostess.

Just outside, between the kitchen door and the terrace where we were laying the table for lunch, Henry stood studying the grape arbor. He had found a young bird on the ground. He was trying to find the nest it had fallen from so he could put it back.

By three o'clock, as planned, lunch was over. All the shutters were tightly closed. The back of the car was packed with flowers and fruits from the garden. We fastened our seat belts and were off.

H. and I sat in the rear seat. Hans drove along side roads on the way to Siena. He wanted us to see the countryside. From there we would join the highway to Florence, Bologna and Venice.

After an hour, Hans pulled off the road at a traffic circle.

"I'm going to sleep," he said. He got out of the car and switched places with Inge.

As she got behind the wheel, Inge said, "I don't like to start from here; I had an accident before."

My chest tightened. Then, as Inge pulled out onto the road, I saw that another car, moving up on us fast, cleared our tail with only inches to spare. Oh dear.

Hans was unfazed, however. He pushed back his seat—at six foot five, he needs all the legroom he can get—and almost instantly he was snoozing.

I chatted to Inge who was sitting directly in front of me. "Let's all hire a boat when you come back to Venice," I said, picking up the thread of a conversation we'd started weeks before. Hans was a skilled sailor and we all wanted to explore the islands of the northern lagoon. There would be time enough for that before we would have to pack up and leave Ca' Donà.

"Yes," she said. But that was it. She didn't continue the conversation. Evidently she wasn't in the mood.

Henry fell asleep next to me. I, a worrier, sat and worried. Was Inge feeling dozy? I wished we had a more casual friendship because, as it was, I didn't feel I could offer to take over driving without it seeming uppity or maybe insulting.

Henry flew toward me moaning. It was a horrifying sound.

My chest was caving in, pushed by a terrible force. I could feel the bones being crushed.

I saw Hans's face covered with blood.

Smoke poured from the hood of the car. A man stood in front of it. In his arms he held an uprooted tree. It was not a sapling.

At half past four the car had driven off the highway.

I wanted to open the door. I must get out. But I couldn't move. I thought we all were dying. Maybe someone was already dead. I couldn't see the others.

Someone dragged me out. I tried to drop down onto the grass. The man holding me wouldn't let go of me.

"You must move away from here," he said.

I understood he was afraid the car might explode. I made all the effort I could and got to his car. He helped me onto the backseat. Liquid was bubbling up in my throat and pouring from my mouth.

"Am I bleeding?" I asked the kind man who was so helpful.

"No you are not."

A doctor appeared. Then Henry. Oh thank goodness. And he was walking. Walking. Imagine it. Now I saw Inge heading toward me.

A collar was fitted around my neck. I was placed on a stretcher, attached to a drip and wheeled to an ambulance. Henry and Inge climbed in and sat next to me. We waited. For what? And then the siren started and a journey began. It seemed to last for hours and hours. I felt every rise and fall in the road, and there were dozens of them. The ambulance bumped over what must have been every hill in Florence.

Amazingly, although I didn't know it until later, Inge had phoned a Florentine colleague of Hans's from the crash site. This doctor arranged for us to be taken to the hospital specializing in orthopedic cases. It was on the other side of town.

"This is like being in a B movie," I thought. But what I felt was "This is hell." The pain was terrible and terrifying.

I had to kick the attendant as he removed me from the ambulance.

If I hadn't called his attention to it, he would have ripped the drip from my arm. I was wheeled into emergency.

I could hear Inge saying over and over, "I want to see my husband. How is Hans?"

I was X-rayed. I suppose I must have been given something for pain. I remained on the stretcher. Waiting. What was taking so long? I wanted to be in a bed. Sleeping. But at the same time I used whatever force there was in me to keep from falling unconscious. Awake meant alive.

A doctor in a green gown walked toward me. He was tanned, in his forties with graying hair. He wore wire-rimmed glasses. He was, in fact, handsome. He bent forward.

"You will recover," he said.

Doctor, I love you still.

It was many, many weeks before I believed that I would recover completely. I was so weak. And scared. But we all recovered in time, even Hans, the most seriously injured of us, whose face was badly smashed as were his ankles and I don't know what else.

I'd fractured my sternum and four ribs. *"Cintura,"* the doctor said when he looked at me. Seat belt injuries, all of them. But if we hadn't been wearing seat belts, I think we would have been killed. For the first two days I was in the hospital I could not lift my head off the pillow. I couldn't raise myself even a little to help the nurses when they changed the linen. My body was like a sack of potatoes, a dead weight, inert. I lay in bed and looked out the windows where I saw the tops of what appeared to be very old trees.

"Will I ever see where they meet the ground?" I wondered. "Will I ever see the grass?"

I could, however, talk. I soon learned that *padella* means bedpan. (Also cooking pot, which usage was then irrelevant of course.) And I learned that *"auguri"* is what the other patients say when you are being wheeled off for diagnostic tests. It is what you say to them when they are. Good luck. I learned, too, that in Italian hospitals the patient is expected to provide her own towels and her own cutlery. I was not yet able to use what I did not have.

We were six in the room. Inge was in the bed next to me. She had fractured her sternum, though clearly not as badly as I had since she could walk. Indeed, Inge, who was being given tests and watched in case of complications, spent most of her time quite naturally downstairs with Hans.

Stubborn Henry had refused to be admitted to the hospital. I could understand that he wanted to feel he was okay. But he had bad bruises and he needed to rest. The day after the crash he felt much worse, of course. One night at the top of a hotel near the hospital that didn't have an elevator made him decide to go back to Venice. He felt Ca' Donà was the only place where he could begin to recover his strength.

Many people came to visit Hans, Inge reported. One or two of the doctors dropped into our room to say hello. Hans was an eminent physician, well-known and much respected. Inge said that one of his Italian colleagues, an esteemed radiologist herself, sat with him studying his X-rays, the two of them discussing what could be done about the damage to his face.

After two days I was given permission to sit up in bed. Inge had to help. By evening I tried to stand. By now, Inge had commandeered extra pillowcases which we used as towels. And the aides had found us plastic knives and spoons and forks.

The following day it was decided that Hans should be flown by air ambulance back to Germany for his facial surgery, to the hospital in Frankfurt of which he had been the director. Inge flew out on a commercial plane.

Each day I talked to Henry on the phone. During one of these conversations he said he had run into Francesco.

"He asked if we wanted to go out on the boat for Redentore."

I had completely forgotten. But Redentore wasn't far away now.

"Please thank him," I told Henry. "Tell him I am in the hospital. It won't be possible."

When I'd been in the hospital almost a week, I'd had enough. It was now Friday. A summer Friday. All the doctors would be away over the weekend. I was alone. I wanted to go home. But I was very weak and terribly frightened. I had not yet even taken a walk out into the hospital's gardens. Though I had managed to find the bar downstairs, where I bought a card for the public telephone.

The doctors were reluctant to let me go. One refused outright. But in the end my doctor, who usually seemed gruff, suddenly showed kindness.

"You can leave," he said. "But only because you don't know anyone here. You must promise you will go into the care of a doctor in Venice immediately."

I phoned Henry. He would take the next train to Florence. He would book first-class tickets on the train to Venice for Saturday morning.

"Please get in touch with Rosella," I said. "Ask her for the name of a doctor."

I was given a prescription to have filled at the farmacia downstairs.

"What is it for?" I asked my doctor.

"You must continue the daily injections of antibiotics," he said. I had some liquid at the bottom of one of my lungs and this was to prevent infection.

"But who will give me injections every day?" I asked. I was too weak to go walking across Venice to a doctor's office.

"Oh, you give them to yourself," he said, looking at me as if my brain had been damaged too. I did not tell him that I could not possibly give myself injections. I wanted to be discharged.

Henry came to fetch me. The taxi driver who took us to the station was gentle. He told me not to think of attaching the seat belt to my broken chest. Piano, piano we drove across Florence. The Eurostar to Venice was very crowded. But we had our seats and I managed to stay awake. I still wasn't taking any chances.

From the ferrovia we took the vaporetto to the Fondamenta Nuove. How did I manage to climb all those stairs to the top of Ca' Donà? But it was so good to be in my own lumpy bed. In the stucchi.

The stucchi. My beautiful stucchi. The most exquisite place in which I had ever lived, or ever would live, now became the place in which I began my recuperation. It proved to suit that purpose as well as it had suited entertaining, daydreaming, boat studies and laboring over Italian verbs. It was so soothing. The butterflies and birds on the ceiling kept me company during the long hours I rested, unable to turn in the bed. I had been forbidden to turn on my side for three weeks. One of our visitors in Florence, a philosopher whose sister had been a pupil of Hans's, was the bearer of this message. I didn't question it. Besides my body had no inclination to roll. It wanted to be still.

Rosella had given us the name of her mother's doctor. She had said he sometimes even made house calls. I phoned him. He said he could come the following day.

"But what about my injection today?" I asked.

I was so unnerved by having been in the car crash and by having my chest crushed. I had been so sure that all of us were going to die, that it took only the very smallest thing for me to fear the worst. If I missed my injection for a single day . . .

Beate telephoned to ask how I was. She had heard the news from Inge who had called her from Frankfurt. I had no doubt Inge had asked Beate to keep an eye on me.

I said I was improving but was worried about the injections. She said she would see what she could do. There were visiting nurses available through the pharmacies as well as nursing orders of nuns.

And as it turned out there were friends.

Michela telephoned. Beate must have rung her to ask for advice. Michela would try to reach Alessandra who worked with her. Alessandra could give shots.

Rosella called to ask how I was. I gave her much the same report.

"But I know how to give injections," she said. "I took a Red Cross course. I cannot come today or tomorrow but I will come the day after."

I went back to bed.

Late that afternoon Alessandra appeared. Before this we had only seen each other on the stairs or out on the landing. Small, redheaded and friendly, she got to work mixing the two different drugs in the packet I had been given by the hospital in Florence. She explained that she had lots of experience with giving injections. Her dog needed a course of shots for a skin condition.

About six in the evening the doorbell rang. It was gray-haired Dottore Sparla. In spite of his saying he could not come, he had. And up all those stairs. I had to explain that someone had already done the deed. And that the remaining injections had been organized also. He briefly examined me. I was to come to his office when the course of antibiotics was finished.

The next day Françoise telephoned to ask after my health. She was

very kind. "If you want to stay longer to rest," she said, "you are welcome."

I was touched and I thanked her.

Françoise then mentioned that the day before an ancient nun had
appeared on the top landing. One of the nursing sisters. Beate must
have called her, too. Her order occupies a building near the church of
the Miracoli. Poor woman. She'd made the trip and climbed to the top
of Ca' Donà and I never heard our doorbell.

It was Saturday. Tonight would be the spectacle of Redentore. Henry
felt well enough go to the Marciana. And he wanted to.

Henry left for the Piazzetta a little after ten. The family I suppose
went off together on the Arzanà outing in the old-fashioned rowing
boat. Ca' Donà was deserted. For the first time since the car crash, I was
entirely alone.

I felt that I was alone not only in the stucchi and the house but that
the whole district had been abandoned, too. I imagined that everybody
was as near as they could get to the coming fireworks show.

Unnerved and exhausted, I willed myself to stay awake. I was determined to have enough energy to push myself up and leave the bed.

At eleven P.M. I went to the window. I stood in my long white night-
dress and looked out over the tiled rooftops toward the Campanile at
San Marco. It was a warm night but I reached for a big woolly shawl
from the chair next to the bed.

"You must not be in a draft," the dear doctor had warned me when
he had made his housecall. "You must not catch cold."

The fireworks began. I could hear them booming. And over the
rooftops I could see the bursting fragments of light. It was so beautiful.
And I felt so terribly alone. I cried. I was sorry for myself and grateful
to have lived to see Redentore again. To be alive.

Henry came home at 12:30. I looked up from the pillow, said good-
night and sank again into dreamless sleep.

I BEGAN BY WALKING THE LENGTH OF THE BEDROOM. I worked my way
up to making a complete circuit of the stucchi. I am not a counter by
temperament, but pacing the floor needs a little accompaniment. I

therefore note that it took seventy-six steps for me to walk from the bed, through the study, into the salone, across to the kitchen, around the dining room table, through the bathroom and back to the bed.

Every day I received a phone call from Inge. She was at home in Frankfurt. Hans was in the hospital. The operation on his face had taken five hours. The doctors were having problems setting his broken ankles properly.

Something strange was happening with my mouth. Everything tasted of salt. Not to mention the fact that I was producing a great amount of saliva. And then I coughed up blood. I nearly passed out from terror.

I telephoned Inge. She had become my physician, once removed. Inge took my various questions to the doctors in the hospital where Hans was being treated. It was helpful and reassuring. But this time I was in a panic and no one answered the phone. I tried her mobile.

Hans answered.

I hadn't known that he was keeping the mobile with him in the hospital. I surely didn't want to bother him with my health worries. But now I was telling him about the blood.

"Don't be alarmed," he said. "This also happened to me. It can occur following an injury to the throat."

Hans suggested I go to the hospital and have a chest X-ray just in case. He gave me the name of a radiologist there. He seemed to know and be known by every radiologist in Italy.

Rosella soon appeared to give me my shot. I told her what had happened and, as I did, I began to cry.

"I am afraid I am going to die," I confessed as I wept.

I was so weak that I felt only a little bit embarrassed.

With Rosella on one side and Henry on the other I walked along the Fondamenta Nuove and then along the Rio dei Mendicanti to the emergency room. I could hardly believe how long it was taking. It was all I could do to keep going. We went into the pronto soccorso. I was told I could not be given an X-ray immediately.

"I would like you to be admitted," said the woman at the desk. "We do not know what has caused this. It could be dangerous."

There was a limit to how authentic I wanted my Venetian life to be and I had just found it. If I had a decent chance of surviving at home, I did not wish to be a patient in this medieval-looking place.

Rosella did not try to convince me I was wrong. Depending on the particular malady, Venetians who are capable of traveling go to hospitals in Treviso or Vicenza or even Mestre. The ospedale in Venice is excellent, however, if you need an operation on your eyes. I did not.

We went back to Ca' Donà. The next morning, I managed to get myself to the radiology department and find the doctor Hans had recommended. The X-ray was fine.

I was relieved, of course. But I still was frightened. In my adult life nothing like this had ever befallen me. I didn't know what my body was telling me or what it was keeping too silent about. I couldn't go on using Inge as my doctor, once removed. I didn't want to.

I sent a fax to Bill Hollis who was back home in Philadelphia. After all, Andrea had been a doctor for years. In a pinch, she could give me advice. Briefly I told Bill what had happened.

The next night about nine the telephone rang. Beate had suggested I get a *telefonino* but I hadn't managed to do anything about it. The nearest phone was in the study and it was hard for me to get out of bed. I had to sort of fling myself forward and then throw my feet over the side of the mattress. Hoisting myself up by holding on to the blankets, I could then begin to slowly shuffle across the floor.

I raised the phone to my ear. It was Bill.

"Andrea came to my office and said, 'There's a fax from Paula. The news is not good.' "

When you are weak, when you are fragile, to hear "the news is not good," meaning you, sounds terrible.

I stood there silently holding the phone. I felt awful.

"When I think about what's happened, I cringe in horror," Bill confessed.

I was frightened for my life and this lonely man in his ritzy suburb was indulging himself in cringing when he thought about what had happened to me.

I now found words.

"I don't need to hear this," I told him.

"Well I guess calling was a mistake," said Bill, almost as quick to take offense as to give it.

I hung up.

All of a sudden, and for the first time since the crash, I felt perky. I really must be improving if I could get so angry.

And I was beginning to feel stronger. The next day I decided to go to Didovich, by myself.

In the stucchi, cooled by the cross breezes, I hadn't realized how hot it was outside. Twice, I had to stop and rest before I reached Campo Santa Marina. When I got there, I had to sit down on a chair outside the pasticceria, along with the other old ladies.

I ordered a coffee. But I didn't care what I was eating or drinking. What I needed was to catch my breath. I had to collect enough energy to see me home again.

Vivian called. When she heard what had happened, she asked if I would like her to come over and we could go out together. She would hold my elbow while I walked. How considerate she was to suggest this, I thought, and I accepted.

As we walked, she told me that she had a large terrace separate from the one used by her guests. If I liked, I could use it. From then on, I went there every afternoon. I had a conviction that if I sat in the sun, wellness would bake into me.

I was just strong enough to begin making piles of the belongings that later would be packed. I'd talked with the people in England who would arrange for my trip back through my travel insurance company. A wheelchair would meet me at the plane at Heathrow. A car would drive us to our house. Beate booked a taxi to pick us up from Ca' Donà and take us to Marco Polo Airport. Everything was arranged.

Just thinking about the trip made me tremble. I couldn't imagine how I would be able to do it. I had to trust that adrenaline would see me through.

I slowly packed every item. The phone calls from Inge became less frequent. This was a good sign. We could not go on being connected umbilically by her guilt and my dependence. I knew that as I got stronger, the resentment that I had submerged would come out. And the fury.

I went on increasing the number of circuits I made around the stucchi. My lung power was improving.

Vivian came over again. She collected a cooking pot I had borrowed and a large white porcelain platter I'd bought, which I wanted her to have. We said goodbye. Twenty minutes later there was a knock at the door.

Gaia was outside with a fellow close to her in age. He was tall and thin and had dark hair and a narrow face. A camera hung around his neck.

I was introduced to Leo Schubert, the architect. He was examining the beams in the attic as part of the preparations for the eventual repair of the roof. (One day there would be no more leaks. I hoped this would happen before the stucco decorations were washed away.)

Henry and I sat on the sofa in the salone while Gaia and the architect were upstairs in the hunting lodge looking at the beams. Henry, too, was recuperating. Though he could walk greater distances than me, it was painful for him. He'd spent most of the time since the accident moving between the bed and the couch in the salone. Neither of us had stamina. Sitting for short periods and sleeping a lot were our two main occupations.

We heard a crashing sound. It was coming from the study. Henry who could move more quickly got up and went to see what it was.

"You won't believe it," he said. "Come look."

The architect had put his foot in it, literally. There was a hole in the study ceiling. Plaster dust filled the air. I started coughing.

Soon the two of them reappeared. They studied the damage. Gaia's sister Chiara arrived ten minutes later to patch it up temporarily. We had never seen her before. She was not now introduced to us. In fact she acted as if we didn't exist. We were merely the tenants who would soon be disappearing and who meantime were an inconvenience.

FRANCESCO TELEPHONED. He asked how I was feeling. We set a time for him to come round so that all of us could read the various meters, check the number of telephone calls we'd made and settle up the final bill. He said his mother would like to stop by also to see us before we left.

"If your father is in the house, I would also like to say goodbye to him," I said to Francesco.

The following afternoon, Francesco, Françoise, Henry and I sat at the dining-room table in the salone.

"I hope you were able to work in the stucchi," Françoise said.

"Yes, I did work here," I answered. "But it didn't go so well in the winter. The stucchi is cold but the studio is like an icebox."

She seemed surprised. We began to talk about how the heating might be improved. I'd had lots of opportunity to work on the problem.

"Perhaps you will come back next year?" Françoise proposed.

Six months earlier, I would not have believed it. Françoise inviting us back? But she meant it now. If before she often had made me feel like crying, this time it wasn't frustration or fury that brought the tears to my eyes.

Would we return? I had no idea. Even stranger, I didn't find this upsetting. I had become a creature mending. Tomorrow and the day after were as far ahead as I looked.

Nicolò Donà came into the room.

He and Françoise were together in the salone of this apartment where they had lived as a young couple when their children were small so many years before. How often had they been together in this room since their divorce, I wondered.

"I am sorry you are leaving," il conte said to me and Henry. "But I am glad that you stayed here."

We told him how very glad we were too.

The three of them stood up.

Françoise, with whom I had previously shaken hands, now kissed me. My eyes were wet again.

"Goodbye," said the Donà as they walked toward the door.

"Goodbye," we murmured.

BASTA COSÌ.